The Buddhist Tantras

GUIDES TO SACRED TEXTS

THE DAODE JING: A GUIDE
Livia Kohn

THE RIGVEDA: A GUIDE
Stephanie Jamison and Joel Brereton

THE BOOK OF COMMON PRAYER: A GUIDE
Charles Hefling

THE ANNALECTS: A GUIDE
Erin M. Cline

THE NEW TESTAMENT: A GUIDE
Donald Senior, C.P.

THE YIJING: A GUIDE
Joseph Adler

THE BUDDHIST TANTRAS: A GUIDE
David B. Gray

The Buddhist Tantras

A Guide

DAVID B. GRAY

OXFORD
UNIVERSITY PRESS

OXFORD
UNIVERSITY PRESS

Oxford University Press is a department of the University of Oxford. It furthers the University's objective of excellence in research, scholarship, and education by publishing worldwide. Oxford is a registered trade mark of Oxford University Press in the UK and certain other countries.

Published in the United States of America by Oxford University Press
198 Madison Avenue, New York, NY 10016, United States of America.

CIP data is on file at the Library of Congress

ISBN 978-0-19-762384-8 (pbk.)
ISBN 978-0-19-762383-1 (hbk.)

DOI: 10.1093/oso/9780197623831.001.0001

The manufacturer's authorised representative in the EU for product safety is Oxford University Press España S.A. of El Parque Empresarial San Fernando de Henares, Avenida de Castilla, 2 - 28830 Madrid (www.oup.es/en or product.safety@oup.com). OUP España S.A. also acts as importer into Spain of products made by the manufacturer.

Contents

Guides to Sacred Texts vii

Introduction: Introducing the Buddhist Tantras 1

1. Dates, Authorship, and Historical Contexts 5

2. Structure and Contents 48

3. Dissemination and Reception of the Tantras 107

4. Canonical Status of the Tantras 141

5. Transgression, Censorship, and Interpretation 167

Notes 209
Bibliography 243
Index 271

Guides to Sacred Texts

What is a sacred text? The *Oxford English Dictionary* offers a definition of "sacred" as "set apart for or dedicated to some religious purpose, and hence entitled to veneration or religious respect." The definition is necessarily vague. What does it mean to be "set apart?" What constitutes a "religious purpose?" How formal is "veneration?" Does minimal "religious respect" qualify? The sphere of meanings surrounding the word "sacred" will depend on the religion involved. For that reason "sacred texts" in this series is a term conceived broadly. All the texts covered by this series have held special regard—they have been "set apart"—in a religion either ancient or modern. Such texts are generally accorded more serious attention than other religious documents. In some cases the texts may be believed to be the words of a deity. In other cases the texts may be part of an atheistic religion. This breadth of application indicates the rationale behind Guides to Sacred Texts.

This series offers brief, accessible introductions to sacred texts, written by experts. While allowing for the individuality of each text, the series follows a basic format of introducing the text in terms of its dates of composition, traditions of authorship and assessment of those traditions, the extent of the text, and the issues raised by the text. For scripture that continues to be utilized, those issues will likely continue to generate controversy and discussion among adherents to the text. For texts from religions no longer practiced, the issues may well continue to address concerns of the present day, despite the antiquity of the scripture. These volumes are useful for introducing sacred writings from around the world to readers wanting to learn what these sacred texts are.

Introduction

Introducing the Buddhist Tantras

The Buddhist tantras are one of the least understood bodies of scripture—with good reason: they are deliberately obscure to maintain the secrecy that traditionally surrounds the teachings and practices of tantric Buddhist traditions. Tantric Buddhist traditions are conceived as a distinct path to awakening, the goal of Buddhist traditions, and it is usually termed either the "adamantine path" (*vajrayāna*) or the "mantric path" (*mantrayāna*), the latter highlighting a key feature, that is, *mantra*s, or sacred formulas, which are recited in tantric ritual and contemplative practices. While they are part of the larger "Greater Path" Mahāyāna Buddhist tradition, the Buddhist tantric traditions are, more accurately, offshoots of this larger tradition. They accept the basic premises of Mahāyāna Buddhism but claim to possess secret teachings that enable awakening in as short as one lifetime.

This volume will attempt to introduce this genre to interested readers, and it presupposes no prior understanding of Buddhism. As a result, the volume will use the English language whenever possible, translating and explaining Buddhist titles and technical terms when they are first introduced, excepting only those Buddhist terms that have entered English and are generally well understood, such as buddha, mantra, karma, and so forth. To best introduce the tantras, many passages from tantric scriptures and commentaries will be included and translated into English in the clearest manner possible. On rare occasions Buddhist terms from other languages, such as a Sanskrit, are used, due to the ambiguity of their meaning

The Buddhist Tantras. David B. Gray, Oxford University Press. © Oxford University Press 2023.
DOI: 10.1093/oso/9780197623831.003.0001

in context, but the reason for this and the possible range of the term's meanings will be explained.

The first chapter of the volume begins by defining terms, indicating what is meant by terms like "tantra" and "tantric Buddhist traditions." It then moves on to introducing them, focusing on their emergence in India during the seventh century CE. The chapter traces two main sources for the development of these traditions. One, the gradual development of traditions of magic and ritual practice in Buddhist traditions, and, two, the tantric traditions that appear to have emerged first among the Śaivas, namely, the Hindus who take the god Śiva to be the supreme creator god. Following this historical overview, the chapter explores the two main types of origin myths for the Buddhist tantras and looks closely at the narratives produced by Buddhists from the seventh century to explain the emergence of the tantras.

The second chapter provides an overview of the contents of the Buddhist tantras. It begins with the background verse that traditionally opens Buddhist scriptures, which relate the contexts in which the texts are taught. These opening passages establish that the work is the speech of an awakened one, the traditional Buddhist understanding of scripture. As this entails a lineage claim, the importance of lineage in tantric Buddhist traditions are also introduced. The chapter also covers the language and style of the tantras, as well as overviews their contents, which are typically ritual and contemplative practices, focusing on the mandala, the circle of awakened beings that features prominently in tantric practices as well as art, iconography, and architecture. The chapter concludes with a brief look at tantric ritual magic.

The third chapter summarizes the dissemination of tantric Buddhist traditions, via maritime routes to Southeast Asia and China, and thence to Korea and Japan, as well as overland from India and Nepal to Tibet and eventually the ethnic Mongolian regions of Central Asia. The chapter argues that tantric Buddhist ritual and magical practices were a major appeal that facilitated their transmission in Asia. The chapter concludes with a look at tantric Buddhism in the contemporary world. It summarizes the travails to which tantric Buddhists were subjected in Tibet and Mongolia, under communist rule in China and the Soviet Union, as well as the global spread of tantric Buddhism from the 1960s onward, facilitated by the diaspora of Tibetan and Mongolian lamas.

The fourth chapter looks closely at tantric literature. It introduces the different genres of tantric literature, including different types of tantras as well as commentaries and ritual texts and meditation manuals. It surveys attempts to classify the tantras and to distinguish them from exoteric Buddhist works, which were developed in India, Tibet, and East Asia. It then relates the attempts to develop canons of tantric literature and how these canons were organized.

The final chapter addresses the unmistakable "red thread" that runs throughout the rest of the chapters, which is the presence of transgressive rhetoric in the tantras, particularly the description of sexual and violent rituals.[1] This is a notable feature of the tantras from their first appearance in the seventh century, and it became more prominent over time. This was a serious issue since Buddhist identity was traditionally defined in terms of nonviolence, and spiritual authority was associated with monastic celibacy. The chapter explores how transgressive content affected the reception of the tantras. It compares their translation in the Tibetan and Chinese contexts, and it argues that it affected how they were received, which led both to efforts to block the transmission and translation of tantras, as well as influenced the translation style, with transgressive passages far more likely to be creatively translated to mitigate the impact of this content. It explores the sophisticated exegetical strategies that Buddhist commentators developed to explain this content. In conclusion, it suggests that transgressive rhetoric in the tantras may have had the effect of challenging Buddhist constructions of identity to facilitate the transformation in self-identification that is required for success in tantric Buddhist contemplative practices. If so, this represents a very risky strategy, given the challenges this rhetoric posed to the dissemination and survival of these texts and associated practice traditions.

While this volume makes a small contribution toward our understanding of what is a vast and complicated body of thousands of works, it will hopefully give the reader with no prior study of Buddhist tantras a solid understanding that can serve as the basis for further study if so desired. Those who have studied them may find that the broad range of topics covered and texts translated will open their eyes to aspects of these traditions they were previously unaware of. Hopefully it will inspire further study of the fascinating array of religious literature, most of which remains unstudied and untranslated in Western-language contexts.

Since this volume is oriented toward readers interested in Buddhist tantras but without specialized training in their study, as mentioned, English translation will be used as much as possible. For technical terms, the equivalent in the original language will also be given in parentheses when first used. The titles of tantric works will also be given in English translation, with their title in the original language also given in parentheses when first introduced. Sanskrit terms will be given in roman transliteration with diacritics, except for terms that have entered the English language, hence "mandala" and "sutra" rather than "maṇḍala" and "sūtra." The only exception is when relating the names of Sanskrit texts; in this case, diacritics are provided for all terms in the title. Tibetan terms will be given using Wylie transliteration. Chinese characters are used for the sake of clarity.

1

Dates, Authorship, and Historical Contexts

1.1 Defining Terms

This volume provides an introduction to the Buddhist tantras. At first glance, the juxtaposition of these terms may seem paradoxical since Buddhism is associated in the West with monasticism and celibate renunciation, while the term "tantra" is strongly associated with sexuality, as anyone who has done an internet search for the term can attest. While there is some truth underlying these associations, they obviously do not adequately relate the meaning of these terms. While the monastic vocation is held in high regard by many (but not all) Buddhist traditions, it never fully encapsulated the Buddhist path because the Buddhist community since early times included the laity. Buddhist tantric traditions, in fact, challenged the authority of monks through the development of a spiritual path that was arguably better suited for the laity. Moreover, while the association of tantra with sexuality is rooted in the erotic discourse contained within many Buddhist and Hindu tantric scriptures, the term's blanket association with sexuality in the West is a modern phenomenon and the result of attempts by Westerners to appropriate and transform elements of Asian religious traditions from the nineteenth century up until the present day, as Hugh Urban has convincingly argued.[1] Given the misunderstandings that surround these two terms, an introduction to the "Buddhist tantras" is needed.

The Buddhist Tantras. David B. Gray, Oxford University Press. © Oxford University Press 2023.
DOI: 10.1093/oso/9780197623831.003.0002

The Buddhist tantras are a genre of works produced by Indian Buddhist communities from the mid-seventh century up until the decline and disappearance of Buddhism in most of South Asia by about 1500 CE, although they continue to be revealed in the Tibetan Nyingma tradition. These works are Buddhist manifestations of the larger tantric movement, which thrived in India during the medieval period, an era spanning from the fall of the Gupta Empire circa 550 CE up until the founding of the Mughal Empire in 1526 CE.[2]

The Buddhist tantras remain one of the least studied sections of the Buddhist canon. This is partially because the Buddhist tantras are the latest additions to the Buddhist canon and that they tend to focus on ritual practices, including those that most would deem "magical" insofar as their operation depends on metaphysical forces, such as deities and spirits. Due to these factors, many European scholars tended to focus on the pursuit of early Buddhism and the "original" teachings of the Śākyamuni Buddha, rejecting later developments as "degenerate," motivated in part by Protestant critiques of the Catholic Church and the concomitant drive to discover the original teachings of Jesus.[3]

The ritual complexity of tantric Buddhism, which was viewed as a sign of degeneracy by Western scholars during the colonial era, was viewed more positively in the Asian cultural contexts in which this form of Buddhism developed, spread, and thrived for centuries. Charles Orzech argued:

> It is no exaggeration to say that the Buddhist tantras were among the most important vehicles for the spread of Indian political and religious ideas throughout East, Central, and Southeast Asia. The literal English rendering of its common East Asian name (*Mi-chiao*, "esoteric teaching") gives the misleading impression that it is practiced only in secret, occult groups. While access to the most profound of its "mysteries" is indeed given through initiation, most of these initiations are quite public in character, and its mysteries are of the same sort as those found in Catholic or

> Orthodox sacramental theology. Like the Catholic traditions of Europe, Esoteric Buddhism was patronized by kings, courtiers, and aristocrats in grand temples with elaborate public ceremony.[4]

Ritual was one of the most important factors contributing to the prestige of the tantric Buddhist traditions, facilitating their spread throughout Asia during the medieval period.

The Buddhist tantric traditions are part of the larger Indian tantric movement. Although the early history of tantrism is unclear, it appears to have emerged within Śaiva traditions of Hinduism circa the fifth or sixth century. Buddhists quickly adopted and adapted many elements of Śaiva traditions, producing their own traditions by the seventh century. Generally speaking, tantric traditions borrowed extensively from classical Indian religious movements, drawing heavily from the ritual practices of the Hindu Vedic tradition as well as the contemplative practices of the ascetic traditions of Hinduism, Buddhism and Jainism. However, they tended to reject the former's focus on ritual purity and the latter's focus on renunciation, instead advocating engagement with the world and with the senses as a path to liberation.

The textual focus of these traditions is a genre of scriptures known as *tantras*. While the term "tantra" has multiple meanings, its most common meaning in classical Sanskrit is a "book" or "treatise."[5] Tantras are scripture insofar as they are understood to be revealed teachings by divine or awakened beings. They are often structurally dialogical, portraying themselves as the written record of an oral teaching, typically between a divine couple, such as Śiva and Pārvatī in Hindu contexts, or between a buddha and his or her interlocutor, usually another buddha or a bodhisattva (an aspiring buddha) in Buddhist contexts. Tantras tend to be rather technical works, relating details of ritual and contemplative practice, unlike the more narrative or philosophical genres of literature, such as Buddhist sutras or Hindu *upaniṣads* or *purāṇas*.

Tantras are the scriptural touchstones for the tantric traditions. The English term "tantric," a derivation from the Sanskrit *tāntrika*, means simply that which relates to the *tantras*, so the term *tantric* also envelopes the practices associated with these scriptures and were traditionally disseminated by the *tāntrikas* (the Sanskrit term also designates tantric practitioners), along with the texts.[6] Therefore, as I have argued elsewhere, "tantric traditions" are "the communities of practitioners who practice, preserve, and transmit through both time and space both the texts and the practices that are traditionally associated with them."[7]

Here I define Buddhist tantric traditions as those communities who

1. take as their central scriptures the "tantras," a term that includes those texts that are called tantras, and which by extension should include closely related, ritually focused texts, such as the esoteric sutras, dhāraṇī collections, and *kalpa* ritual texts,
2. which are Buddhist insofar as they are understood to be *buddhavacana*, the speech of a Buddha.
3. These communities understand that, insofar as these texts contain imagery and descriptions of ritual practices that transgress Buddhist ethical norms, such content is understood to be the result of the founding Buddha employing skillful means (*upāya*) to instruct sentient beings who are inclined toward such transgressive imagery and activities.
4. Partly as a result of transgressive content, the practices revealed in these texts are understood to be secret, not appropriate for everyone, and should be revealed only to properly prepared disciples.
5. When practiced correctly under the guidance of a qualified guru, these traditions claim that one can attain awakening in as little as one lifetime; the traditions lionize the great adepts

(*mahāsiddha*) of the past who are believed to have accomplished this.

In other words, Buddhist tantric traditions are those traditions that take as their central scriptures tantras that are Buddhist insofar as they are understood to encapsulate the secret teachings of a buddha that, if practiced properly, are believed to enable awakening in as little as one lifetime.

1.2 Dating the Tantras

While the origins of tantric traditions are unclear, available evidence indicates that distinctly tantric forms of Hinduism emerged first among unorthodox Śaiva Hindu traditions around the fifth century CE. Thence it spread to other Hindu traditions, as well as to Buddhism. It is impossible to precisely date the emergence of tantric Hindu traditions due to the poor state of textual preservation in these traditions; no complete Hindu tantric manuscripts from earlier than the ninth century have been preserved, although two folia of a Śaiva tantric work were preserved among the Gilgit Buddhist manuscripts, dating to approximately the mid-sixth century.[8]

Epigraphic evidence points to the fifth century as the most likely time when Śaiva Hindu tantric traditions first emerged. One of the earliest references to tantric texts and/or practices is found in a 423 CE Gaṅgdhār stone tablet inscription. The inscription includes the following reference to a temple to the Mothers (*mātṛ*):

> Also for the sake of religious merit, the king's minister caused to be built . . . this most terrible of abode, strewn with a multitude of [images of] Ḍākinīs [i.e.,] of the Mothers, that drove of joyous over-the-top gong-bangers who are pumped up to the rain clouds [on] the powerful winds raised by the Tantras.[9]

This is the earliest datable reference both to the term tantra qua "ritual manual" and to the *ḍākinī*s, a class of goddesses who are closely linked to the tantric traditions. While we do not know exactly what texts or ritual traditions were being deployed in early fifth-century Gaṅgdhār, it was almost certainly Śaiva. This is because the Śaiva tantric tradition is the only tradition for which there is reliable evidence dating to the fifth century.[10]

The early association of tantras relating to the ḍākinīs and the Śaiva tradition are also confirmed by Buddhist sources. The Buddhist philosopher Dharmakīrti, who was active circa 550–620 CE,[11] mentions in his "Commentary on Epistemology" *Pramāṇavārttika* a genre of texts he calls *ḍākinī tantras*. He does this in the context of a passage addressing the issue of whether "success" (*siddhi*) in magical procedures involving mantras is dependent on adherence to ethical norms (*dharma*). His answer: "No, for it is evident that there are observances in the *ḍākinī* and *bhaginī tantras*, etc., which are incompatible with ethical norms and are replete with violence, theft, sexual intercourse, perverse actions, and so forth, and through which there is distinctive success."[12] As Alexis Sanderson has argued, the texts to which he refers were almost certainly Śaiva texts.[13] Within about a century after Dharmakīrti's death, Buddhists would develop their own versions of *ḍākinī tantras*.

The early history of Buddhist tantric traditions is relatively clear, despite the paucity of historical sources from the early medieval period in India. This is due to the international Buddhist network that led to the rapid dissemination of new Buddhist works. Many works of Buddhist tantric literature were quickly translated into Tibetan and Chinese, and the date when a translation was made can help us estimate when the text was compiled. The earliest known dateable tantric Buddhist text is the "Awakening of Mahāvairocana" *Mahāvairocanābhisaṃbodhi Tantra*, which was composed circa the mid-seventh century, and it was reportedly one of the texts collected by the Chinese pilgrim Wuxing (無行) circa 680 CE.[14] Wuxing also commented on the emergence of a new "teaching about mantra" (*zhenyan jiaofa* 真言教法) which was very popular during his time in India,[15] a fact confirmed in the account of another Chinese pilgrim who journeyed in India during the late seventh century, Yijing (義淨, 635–713).[16]

These seventh-century reports of the development of a new form of Buddhism in India, along with new scriptures such as the *Awakening of Mahāvairocana Tantra,* was followed by the rapid development of new scriptures and practice traditions in the eighth century, as the newly established tantric form of Buddhism rapidly developed in India and abroad.

1.3 Early Influences on Tantric Buddhism

The development of the Buddhist tantras was influenced by two major textual genres. These include the genre of literature on magical and ritual practices in Mahāyāna Buddhist circles that developed over the course of the first half of the first millennium CE, as well as the prior Hindu tantric texts and traditions.

While Buddhists were certainly influenced by the development and growth in popularity of Śaiva tantric traditions, they also had their own growing body of esoteric lore that offered a native rootstock onto which tantric traditions could be easily grafted. Most if not all of the early Buddhist traditions had collections of protective formula (*rakṣā*) to be recited by monks and nuns when needed. Protective formula collections are found in many of the early schools and reflect an important role played by monks and nuns, who, in exchange for the material support provided by the laity, were expected to use their spiritual power to benefit them.[17] The engagement of the monastic community in magical practices was common enough that Buddhist communities felt it necessary to regulate it. The Vinaya literature on the monastic code of conduct relates "many and often curious instances of monks and nuns employing mantras [that] are indicative of the pervasion of mantra-related practices in several of the early schools."[18]

Over time, within Mahāyāna communities, Buddhists began compiling ritual texts that contained magical formula or spells, known as mantras, *dhāraṇīs*, or *vidyā*, as well as instructions on the rites in which they are employed to achieve various worldly ends. This, properly speaking, is the origin of the Buddhist tantras. Tantras are primarily ritual texts, and they arose from and with the evolution of Buddhist ritual practices. Buddhist traditions tend to ascribe to tantras primary status as the origins of their practice traditions, as indicated both by the term commonly applied to them, "root tantras" (*mūlatantra*), and the myths describing their revelation by awakened beings. Connected with them are various ritual manuals to facilitate the performance of the many rites in a master's repertoire.

The relationship between the tantras and the ritual texts associated with them is almost certainly iterative. Rather than being origin points in and of themselves, tantras are just simply textual records of certain points in the evolution of Buddhist ritual and contemplative practices. That is, they depend on prior ritual texts, which are important sources for their composition, and then, when accepted as root tantras, become the basis for new ritual textual production. As Jacob Dalton has argued:

> Ritual manuals were in fact the principle creative source for early tantric innovation, and the tantras were written, and rewritten, to encapsulate and canonize these ritual changes. Ritual manuals were . . . a particularly creative source of innovation, thanks to their extraordinary creativity. They could be composed or altered by anyone claiming the necessary qualification (or, more specifically, who had received the *ācārya* initiation that consecrated one as a teacher). They could declare allegiance to any given tantra, and they could be easily updated to include the very latest ritual techniques.[19]

Koichi Shinohara, studying "*dhāraṇī* collections," Mahāyāna ritual texts translated into Chinese from the fifth through ninth centuries, traced the gradual growth in the complexity of the rituals described in these texts, which include the development of the mandala initiation rituals as well as rituals involving image worship and visualization.[20] These texts gradually became more complex, reaching a critical mass in the seventh century, becoming the textual basis for a new Buddhist tradition that was deemed by its advocates to be distinct from the larger Mahāyāna tradition from which it emerged.

Since early times Buddhist monastics were thought to have worldly powers (*laukikasiddhi*) by virtue of their spiritual practice, such as the power to protect against evil influences, and the early protective formula literature is a record of this lore. However, by the mid-seventh century, Buddhists began to claim that there existed secret teachings that could also enable the ultimate achievement (*lokottarasiddhi*) of awakening in as short as one lifetime. Since these new teachings dealt with the ultimate accomplishment, they had to be attributed to an ultimate source, an awakened buddha. And secrecy provided a convenient explanation for the relatively sudden appearance of these new teachings, which could be explained as either teachings of Śākyamuni Buddha that were hidden until a preordained time of revelation or new revelations from other awakened beings.

There was rapid growth and dissemination of the newly emerging tantric Buddhist traditions. Within a few decades after their initial composition early tantric traditions of text and practice were disseminated to East and Southeast Asia through maritime trade routes.[21] Moreover, the Central Asian monk Amoghavajra (不空金刚, 704–774), who journeyed from China to India and back via the maritime route during the mid-eighth century, reported that there was a new canon of eighteen tantras that his master Vajrabuddhi (金刚智, 671–741) attempted to convey back to China and which he partially translated into Chinese.[22] This suggests that there was a very rapid production of new tantric texts and practice traditions circa the mid-seventh century through the mid-eighth century. From this point onward, Indian Buddhists would continue developing new tantric traditions and revealing or compiling new tantric texts, until the destruction of Buddhist centers of learning and the disappearance of Buddhism from most of the subcontinent by circa 1500 CE.

1.4 Historical Contexts for Tantric Production

The seventh century CE was a challenging period for Buddhists in India. As Ronald Davidson has argued, with the downfall of the Gupta Dynasty and the concomitant social and political upheaval that afflicted much of the subcontinent, the patronage system from which Buddhists benefited for several centuries was severely disrupted. This system included the guilds involved with national and international commerce, with which Buddhists were closely aligned, and which were powerful and influential under the Gupta Dynasty. The decline of these guilds, in part due to predatory policies targeting them implemented by early medieval rulers, removed an important basis of economic support for Buddhist monasteries.[23]

Another base of support for Buddhists was alliances with new groups, outside the orthodox Vedic Hindu system, such as the ethnic Greek and Persian polities who controlled significant areas of Northwest India in the late first millennium BCE and early first century CE. Buddhism offered these groups religious legitimacy in exchange for patronage. However, by the mid-first millennium CE, Buddhism faced a serious challenge in this arena from new groups strongly associated with the rise of Śaiva Hindu tantric traditions, such as the Pāśupatas and Kāpālikas, who became increasingly active in pursuing patronage from outsider or marginal groups.[24]

Since the system of patronage from political and economic elites was deteriorating, Buddhists were faced with the necessity of competing with the new Śaiva traditions, the prestige of whom was based in part in the perception that they were spiritually powerful. One of the Buddhist responses was the venerable practice of imitation and borrowing, developing new traditions in part by copying elements of rival traditions that were popular. A number of Buddhist tantras were produced via what Phyllis Granoff (2000) termed "ritual eclecticism," incorporating practices from a wide range of preexisting and sometimes rival traditions.

Although tantric Buddhists were compiling new scriptures from the seventh century onward, they could not openly acknowledge this. This was not only because they were borrowing elements from rival traditions but also due to the inherent conservatism of Buddhism and other Indian traditions. Consequently, they needed to develop origin myths for these new traditions, displacing their revelation in most cases to the distant past, and attributing them to buddhas. There are two basic forms of these origin myths. The first are myths that the revelation of the tradition to the distant past and claim a contemporaneous rediscovery of the tradition. The other type are conversion myths that tend to focus on a contemporaneous "problem," namely non-Buddhist competitors. These depict the Buddha as motivated by a desire to discipline "heretical" and sinful sentient beings, who turn out to be Hindu deities. These myths serve a double role, both relating the origin of the tradition and accounting for the fact, which would have been obvious to many contemporary Buddhists, that the texts are dependent on rival traditions.

While the earliest firm evidence for Buddhist tantric tradition dates to the mid-seventh century, there is interesting evidence suggesting its presence in India a bit earlier, reported by the famous Buddhist pilgrim Xuanzang (玄奘, c. 602–664), who was famous for his account of his journey to India, *Great Tang Records on the Western Regions* (大唐西域记),[25] relating his travels in India between 626 and 645 CE. Now, Xuanzang spent considerable time at Nālandā and was evidently unaware of any new teachings being taught there. However, Hui Li's biography of the Xuanzang contains a remarkable passage recording the complaint made by a group of monks from Orissa from one of the older, more conservative traditions concerning Nālandā Monastery to King Harṣa Śīlāditya (r. 606–647 CE). It occurs as follows:

> King Śīlāditya had constructed a bronze temple over a hundred feet high beside Nālandā Monastery. It was well known in various countries. Afterward the king went personally to conquer Koṅgoda, and crossed the country of Uḍra,[26] where all monks were Hinayana adherents and did not believe in Mahayana teaching, saying that they were the views of Śunyapuṣpa[27] heretics and were not taught by the Buddha. When they saw the king, they sneered at him, saying, "We have heard that Your Majesty has constructed a bronze temple beside Nālandā Monastery. It is indeed a magnificent work of great merit, but why did you build it there and not near some heretical temple of the Kāpālikas?" The king said, "What do you mean by saying so?" The monks said in reply, "Because the friars of Nālandā Monastery being Śunyapuṣpa heretics, they are not different from the Kāpālikas!"[28]

It cannot be an accident that monks in Orissa would identify a rival Buddhist group, the monks of Nālandā, with the Kāpālikas, a Śaiva group closely associated with the rise of Hindu tantric traditions, who were notorious for their antinomian behavior. As David White relates, "Kāpālikas, fornicators with menstruating women, cremation-ground consumers of human flesh, worshippers of the female sexual organ, brahman murderers, were the Hell's Angels of medieval India."[29] This is hostile rhetoric, but the comparison itself is interesting, and it suggests that tantric practice may have been taken up in Nālandā during the first half of the seventh century, which more or less accords with Stephen Hodge's estimate that the "Awakening of Mahāvairocana" *MahāvairocanābhisaṃSET Font:"Ti* was composed circa 640 CE in northeastern India, where Nālandā is located.[30]

It is also necessary to address the issue of authorship. Since tantric Buddhists believe that their texts are records of the revealed teachings of awakened beings, there are technically no authors for these works, rather compilers who received the teachings and put them in writing. Although it is tempting to view these figures as "authors," who appear in many instances to have committed "plagiarism" by borrowing textual passages wholesale from earlier works without acknowledgment, this is not a reasonable standard by which to evaluate the development of these works. As Robert Mayer has argued with respect to the revelatory "treasure text" (*gter ma*) genre of the "Ancient" Nyingma (*rnying ma*) school of Tibetan Buddhism, a better standard is that developed for the study of Judaic and Islamic scripture. Scholars in these fields have replaced the problematic term "author" with "tradent," in the sense of a person who plays a central role in the transmission of a scriptural tradition. Mayer elaborates as follows:

> The term "tradent" indicates a producer of sacred text, who claims not to invent new doctrines but merely to pass on established, authentic, ancient ones. It applies particularly to contexts of religion and scripture, where producers of sacred text must take great pains never to seem to innovate nor invent, but only faithfully to pass on ancient truths.[31]

Tradents, who envision their role as primarily focused on passing down received traditional texts, in both oral and written forms, often produce texts by cobbling them together from various sources, including oral teachings, received from living teachers or possibly from supernatural beings received in dreams, visions, or meditative states, along with passages from other texts, including previously composed tantras, ritual works, or commentaries.

Properly speaking, this was not seen as plagiarism as we conceive it. While modern scholars see this as an intellectual crime and feel compelled to produce something "original," a tradent has the exact opposite orientation, favoring what has been written in the past and reproducing it, while seeing originality as a sin to be avoided. What need is there to write something anew that has already been written well by past masters? Even the works of non-Buddhists were fair game, if well stated, an attitude made possible by the famously lax Mahāyāna definition of authoritative scripture, namely "whatever is well spoken is spoken by a Buddha" (*yat kiṃcin . . . subhāṣitam sarvaṃ tad buddhabhāṣitam*).[32]

Mayer, following Peter Schäffer (1992), argues that tantras should be understood as modular in nature, with completed texts seen as "macroforms," composite texts, composed of "microforms," textual modules that cannot stand alone, and lastly "lemmata," discrete, conventional units that tend to be repeatedly found in works across a tradition. Mayer explains this in the context of a treasure text as follows:

> To apply this nomenclature to the *Meteoric Iron Razor* main ritual manual (*las byang*), the work as a whole would be the macroform; its several dozen conventionally required sections, such as the refuge and bodhisattva vows, the praises, the offerings, the feast, the liberation rite, the fulfillment, the four activities and the dedication of merit, would each be microforms; while isolatable standard categories, such as the seed syllable, the deity Vajrakīlaya, his consort, his throne, the protective vajra tent, the four gates of their visualized palace, their four gatekeepers, the visualized weapon wheel and so on, would all be analysable as lemmata.[33]

Much like the treasure text tantric works that Cathy Cantwell and Robert Mayer study, the "Supreme Bliss of the Wheels" *Cakrasaṃvara Tantra* also shows signs of being a modular text, as

I have argued elsewhere.[34] Additional research on tantric textual history may show that many Buddhist tantras were composed in this manner. For this reason, in this volume the idea of "authorship" will be jettisoned when discussing texts deemed to be revealed scriptures.

Unfortunately, very little is known about the tradents of the tantras composed in India during the early medieval period, since they functioned anonymously. Moreover, the period of active production of Buddhist tantras in India was quite lengthy, spanning over five centuries, from about 650 to 1200 CE. Since the production of tantras in India more or less ceased when the great Buddhist tantric centers of learning were destroyed in the twelfth and thirteenth centuries, it seems safe to assume that most of the tantras were composed in monastic settings. However, there likely were some exceptions. I argued previously that the *Cakrasaṃvara Tantra,* a macroform with many microforms drawn from Śaiva tantras, and relatively few microforms and lemmata drawn from Buddhist sources, was probably composed outside of the monasteries, most likely in a liminal setting in which Buddhist and Śaiva yogis intermixed and interacted. The Buddhist commentator Padmavajra, who was active during the late eighth or early ninth century,[35] relates a scenario in which such cross-traditional exchanges would have been quite likely. It occurs as follows in his "Esoteric Achievement" *Guhyasiddhi:*

> He should wander in other lands, in which he is known nowhere. With firm resolve the Sādhaka should enter among untouchables who are devotees of Śiva and recognize no other deity as absolute, who are inspired by the Siddhānta, always attached to [the rituals of] bathing and deity-worship, and dedicated to the doctrines of its scriptures through some slight degree of literacy. After entering among them in the guise of an untouchable votary (*caṇḍālagaṇaḥ*), he should, while cultivating insight into the highest wisdom, instruct them in the religion of the Siddhānta

> established in such scriptures as the *Kālottara*, or the *Niśvāsa*; and in order to win their trust he should take as his disciples all those who are enjoined by the Tantra after [initiating them before] the Initiation Maṇḍala [of Śiva]. Then he should give back to them all the goods and money that they will previously have gathered and given him as their offering to their Guru and take [instead] a girl of theirs with a beautiful face and eyes. After acquainting her with the essence of the Mantras and making her adhere to the rules of an initiate that wise one should practice the Vidyā observance [with her], after resolving to become a Buddha.[36]

Why would a Buddhist yogi do this? Padmavajra does not address this question, but we can infer a possible answer. Padmavajra narrates this in the context of a verse on the "consort observance" (*vidyāvrata*) in the "Esoteric Community" *Guhyasamāja Tantra.* The passage occurs as follows:

> [93] Having obtained a sixteen-year-old girl
> Who has both a lovely face and large eyes
> And who is adorned with all ornaments,
> One should practice the consort observance.
>
> [94] Visualize her with the vajra signs
> Enjoying the status of Locanā,
> [95] Knowing the rites of gesture and mantra,
> And instructed in tantra and mantra.
> Make her the wife of the Tathāgata,
> Set up in a buddha's awakening.[37]

In the *Esoteric Achievement,* Padmavajra was commenting on the first verse translated above, which instructs the yogi to obtain an attractive sixteen-year-old girl to practice the "consort observance," in other words, sexual yogic practices. The two verses that follow contain the additional instructions that the yogi should visualize her as the female buddha Locanā and that she should be well educated in tantric practice. In other words, this seems to have been presented as a strategy for the yogi to find a suitable consort. Why would this elaborate ruse be needed? It may simply be because this behavior was expected of Śaiva yogis and thus tolerated in communities inclined toward Śaivism. In eighth-century Indian Buddhist communities, on the other hand, there may have been much less tolerance for such behavior, given that the celibate monk was long the standard for ideal behavior among Buddhist authority figures. While we do not know if Padmavajra was describing an actual practice in which he or other Buddhist yogis engaged at the time, it is likely at the very least that some practitioners might have tried it after his text was written. Such a figure, who by necessity would be very familiar with Śaiva texts, would be the exact sort of tradent who would be able to draw from Śaiva sources while compiling a scripture. As we will see, such tradents, who themselves were masquerading as Śaiva, might very well have come up with the origin myths of the Buddhist tantras that hold that they were taught by buddhas masquerading as Śaiva deities, who are thus imagined as engaging in the very behavior in which these intrepid hybrid Śaiva-Buddhist yogis were preoccupied.

1.5 Tantric Origin Myths

1.5.1 Myths of Rediscovery

There is other evidence connecting the rise of Buddhist tantric traditions with the Nālandā Monastery. One of the earliest accounts of the origin of new tantric textual collections is preserved in Yijing's (義淨) *Records of Eminent Monks of the Great Tang Who Sought the Dharma in the Western Regions* (大唐西域求法高僧傳). In this collection of short biographies, Yijing recounts the story of a Chinese monk named Daolin (道琳), who traveled to India during the seventh century, prior to Yijing's arrival there in 671 CE. While in India, Daolin studied an esoteric Buddhist text, the *Wizardry Collection* (*vidyādharapiṭaka*). Yijing relates Daolin's sojourn in India as follows:

> The Dharma Master Daolin was a native of Jiang-ling in Jing-zhou.[38] His Sanskrit name was Śīlaprabha, which means "Light of Discipline." Before coming of age,[39] he put on the robe and renounced the world. When he reached adulthood, he called on his friends in search of the truth. He sought the treasury of the Vinaya and an explanation of the lustrous pearl that is the discipline. He sat in meditation and calmed his mind. [Recognizing that things are] naturally empty, pure, and refined, he maintained incorruptible chastity. He bathed in the azure spring and scoured the jade fountain with his quiet determination, and he was nourished with spiritual power. He always sat and did not lie down, ate once a day, and was thoroughly honest.
>
> Later he was saddened [by the fact that as] the great Teachings spread east many sutras had been recorded, but few of the teachings on meditation had made it, and there had been some loss in the Vinaya canon. Consequently, he desired to travel and seek out their source, to journey far to the Western Countries. So staff [in hand], risking death, he set out on a boat for the southern deeps. Passing the bronze pillar he arrived at Sri Lanka. They passed through Kaliṅga and the Land of the Naked People.[40] The king there treated him with respect and extended to him the highest degree of generosity. After a few years he reached Tāmralipti in East India. He lived there for three years studying Sanskrit. Then he gave up serious undertakings, studying all of the divisions [of knowledge]. The discipline, however, [involves] not only study but also meditation on wisdom. Now there also happens to be the *Wizardry Collection* of erotic pleasures. Later in Central India he observed an excellent ritual, the rite of Awakening on the Adamantine Throne.

Subsequently he reached Nālandā Monastery, where he studied the Mahāyāna treatises. He fixed his mind and resided there, and staying a few years. He went to Gṛdhrakuṭa Peak and Yaṣṭivana Monastery. Exerting himself to the upmost, he raised his head, exhibiting total sincerity. Then he went to Southern India in search of the profound arts. He spent a year in Lāṭa in West India practicing.[41] Standing before the divine altar he received again the spell (*vidyā*). It says in the treatise that there are [texts] that contain the *vidyā*, called in Sanskrit the *vidyādharapiṭaka. Vidyā* means "that which illumines," and *dhara* "to hold," *piṭaka* means a "treasury." One could say that it is the treasury which contains the spells.

Moreover, traditionally it is said that the *Wizardry Collection* in Sanskrit consisted of one hundred thousand stanzas, which in Chinese translation would amount to three hundred fascicles. Nowadays, if you search for [these texts] it is evident that many have been lost and few are complete. After the death of the great sage, Ārya Nāgārjuna bodhisattva in particular mastered them. At that time, he had a disciple named Nanda who was bright, very learned, and thoroughly steeped in this text. He spent twelve years in West India, and single mindedly practiced the spells, whereupon he was experienced [supernormal] effects. Whenever it was mealtime, his food descended from space. Also, once while reciting spells he prayed for a wish-fulfilling vase, which he obtained after a little while. And within the jar he found a scripture, which delighted him. But since he failed to bind his vase with a spell, it disappeared. The Dharma Master Nanda, fearing that the spells would be scattered and lost, gathered them together to form a single compilation of about twelve thousand stanzas. Within each stanza he paired the text for the spell with a gesture (*mudrā*). But although the letters and words [of this text] are the same [as those of ordinary writing], their meaning and usage are in fact different. There is actually no way that these can be understood without receiving the oral transmission. Later the

> commentator Master Dignāga saw that it was written so artfully that [it required] the intelligence of extraordinary people, since its import reached the limit of the sensible. Clasping the book he sighed, saying, "Had this sage applied his intellect to the science of reasoning (*hetuvidyā*), what would there have been for me [to do]?" From this it is evident that the wise recognize their own capacity, while fools are blind to the differences between themselves and others!
>
> This *Wizardry Collection* has not yet been transmitted to the East, and Daolin was deeply impressed by its subtleties. For the *Wizardry Collection* says that "Only with the spells may one access the way of ascending into the heavens, riding a dragon, controlling one hundred spirits, or benefiting sentient beings."[42] When I, Yijing, was at Nālandā, I repeatedly tried to enter the mandala, but my hopes were vain as I was unable to produce sufficient merit, which shattered my aspiration to propagate these extraordinary teachings.
>
> Daolin then turned from the Western regions and proceeded to North India. He visited Kashmir and then entered the land of Udyāna to inquire about meditation methods and seek wisdom (*prajñā*).[43]

This passage is remarkable for many reasons. It seems to confirm that not only was Nālandā an early center for tantric Buddhist practice in seventh-century India but that the practice was also found in several other regions, such as Lāṭa in western India, where he spent a year engaged in tantric practice. The text's indication that after studying there, Daolin proceeded north to Kashmir and Udyāna, the Swat Valley in what is now Pakistan, is interesting in that both would later be major sites for tantric Buddhist practice in India, the latter being associated with the great adepts Indrabhūti and Padmasambhava.

Yijing introduces the text as the "*Wizardry Collection* of erotic pleasures," which points to the transgressive nature of tantric practice from a very early stage of its development. While the text does not clarify what it means by this, it seems to foreshadow the importance of sexual practices in many of the later tantric traditions.

Yijing's biography of Daolin contains what is also likely the earliest origin myth for a tantric tradition. This origin myth is remarkable on many grounds. As is typically the case, it displaces the origin of the text to the distant past. Unlike many myths, however, it does not discuss its actual origin or name the buddha who revealed it, although it implies that it was taught by the "great sage" Śākyamuni. It also claims that it was practiced by the famous Mahāyāna Buddhist philosopher Nāgārjuna, who lived circa the second to third centuries CE. The attribution of the text to Nāgārjuna is certainly no accident. This choice was almost surely inspired by his fame in Mahāyāna circles, particularly his role in the "rediscovery" of the Perfection of Wisdom (*prajñāpāramitā*) scriptural collection.[44] In a myth of the rediscovery of a tantric scripture, this choice makes great sense.

The name of the text also implies canonical status. The term *piṭaka,* literally meaning "basket," was long used by Buddhists to refer to a collection of scriptures, as used in the expression *tripiṭaka,* "Three Baskets," to refer to the Buddhist canon.[45] The canon was thus understood to be tripartite, consisting of discourses attributed to the Buddha (*sūtra*), teachings on monastic discipline also attributed to him (*vinaya*), and scholastic works (*abhidharma*). The tradents of this work thus proposed a fourth division of the canon, the *Wizardry Collection,* which would be the collection of tantric works. This was evidently not a radical claim; one Buddhist tradition, the Dhammagutta, compiled a *vidyādharapiṭaka* as a division of their canon.[46] The text Daolin encountered could very well have been the esoteric lore collection compiled by members of this tradition or another related tradition. The term *vidyādhara* is an important term in tantric traditions. Literally translated as "spell holder," it is perhaps best translated as "wizard," since these beings, like the wizards of Western folklore or Daoist immortals (仙), were thought to be immortal and removed from the mortal world of cyclic existence, yet capable of intervening in it.

While a single text of 12,000 stanzas is hardly sufficient to constitute in and of itself a scriptural collection, the myth explains this by claiming that the original text was a massive text of 100,000 stanzas, which was lost but fortunately was revised and abridged by Nāgārjuna into the shorter text that was available when Daolin studied in India. This certainly was a convenient myth for the founders of the early tantric traditions, who cobbled their texts together from various diverse sources. The myth thus portrays the fragmentary and incomplete state of seventh-century tantric literature as not the result of it being a new tradition in its formative stages (a portrayal that would clearly be problematic for advocates of the tradition) but rather as the result of inevitable loss and decline from a prior golden age. The rapid appearance of new works was thus the rediscovery and partial restoration of this mythic, glorious canon. The number 100,000 here is aspirational; a text of this length would be massive, consisting of many volumes. There is in fact a Buddhist text of this length, the "One Hundred Thousand [Stanza] Perfection of Wisdom" *Śatasāhasrikā Prajñāpāramitā Sūtra*, which set the standard for massive Buddhist texts.

This narrative indicates that secrecy was a feature of tantric Buddhist from very early on in its development. Yijing provided eyewitness testimony that access to the mandala, the premier site of tantric practice, at Nālandā was not open but was restricted to those deemed "worthy," and his account of the *Wizardry Collection* shows that it exhibited the textual esotericism that is typical of the genre of tantras. That is, this literature often uses coded language, such that the "meaning and usage" of words in the text differ from ordinary, conventional usage, and that oral commentary from a master is needed to understand it. This commentary would also entail matching the written text to elements of ritual practice, such as the deployment of ritual gestures (*mudrā*). Like many texts that are practice oriented, it is often not enough to just read the text; one also needs practical instruction in the rituals that are obliquely described therein.

This textual esotericism is a distinctive feature of the tantras, including the oldest Buddhist tantra, the "Awakening of Mahāvairocanā" *Mahāvairocanābhisaṃbodhi Tantra*. The Japanese Buddhist master Kūkai (空海, 774–835) was inspired to go to China for further study when he encountered a copy of the Chinese translation of this work but was unable to makes sense of its ritual passages.[47] Many of the elements of the origin myth related by Yijing are repeated by Kūkai in his early ninth-century "Introduction to the Mahāvairocana Sūtra" (*Dainichikyō-kaidai*, 大日經開題),[48] as follows:

> Overall this sutra has three texts. The first, the eternal text that accords with reality (法爾常恆本), is the dharma mandala of all buddhas. The second, the manifest extensive text (分流廣本), is the sutra of one hundred thousand stanzas disseminated by Nāgārjuna. The third is the abbreviated text (略本) of just over three thousand stanzas. While this sutra has three thousand stanzas in seven fascicles, in its brevity, however, it remains true to the extensive [text], expressing much with few [words]. A single word contains infinite import, and a single dot encases principles as numerous as atoms. Why then could the hundred-syllable wheel (百字字輪, *śatākṣaracakra*) not completely express this sutra? What principles are not manifest in its more than three thousand stanzas? The extensive and abbreviated [texts], though different, are of identical import.[49]

Here we see the elaboration of the myth into a threefold structure of textual manifestation and decay. Kūkai adds an additional level of textuality, an ultimate level of an eternal, transmundane text, which arguably is a Buddhist transformation of Vedic strategies of textual legitimation.[50] This manifested in history as a massive ur-text, here again brought to light by Nāgārjuna. And lastly, the final manifestation is the more modest text that is available at the present time. While this text is arguably the result of a process of degeneration, Kūkai employs what might be termed a tantric philosophy of language to defend the shorter version of the text. If a single word possesses infinite signification, then clearly the depths of even the short version of the scripture can never be fully plumbed.[51]

Tantric Buddhism rapidly developed in the late seventh and early eighth centuries, with the production or discovery of many more tantras. Vajrabuddhi,[52] a south Indian monk who studied at Nalandā Monastery, journeyed to China via the ocean route, arriving in southern China in 719 CE.[53] He brought with him an account of a collection of eighteen esoteric scriptures, called the "Assembly of the Eighteen Adamantine Pinnacle Yoga Scriptures" (金剛頂經瑜伽十八會), which reportedly amounted to 100,000 stanzas, a claim that is not preposterous for what is in effect a substantial textual collection.[54] Vajrabuddhi reported that these scriptures were evidently discovered within an iron stūpa, or reliquary monument, by Nāgārjuna, a figure who is central to many Mahāyāna textual discovery legends, including the one related by Yijing as discussed above. Amoghavajra related the story of the massive text interred in the reliquary monument and later discovered there by Nāgārjuna:

> The one-hundred-thousand-verse text is, moreover, just the outline of the great treasury scripture of the bodhisattvas, [and] this great scripture is the scripture the teacher (*ācārya*, that is, Vajrabuddhi) spoke of bringing [here]. Broad and long like a bed, and four or five feet thick, it has innumerable verses. It was enclosed in an iron stūpa in south India and during several hundred years after the Buddha's extinction, no one was able to open the stūpa [because] iron gates and locks were used to secure it.[55]

The authors of this work present a remarkable image of a massive text: the size of a bed and four- to five-feet thick. At the root of this story is the fact that Buddhists often interred scriptures in reliquary mounds. As records of the Buddha's teaching, they were considered "reality body" *dharmakāya* relics of the Buddha and sometimes interred in place of corporeal (*rūpakāya*) relics, although this text magnifies this into a massive, hidden text. The text goes on to relate that a "great worthy," later identified with Nāgārjuna, recovered this text using magical practices and extracted from it the hundred-thousand stanza Adamantine Pinnacle collection, which Vajrabuddhi claims to have brought from India, but which he lost enroute when his boat was hit by a typhoon, leaving him with an abbreviated version of the collection.[56]

Interestingly, there are multiple accounts of an eighth-century collection of eighteen tantras. Tibetan sources also record a collection of eighteen "Great Yoga" (*mahāyoga*) tantras dating from the same era of time. There is also substantial overlap between the Adamantine Pinnacle collection documented by Vajrabuddhi's disciple Amoghavajra, and Tibetan records of the Mahāyoga tantra collection.[57] Probably the earliest reference to the latter source is found in the *Commentary on the Method of the Perfection of Wisdom in 150 Stanzas* (**Prajñāpāramitānayaśatapañcāśatkāṭīkā, 'phags pa shes rab kyi pha rol tu phyin pa tshul brgya lnga bcu pa'i 'grel pa*), a commentary on one of the esoteric sutras, composed circa 800 CE by Jñānamitrā. At the opening of the commentary, he recounts an origin myth for this collection, as follows:

> Regarding the history of this scripture, when the Buddha had previously lived for eighty years in the human world, there was not yet in the human world of Jambudvīpa anyone who was a suitable vessel for practice on the paths of the "Union of All Buddhas" *Sarvabuddhasamāyoga*, "Esoteric Community" *Guhyasamāja* [tantras], and so forth. These scriptures existed at that time in Cāturmahārājakāyika, Trāyastriṃśa, Tuṣita [heavens], etc.,

> where there were gods and fortunate bodhisattvas who were suitable vessels. Later, after the Buddha's complete cessation (*parinirvāṇa*), there were some persons in the retinue of King Indrabhūti of Zahor who had faith in the miraculous Dharma, who were destined for the practice of this vehicle and who were suitable vessels [for this]. The eighteen classes [of scripture] such as the *Union of All Buddhas* thus came to Zahor through the blessings of Vajrapāṇi.[58]

Jñānamitrā attributes these works to Śākyamuni Buddha, who evidently taught them to the gods in heaven but not to humans on earth, due to the latter lacking any "suitable vessels" for their practice. "Suitable vessel" is a Buddhist term that refers to those who have the proper training and prior experience, enabling them to understand and put into practice a teaching. The first person on earth to be such a suitable vessel was King Indrabhūti, a famous figure in Buddhist legend who is usually associated with the region of Oḍiyāna, or the Swat Valley, in the Northwest, the region to which the Tibetan placename Zahor here refers.[59] His reception of these works was made possible by "the blessings of Vajrapāṇi," an extremely important bodhisattva who plays a major role in many tantras as the interlocutor of the Buddha, whose questions prompt the teaching. This short narrative thus implies a process of revelation, of tantras being divulged to humans at preordained times by awakened or awakening beings. It also appears to be the earliest known instance of a narrative of the revelation of tantras to a king. In the Tibetan context, there are many variations of this myth, focusing on a legendary figure known as King Dza, to whom Vajrapāṇi also imparted tantric teachings. This narrative played an important role in the Nyingma school of Tibetan Buddhism.[60]

Narratives of revelation of tantric texts became relatively common as tantric traditions developed over time. Many of the great adepts who are key figures in the early dissemination of the tantras reputedly received their texts via revelation by divine figures such as Vajrapāṇi and Vajradhara. Often such revelation required travel to inaccessible realms, following the example of Nāgārjuna's descent to the subaquatic realm of the Serpent Deities (*nāga*) to recover the *Prajñāpāramitā Sūtra*s or his penetration into the iron reliquary monument to reveal tantras hidden there, as discussed above.

Such feats were repeated by some of the later adepts. The "Kiss Drop" *Sampuṭatilaka Tantra* was recovered by the great adept Kāṇha from the ḍākinī Bhadri in "Pretapuri," somewhere on the Tibetan plateau.[61] A particular striking example of such recovery is relayed in the origin myths of the "Black Bane of Death" *Kṛṣṇayamāri Tantra*. These accounts claim that Lalitavajra traveled to Oḍiyāna, where the ḍākinīs gave him temporary access to a treasury of tantras, permitting him to "withdraw" as many texts as he could memorize in seven days. He was able to memorize during this time the *Kṛṣṇayamāri Tantra* and several other texts.[62]

As the number of tantras grew, and as most made similar claims regarding their revelation by awakened beings and/or derivation from amazingly large source texts, advocates for some traditions began making even more dramatic claims regarding their tradition's origin, perhaps to bolster its prestige. For example, one of the tantras included in the eighth-century lists of eighteen tantra collections was the "Ḍākinīs' Network That Unites All Buddhas" *Sarvabuddhasamāyoga-dākinījālasaṃvara Tantra*. An Indian commentator on this tantra, Indranāla, claimed that it originated in a much larger work called the "The First Buddha" *Ādibuddha Tantra*, which ups the ante on early origin claims, attributing it to a primordial buddha rather than a latecomer like Śākyamuni Buddha. Indranāla related the following account of the origin of the *Ḍākinīs' Network That Unites All Buddhas Tantra* in his "Detailed Exegesis of the Import of the Sarvabuddhasamāyogaḍākinījālasamvara Tantra" *Sarvabuddhasamāyogaḍākinījālasaṃvaratantrārthodaraṭī kā* commentary:

> Vajradhara, the embodiment of all Victors, at the beginning of the fortunate eon created the mandala, emanated by means of his compassion, in order to purify things in the animate and inanimate worlds. Thinking that he should clearly explain the import of the tantra in accordance with his previously formed intention to teach, he manifested the mandala on the peak of Mount Sumeru, in order to please his fortunate followers and deity hosts. He progressively explained the yoga of purification and so forth, in accordance with the Great *Āditantra*, etc.[63]

Indranāla supported his claim that the *Sarvabuddhasamāyoga Tantra* was derived from a larger root text by providing quotations from it.[64] He did so shortly after relating the origin of the work, as follows:

> The *Ādibuddha Tantra* states: "The meaning of the mantra and tantra is very hard to understand, but it is realized with recourse to the explanatory tantras such as the ancillary [tantras], etc. Seeking out the lineage instructions, one should give rise to, settle, and realize a vast expanse of certainty. The intelligent beings of the future will take delight in the meditation manuals (*sādhana*) and the abbreviated commentaries, so to begin with they were condensed at my command: uphold them reverentially so that they will last long."[65]

The quoted passage is a prophesy, explaining how beings of future eons, who will have much shorter life spans, will out of necessity prefer much shorter works, thus necessitating their condensation, as the primordial buddha wisely realized. Since only the shorter texts survive, we have no way to confirm that such texts actually existed but have to take this on faith if so inclined.

While the movement in the myths is from a past full of massive tantras to a present in which only their abbreviated remnants survive, looking diachronically, one can see an inflationary trend, in which claims are made for increasingly grandiose source scriptures. This was likely motivated by one-upmanship, a desire to exceed claims made for rival traditions. For example, the "Supreme Bliss of the Wheels" *Cakrasaṃvara Tantra* is a relatively short work of only about 700 Sanskrit stanzas, for which reason it is also called the "Supreme Bliss Light" *Laghusaṃvara Tantra*. It was composed circa the ninth century.[66] It became the basis of a popular tradition in India, and, as a result, there were new scriptures composed that expanded on this short and cryptic work that were deemed "explanatory tantras," *vyākhyātantra*, being exegetical by nature. The consensus among the commentators was that it was derived from a much larger source text, variously named the "Discourse" (*abhidhāna*) or "Sky-like" (*khasama*) tantra. Following what was by the ninth century a venerable pattern, the length of this source text was deemed to be 100,000 stanzas.

Some sources inflated the size of the source text. The "Ocean of Warlocks" *Ḍākārṇava Tantra*, an explanatory tantra of the *Cakrasaṃvara Tantra* likely dating to the tenth century, says the following regarding the latter's derivation: "Thus the *Supreme Bliss Light* was condensed from the *Discourse* of three hundred thousand [stanzas], and its chapters accord with [the fifty letters], beginning with *a* and ending with *kṣa*."[67] However, an eleventh-century commentator on the *Laghusaṃvara Tantra*, Vīravajra, took one-upmanship to an extreme level. Commenting on text in the first chapter of the text, "more lofty than the lofty" (*uttarād api cottaraṃ*), he took the word "lofty" (*uttara*) as a reference to a textual genre, the *uttaratantra* or "appendix tantra," a tantra that is deemed to serve as an appendix to a typically larger root tantra text. He commented as follows: "Why is the appendix also [derived] from an appendix? There is the Root Tantra of one hundred thousand chapters, and subsequent to it is the one hundred thousand stanza *Skylike [Tantra]*, and the fifty-one chaptered *Supreme Bliss Light* is the subsequent appendix."[68] Here the expansion reaches an staggering level; a text of 100,000 chapters would be inconceivably large. Here Vīravajra seeks to astound the reader with the vision of the expansive canon that existed either in the distant past or in alternate spheres of reality, such as the treasury of tantras protected by the ḍākinīs in a celestial realm.

Over time there was an increase in tantric literature, with explosive growth in the seventh through ninth centuries followed by gradual decline in the subsequent centuries until Buddhism disappeared from most of South Asia. Tantric Buddhists, however, envisioned a golden age replete with massive tantras followed by gradual loss and decline. This accorded with the general Indian cosmology envisioning a golden age, when people enjoyed very long lifespans replete with sensual enjoyment, followed by a gradual decline through three subsequent eras, in which both lifespan and quality of life diminish, much like the Greek system of the four ages correlated to metals, gold, silver, bronze, and iron, of decreasing value, while the last two evoke conflict. The Indian system is almost identical, but rather than being equated to metals, they were equated to the throws in the ever-popular game of chance, dice. Accordingly, the golden age is named after the best or "perfect" (*kṛta*) throw, in which one scores the best possible score of four. Accordingly, it is followed by the "triples" (*tretā*) age, and then by the "doubles" (*dvāpara*). The final age is named after the worst possible throw, "snake eyes" (*kali*). The latter age is characterized by short life spans and low quality of life due to rampant disease, poverty, and conflict, as well as the decline of Buddhism and righteousness (*dharma*) in general. Needless to say, Buddhists typically envisioned themselves as suffering in the end time, and they thus imagined that religion too was in a state of decline, a faint shadow of the glories of the golden age, even if the "fast track" of tantra is the tradition best suited to the short life spans of denizens of the Snake Eye Age.

For example, Tāranātha reported that there was a tradition that the *Tārā Tantra* underwent a gradual diminishment over the course of the four ages, starting out as a 10 million stanza text

(!) in the Perfect Age, condensed into a 600,000-stanza text during the Triples Age, further condensed to 12,000 stanzas during the Doubles Age, and finally resulting in a 1,000-stanza verse text during the current Snake Eye Age.[69] Such myths offered solace, portraying tantric Buddhism as a venerable tradition that simply adapted as times changed. The alternative view, that it was a new tradition developed in response to changing times, would not have been acceptable in the religiously conservative milieu of early medieval India.

1.5.2 Śaiva Conversion Myths

There is another major genre of tantric Buddhist origin myths, which we might term "conversion myths" since they feature the founding figure, an awakened buddha, converting Śaiva Hindu deities to Buddhism. These myths address a central problem faced by early tantric Buddhists: they were borrowing extensively (both texts and actual ritual practices) from rival Śaiva groups, and this borrowing was recognized and called out by intragroup rivals, such as the conservative Buddhist monks in Orissa who called out the monks of Nālandā for following "heretical Kāpālika" teachings, as discussed in section 1.4. The conversion myths represent an attempt to explain this discomfiting appearance of appropriation from rival groups by explaining it as the skillful means of an awakened being. Both evidence for such borrowing and the conversion myths that attempt to account for it are found in the earliest strata of tantric Buddhist literature.

Here we might recall Dharmakīrti's mention of non-Buddhist *ḍākinī tantra*s circa the late sixth or early seventh century. This was probably the earliest mention in Buddhist literature of this genre of texts. However, there are earlier mentions of the beings known as *ḍākinī*s. This term is difficult to translate, and probably the closest English term that encompasses the same scope of associations is the term "witch." Ḍākinis are female; the related male term, *ḍāka*, which occurs much less often, might be translated as "warlock." While female *ḍākinīs* could evidently be seen as either human or nonhuman, in which case they might be classified as a type of evil spirit. However, in later tantric Buddhist literature they become lionized as awakened deities. The English term "witch," however, works well, with all its negative associations, which the ḍākinīs of Indian mythology share. But the term was appropriated and given positive associations by Buddhists, much as the English term "witch" has been taken up as a positive marker of religious identity by some practitioners of neopagan religions.[70]

Earlier mentions of ḍākinīs in Buddhist literature presented them as nefarious evildoers. For example, the "Descent to Laṅkā" *Laṅkāvatāra Sūtra,* a Mahāyāna scripture composed in India during the fourth century, makes the following warning in its eighth chapter about meat eating: "The [carnivore] is born again and again as one who is ill-smelling, contemptuous, and insane among the families of the caṇḍāla, the pukkasa, and among the ḍomba. From the womb of a ḍākinī he will be born into a carnivorous family, and then into the womb of a rākṣasī and a cat; he belongs to the lowest class of men."[71] Here carnivores are threatened with rebirth in lower caste groups, which makes sense in the logic of the Indian caste system, which associates "purity" with the higher castes and allegedly impure activities, such as meat eating, with lower castes. They are also threatened with rebirth in the wombs of a ḍākinī "witch" and a *rākṣasī* "demon girl"; both here appear to be evil spirits renowned for their desire to eat human flesh. Lastly, one ends up in the womb of an obligate carnivore, a cat, fully reaping the karmic consequences of one's dietary proclivity.

Given the lowly portrayal of the ḍākinī in Buddhist texts such as the *Laṅkāvatāra Sūtra,* it is interesting to note that they make a small appearance in one of the earliest Buddhist tantras, the "Awakening of Mahāvairocana" *Mahāvairocanābhisambodhi Tantra.* The fourth chapter of this work, entitled the "General Mantra Treasury," contains a long list of mantras associated with various classes of nonhuman entities, including gods, titans (*asura*), and a host of nonhuman spirits known for their fondness for human flesh, such as the *rākṣasa* "demons," *yakṣa* "dryads," and *piśāca* "goblins" in addition to the ḍākinīs. This ḍākinī mantra is simply named and listed; it is *hrī haḥ*. Buddhist mantras are "spells," that is, they are carefully structured verbal utterances recited in conjunction with ritual practices to produce a desired magical effect. In the *Awakening of Mahāvairocana Tantra*, these are presented devoid of any contextualization, with no explanation of their history, ritual use, or the magical effects of their successful application.[72] This lack of contextualization is common in esoteric Buddhist literature, which typically describes practice elements in a sufficiently cryptic way to prevent one from putting them into practice through reading the text alone. The obscurity of this text was, as noted above, what motivated Kūkai to travel to China to gain the instruction that he needed to put the text into practice.

The Indian master Śubhakarasiṃha (善无畏, 637–735) and his Chinese disciple Yixing (一行, 683–727) addressed this lacuna in their extensive *Running Commentary on the Awakening of Mahāvairocana Sūtra* (大 畏 盧 遮 那 成 佛 經 疏), which they composed in the early eighth century in Chang-an, China.[73] In this work they relate a fascinating myth concerning the revelation of the ḍākinī mantra, which occurs as follows:

> Next is the *ḍākinī-mantra*. There are those in the world who are well-versed in this technique, and are practitioners of Īśvara's esoteric lore (*vidyā*, 咒 術), who are able to know when a person's life is about to end. Knowing this six months in advance, they immediately apply the spell to extract a person's heart and eat it. It turns out that within the human body there is a concretion, which is thus called human concretion (人 黃). It is like the concretion found in cattle.[74] One who is able to eat it attains the greatest powers (*siddhi*, 成 就), [such as] circling the world in one

day, obtaining anything which one desires, and being able to control people in various ways. If they have an enemy, they can use this spell to punish him, causing extreme sickness and suffering. However, this method cannot kill people. Should they follow this self-devised method, they know when a person is to die six months in advance. Knowing this, they use this spell to extract his heart. Although they take his heart, there is [another] procedure, [whereby] they must replace his heart with something else. [Thereby] this person's life does not [prematurely] end. When he reaches his time of natural death, then [the heart simulacrum] malfunctions.

Their chief was the dryad (*yakṣa*) Maheśvara, who worldly people say is the ultimate [god]. They were subject to Mahākāla, the god called the "Great Black One" (大黑). Vairocana, employing the method of Conquering the Triple World (*trailokyavijaya*)[75] and wanting to exterminate them, transformed himself into Mahākāla, exceeding him in an immeasurable manifestation. His body smeared with ashes in a desolate place, he summoned with his magical art all the *ḍākinī*s, who had all of the magical powers [such as] flying, walking on water and being completely unhindered. He upbraided them, saying: "Since you alone always devour people, now I will eat you!" Then he swallowed them, but did not allow them to die. Once they had submitted, he released them, completely forbidding them to [eat] flesh. They spoke to the Buddha saying, "We presently eat flesh to survive. How can we sustain ourselves now?" The Buddha said, "I will permit you to eat the hearts of dead people." They said, "When a man is about to die, the great dryads (*mahāyakṣa*) and so forth know that his life is exhausted, and they race there to eat him, so how can we get [our share]?" The Buddha said, "I will teach you the mantra procedures and gestures (*mudrā*). You will be able to know six months before someone dies, and knowing this, you should protect him with this method, so he will not fear being injured. When his life has expired, then you can seize and eat [his heart]." In this way, they were gradually induced to embark upon the path. Thus there is this mantra, *hrī haḥ*, which removes the taint of heretical practices.[76]

Features of this text are also found in other Buddhist conversion myths worthy of note. First, the chief rivals of the Buddhists for patronage, the Śaivas, are portrayed as immoral. In this case, the Śaiva ḍākinīs are portrayed as murderous cannibals, who ritually kill those whose bodies hold the valuable concretion so they might consume it and thereby attain supernatural powers. It is worth noting that Iśvara or Śiva is belittled as well; Śubhakarasiṃha downplays the claim that he is the ultimate god, referring to him instead as a "dryad," or *yakṣa,* a demigod of dubious moral character. Second, the Buddhist deity *assumes Śaiva guise* to subdue them. This is a very important detail as it is likely a mythical explanation for Buddhist adoption of Śaiva iconography and ritual practices. Here Vairocana transforms into Mahākāla, a fierce manifestation of Śiva particularly associated with Śaiva tantric traditions. While his motivation is supposedly compassionate, he assumes not only the fierce appearance but also the violent behavior of those he is trying to discipline. To stop the ḍākinīs from consuming people, he consumes them, stopping short of killing them. Lastly, once they are intimidated, the Buddha convinced them to modify their practices, such that they consume the power substance without prematurely killing people. This represents an appropriation and adaptation of a violent Śaiva ritual, one that modifies it so actual killing is avoided, without eliminating the violent imagery of the practice.

In this commentary, Śubhakarasiṃha and Yixing mention "the method of Conquering the Triple World," which is a reference to another early tantric work, the "Compendium of the Realities of All Tathāgatas" *Sarvatathāgata-tattvasaṃgraha-nāma–Mahayana-Sūtra,* an esoteric sutra that was included in the Adamantine Pinnacle collection. This work contains a detailed conversion myth that was extremely influential, serving as the paradigm for other myths of this type that were developed later. It is also a very long myth that would take up many pages in translation.[77] Fortunately, the tenth-century scholar Indrabhūti, named after the eighth-century king of Oḍiyāna, includes a summary of this myth in his *Commentary on the Glorious Binding of the Wheels King of Tantras Called the Assembly of Supreme Bliss,* as follows:

> To summarize, in the beginning—in accordance with the previous origination of the wheel of wisdom the Buddha created the palace of the sphere of reality in the expanse of pure wisdom. From the inseparable sphere of the reality body and wisdom inseparable, there was the glorious communal enjoyment body, Mahāvajradhara in Akaniṣṭha, the realm of great happiness. There dwell changelessly, through the method of inseparability, measureless great bodhisattvas of the ninth stage goddesses who are bodhisattvas, and tathāgatas. The lustful ones who are to be disciplined, and their principle teacher, Mahādeva, came to the palace atop Mt. Sumeru, and all of these evil ones were disciplined. The Tathāgata Mahāvajradhara himself, and the Reverend Vajrapāṇi who is inseparable from him, disciplined them as described in the *Śrī Tattvasaṃgraha.*
>
> Vajrapāṇi asked Vajradhara, "Lord, How should I proceed with the criminal sentient beings such as Mahādeva and so forth, who have not been peacefully trained by all Tathāgatas?" Then the Lord Vairocana, through the blessing of all tathāgatas, settled into the concentration called the "Gnostic Vajra of the Great Skillful Means of All Tathāgatas." As soon as he was equipoised, the atoms of all of the spheres of the tathāgatas burst forth, and they assembled on the peak of Mt. Sumeru as a palace made of vajras and precious jewels. It was perceived in the same way by all of the tathāgatas and resided in the curl of hair at the heart of the Lord Vairocana. As soon as he uttered [the syllable] *hūṃ*, luminous light from the heart of Vajrapāṇi pervaded all of the three realms.

The great god Mahādeva, and so forth, surrounded by a great host of [beings] who dwelt everywhere, in all of the realms, far-flung clouds and oceans of the world,[78] were summoned by the iron goad of the commitment of all tathāgatas, and gathered there. All the lords of the three worlds such as Mahādeva surrounded the palace [on Mt. Sumeru], aghast with their jaws dropping, muttering anxious words, and seeking refuge in Vajrapāṇi. The god known as Mahādeva fell to the ground unconscious.

There Vajrapāṇi called out to all the gods, saying, "Listen to my command! If you all want to live, then take refuge in Buddha, Dharma, and Sangha!"

Then they replied, "We go for refuge in the Buddha, Dharma, and Sangha, together with our consort host." Being pacified, those sentient beings who did not endeavor to turn away from evil were blessed by being annihilated.

Then the Lord said to the Great Bodhisattva Vajrapāṇi, "Great Bodhisattva, if we do not reanimate this Maheśvara or Mahādeva, there will be no point in his striving to listen with a diminished life-force. But if we revive him, even he could become a good person!"

Thinking "So be it!" Vajrapāṇi spoke the essence mantra for reviving the dead, which is: *Oṃ vajrāyur jñāna bhāṃ*. As Glorious Vajrapāṇi uttered these adamantine words, the essence mantra blazed upon the soles of his feet. To purify them, he pressed Mahādeva with his left foot, and the goddess Umādevī with his right. Then Mahādeva, through being touched by the sole of Vajrapāṇi's foot, experienced the bliss of the many concentrations (*samādhi*), spells (*dhāraṇī*), and doors of liberation of all the tathāgatas. Offering up his body at the feet of Vajrapāṇi, Mahādeva passed beyond numerous world systems, as

> many as there are grains of sand in thirty-two Gaṅgā rivers, or as there are atoms in a world system, and he became a buddha known as Soundless Lord of Ashes (*Bhasmeśvaranirghoṣa*) in the world system called Ash Parasol (*Bhasmacchatrā*). Due to this the body of Mahādeva exclaimed: "Ah! The wisdom of awakening of all the buddhas is indeed unexcelled! I have been established in nirvana through being pressed with the mantric words!"
>
> Then that buddha created a manifestation which entered into the body of Mahādeva, who then said, "Ah! What a wonder is the secret wisdom and bliss of all buddhas, on account of which this corpse has returned to the world of the living!" Then the body of Mahādeva was revived and blessed, for the sake of all the beings of this world, so that all the criminals would be disciplined. He was established as the crown prince in Jambudvīpa.
>
> After Vajrapāṇi pressed down the head of Mahādeva, he had a crescent moon on the left side of his dreadlocks. All the tathāgatas gave him a trident to bear and bestowed the adamantine name consecration [calling him] "Excellent Adamantine Spell" (*Vajravidyottama*). Then Vajravidyottama Bodhisattva, circling with his blazing vajra trident like a whirling firebrand, worshipped them with an offering of dance and said, "Ah! Buddhahood is attained through contact with the supreme foot due to the unexcelled spirit of awakening of all buddhas!"[79]

This myth features Vajrapāṇi, the fierce *yakṣa* guardian of the Buddha, who was gradually elevated to a lofty position in the Vajrayāna.[80] He is depicted as possessing cosmic mastery in the following passage in the "Supremely Wonderful Sovereign Yoginītantra called the Gnostic Drop" *Jñānatilaka-yoginītantrarāja-paramamahādbhuta*:

> Then the Lady offered the ambrosial fluid of her lower lip and made offerings of solar and lunar flowers. When the Lord was

> satisfied, she asked the following: "Hey Lord, who will teach this truly secret Tantra in the future to fortunate sentient beings?"
>
> The Lord replied, "It will be taught by the glorious sovereign Vajrapāṇi."
>
> The Lady asked, "You, Lord, have bestowed the marvelous descent of gnostic ambrosia. Tell me, oh King of Knowledge, Lord of Sovereign Might, what is the origin of the great sovereign Vajrapāṇi?"
>
> The Lord replied, "Listen well, Lady, to that which you have requested. The great sovereign Vajrapāṇi is the lord of all Vajradharas, and is the cause of the creation and destruction of infinite worlds and realms. There is nothing which arises apart from him, the self-existing, supreme lord. Vajrapāṇi, who has the twelve gnoses, is unoriginated. At the top the five tathāgatas arose on the five mountain peaks, and at the bottom [arose] the five great elements. In the middle the six realms of living beings developed.[81] In order to preserve all views, he ranges in a variety of forms. He sometimes takes on the form of a Vajradhara, Buddha, Heruka, Tathāgata or Bodhisattva. Sometimes he takes on the semblance of the audience, speaker, reader or author of the tantras and treatises (*śāstra*). [His forms] are too numerous to state, as many as are needed. This is the teaching on the sovereign Vajrapāṇi."[82]

Vajrapāṇi's role as the Buddhist tough guy who subdues evildoers stems from his earlier role as the Buddha's protector and bodyguard. He is depicted in the *Mūlasarvāstavāda,* a text compiled during the early centuries of the common era,[83] as subduing the Nāga Apalāla.[84] This myth was recounted by the Chinese pilgrim Faxian (法显, 337–c. 422), who journeyed in India and Central Asia from 399 to 414 CE.[85] He reported that the conversion took place in Oḍiyāna in Northwest India, a region later associated with Tantric traditions.[86]

Buddhist deities such as Vajrapāṇi are often aggrandized in the tantras; in the "Gnostic Drop" tantra just quoted he is given the title "Lord" (*īśvara*), which is used in Hindu sources either for Śiva or the supreme creator deity, and is likewise granted the divine roles of creating and destroying the universe; to strengthen the notion of his supremacy, he is granted the grandiose title of "self-existing supreme lord," which evokes the discourse found in monotheistic traditions, such as Śaiva Hinduism. The Hindu deities being supplanted by their Buddhist rivals are, not surprisingly, often demonized. In the case of Śiva, this was not a difficult task given his morally ambiguous portrayal in Hindu mythology.[87] He is then violently converted, often by being killed and then revived, before finally submitting to the superior power of the buddhas. These myths attempt to create a hierarchy, one in which the buddhas are in the highest position, and Hindu deities are downgraded via their association with the demonic, which comprises the violent, unordered "lower level" of reality that needs to be kept in its place, and which is an inescapable counterpart to the mastery represented by the buddhas.[88] He achieves this by skillfully adopting whatever guise is needed to discipline beings.

The awakened buddha counterpart to the bodhisattva Vajrapāṇi is Vajradhara, who likewise could take a fierce form to subdue demonic deities. The eighth-century text the

> Noble Supreme Spell Great Tantra" *Āryavidyottama-mahātantra* depicts him in a way that combines both the myths of Vajrapāṇi's conversion of the *nāga* and of Śiva, as follows: "on the northern side of Mount Sumeru is the furious Mahāvajradhara who holds the great serpent deity of the teachings (*dharmanāga*). He has a vajra in his powerful hand. His left foot presses Maheśvara, and his right foot presses Umā.[89]

Buddhists justify the subjugation presented in these myths as a response to violence and other abuses on the part of the Śaivas, but it may also reflect the credibility of their threat as a competing tradition. As David White suggested, "We may attribute the uncanny parallels between the Buddhist and Hindu tantrism of this pivotal [i.e., early medieval] period to the simple fact that the two traditions were, in spite of their professed mutual animosity, so close to one another."[90] This animosity was often very stark. Some myths depict scenarios of considerable violence, such as dismemberment and/or consumption. A relatively mild example is Śubhakarasiṃha and Yixing's myth of Vairocana *qua* Mahākāla's conversion of the ḍākinī, in which he consumed them without killing them. A more graphic scenario is depicted in the "The "Glorious Esoteric Essence that Ascertains Reality," *Śrīguhyagarbhatattvaviniścaya,* a text translated into Tibetan during the imperial period, most likely during the eighth century. In this work, the fierce tantric buddha Heruka is depicted as killing Maheśvara and his band and then processing and consuming them with cannibalistic efficiency, as follows:

> Then the Lord Great Delight, existing in a [form with] nine heads, eighteen arms, and eight legs, very fiercely through the art of disciplining out of compassion in a terrible voice said: "*Hūṃ hūṃ hūṃ ha ha ha khāhi khāhi khāhi.*"
>
> Thereby Maheśvara and his great host of evildoers all lost their minds and senses. Releasing from within he drew them all out, he cut and chopped all of their limbs, drank all of their blood, and split all of their bones.[91]

The brutality of this myth is rivaled by some accounts of the subjugation of the Śaiva deity Rudra by the buddha Hayagrīva, which plays an important role in several early tantras preserved by the Nyingma school of Tibetan Buddhism.[92]

Needless to say, Śaiva Hindus took notice of the pejorative representations of their deities in tantric Buddhist conversion myths and composed their own counter-myths. One of the most notable of these is found in the "Wish Fulfilling Jewel of the Deeds of Hara," *Haracaritacintāmaṇi*, "Hara" being an alternate name for Śiva, a collection of Śaiva mythology composed by the thirteenth-century Kashmiri Śaiva Jayadratha. This collection relates a clever strategy used by Bṛhaspati, the guru of the gods, to deceive the demons, who were empowered due to their devotion to Śiva. His strategy was an old one, often found in Hindu mythology, to weaken them by tricking them into adopting a false teaching, usually Buddhism or Jainism. This version of the myth, however, makes wry note of the Buddhist adaptations of Śaiva tantric texts and practices. Bṛhaspati relates his plan as follows:

> My way of destroying their understanding will be this. I shall call this teaching Buddhist, [appropriately enough] since it will be born of [nothing more than] my intellect (*buddhiḥ*). The well-known Buddha will be conceived therein as the sole lord of the gods. Even the greatest deities will be portrayed as his chowry-bearers. Gods that I shall call Buddhist will be depicted positioned on top of Gaṇapati and others of the highest Śaiva deities. When the demons see these falsely conceived visualization-texts they will certainly make the mistake of thinking that these gods are greater than Śiva. Once these texts have been established and I have accustomed the demons to them I shall introduce Mantras modelled on [those of] the Śaiva Tantras. . . . by redacting various passages from these same scriptures . . . I shall add a worthless, concocted system of [Tantric] observances involving Mantras, ritual, and the rest. The learned [Buddhist] literature that I shall compose to define bondage and liberation will be nourished by higher reasoning of an exceptional degree of rigour. It will explain, of course, that of these two bondage includes such activities as worshipping the Liṅga; and liberation will be [defined

> as] a voidness [of self] that [once accepted] will subvert [their commitment to their] religious duties. Their sacrifices and other rituals will be opposed there; and coming to believe [though this teaching] that there is no soul they will denigrate Śiva himself [for teaching otherwise].[93]

By taking up this cleverly concocted "false" teaching, which simulates the "true" teaching but also contradicts it at key points, the "demons" who made this mistake will lose their spiritual power and can thus be easily vanquished by the gods. As both David White and Alexis Sanderson have argued, tantric Śaiva and Buddhist traditions are closely related, and their hostile portrayals of one another are a result of the fact that they were both competing for patronage with traditions that shared tremendous commonalities and relatively few but stark differences.

Tantric Buddhist textual production was most active from the seventh through the eleventh century, when the last major tantric tradition, that associated with the "Wheel of Time" *Kālacakra Tantra,* was composed.[94] However, tantric Buddhist textual production has never ceased and continues to this day, particularly in the Tibetan Nyingma tradition, in which the rediscovery of tantric texts continues unabated, and in the various communities in which tantric Buddhism is still practiced, where new commentaries and ritual manuals continue to be produced, as will be discussed in chapters 3 and 4.

2
Structure and Contents

2.1 Lineage Claims to Authority

As suggested in the previous chapter, Buddhist tantras appear to have developed from earlier Buddhist magical and ritual texts while borrowing a significant amount of content from rival Śaiva Hindu traditions. Ever since Buddhist traditions began creating collections of ritual literature, such as the *Wizardry Collection,* they attributed these works to Śākyamuni Buddha or other awakened beings. This is because to be considered canonical, a Buddhist scripture must be deemed to be "spoken by a buddha," *buddhavacana.*

To claim that a text was taught by an authority figure located far back in time is to make a lineage claim, that one and one's tradition preserve an unbroken record of teachings going back to that venerable teacher. Buddhists had long privileged the teachings of Śākyamuni Buddha and claim to have passed them down, originally through a lineage of oral recitation and memorization and later via written texts. However, this focus on lineage as the central marker of authority became even more important in India during the early medieval period, when Buddhist tantric traditions emerged.

Brajadulal Chattopadhyaya has suggested that, during the early medieval period, political authority was particularly articulated through the rhetoric of lineage and that this model emerges most noticeably in the seventh century.[1] Tantric Buddhist lineage claims accord with Jiang Wu's rule of marginality, which "stipulates that when a religious tradition is to be systematically reinvented, the provenance of the transmission, which provides the crucial link with antiquity, is always marginal, obscure, and ambiguous."[2] In

The Buddhist Tantras. David B. Gray, Oxford University Press. © Oxford University Press 2023.
DOI: 10.1093/oso/9780197623831.003.0003

other words, one will almost certainly be disappointed if one seeks to historically verify the lineage claims of newly appearing religious traditions. The statement of genealogy, regardless of whether "true" or "fabricated," should more properly be seen as a creative affirmation, a placement of one's self vis-à-vis tradition.

It is also a double-visioned emplacement, one that simultaneously places one in relation to both the transcendent and the mundane worlds, to "true reality," however conceived, and its local manifestations in the social realm. David White argued that "through their systematic genealogies, the tāntrikas at once located themselves within a cosmic chain of being and within a network of socioreligious institutions."[3] Traditions are themselves a product of such verbal acts, of a successful assertion of lineage, one which has been socially accepted and adorned with the resulting intellectual and material accoutrements.

The lineage model proliferates in decentralized political situations; lineage by its very nature is a model for the organization of relatively small groups, at the level of the extended family or clan (*kula*), so its coming to the fore may suggest the breakdown of larger, centralized authority. The development of lineage-centered religious traditions in early medieval India may reflect that period's political fragmentation. Likewise, the rapid proliferation of these traditions in Tibet was facilitated by Tibet's political decentralization.

Buddhist Tantric traditions are transmitted not so much as a part of a monastic curriculum, but as lineages imparted by an "adamantine master" (*vajrācārya*) who embodies it; these lineages are not necessarily restricted to any sectarian or institutional basis. This had the virtue of being a decentralized mode of transmission, not requiring the presence of a sizable monastic community. In the case of Tantric Buddhism, there were in fact multiple lineages, which evidently led to the formation of a decentralized community while imparting, as Daniel Gold noted, "some obvious coherence to the larger community."[4]

In the Indian context there were two types of lineage descents recognized, the spiritual and the biological, the "*nād paramparā* and *bindu paramparā:* succession through the sound (*nād*) of *mantra* and succession through physical seed; spiritual and biological lineage."[5] In contradistinction to the Hindu brahmin priests, who saw the transmission of their authority as occurring solely through biological channels, the Buddhists from the very start sought to create an alternative lineage. As Eric Reinders argued regarding Chinese monastic traditions:

> The monk's disengagement from the family was simultaneous to his placement in a new pseudo-family, in a pseudo-genetic vertical lineage with ancestors, patriarchs, and sibling-like generations of disciples. This distinction involves time differences and transmission through a lineage.[6]

Tantric initiation likewise entailed one's entry into an alternative community, a clan based not on genetic descent but rather spiritual inclination, hierarchically ranked vis-à-vis the guru who serves as one's father, the source of the spiritual "seed" transmitted to one during the process of initiation and subsequent instruction.

Now, this brief survey on the importance of lineage in tantric Buddhism is essential because the structure and contents of the tantras is deeply informed and influenced by the lineage model for the transmission of authority in these traditions. There are three main ways that this manifests. The first is the opening context narratives in the tantras, which usually establish the founder of the tradition, an awakened buddha, and his or her interlocutor and audience, which in effect establishes the founding figures from which the lineage proceeds. This is reinforced in some tantras by a dialogical structure, consisting of questions and answers exchanged between these key figures.

The second important feature informed by lineage is secrecy. The tantras are not cookbooks or technical manuals, attempting to clearly communicate to the reader how to perform complicated tasks. Rather, they deliberately attempt to confound such readers, either by providing unclear instructions or making it impossible to perform the rituals or contemplations described in the texts by reading them alone. They do this through omission—leaving out essential details, misdirection—occasionally giving incorrect instructions, and obfuscation—often by using coded terminology. Instead of being clear instructions for any reader, tantras imply a special sort of reader, an initiated adept studying under a master. The master is expected to fill the gaps left by the text and to decode it through oral instructions provided to the adept along with the text post-initiation. Moreover, the adept is bound by vows to keep these things, the text and oral commentary, secret. The need for secrecy created new imperatives for textual practice. Although tantric traditions often claim that their scriptures descend from a lengthy precursor, the actual texts composed and utilized in these traditions tend to be brief, so that they are more easily employed in ritual uses and more easily hidden. This attitude toward texts is evidenced in a colorful passage in the *Hevajra Tantra*,[7] a tantra composed in the late ninth or early tenth century:[8]

> O listen, Goddess, greatly blessed, and I will speak on the subject of books. The book should be written by one of our tradition on leaves of birch-bark twelve *aṅgula* long, with collyrium for ink and with a human bone as a pen. But if someone unworthy should see either book or painting, one will not succeed either in this world or the next. To one of our tradition it may be shown at any time. On a journey the book should be hidden in the hair or under the arm.[9]

As twelve *aṅgula* is equivalent to the span of one's hand, the text prescribes here a small and easily portable text, which is quite distinct from the immense and often elaborately decorated texts of Mahāyāna sutras, which were to be treated as objects of reverence, and often installed on or above altars, not to mention the massive bed-sized mythical ur-texts discussed earlier. Rather, the text, which appears at first glance to be ideally suited for disclosing secrets, is physically structured so as to preserve them. This points to the paradoxical role of texts with regard to secrecy. As Georg Simmel argued:

> Whereas speech reveals the secret of the speaker by means of all that surrounds it—which is visible but not audible, and also includes the imponderables of the speaker himself—the letter conceals this secret. For this reason, the letter is clearer than speech where the secret of the other is *not* the issue; but where it *is* the issue, the letter is more ambiguous.[10]

In other words, since texts lack the contextual cues of in-person oral discourse, they are more amenable to secrecy because there are fewer cues that might inadvertently disclose secrets.

Lastly, the rituals described in many of the tantras reveal the significance of lineage for these traditions. The officiant for many of them is the adamantine master, the *guru* qua master of ceremonies in major tantric Buddhist rituals. One of the most important of these is the rite of consecration, in which the initiate joins the community centered on the master, which is symbolically represented by the mandala. Many of these texts envision a familial relationship revolving around the guru. And while the rites transmit a spiritual lineage, some of the rituals employ the symbolism of the transmission of biological lineage, namely sexual symbolism, to reinforce this sense of spiritual rebirth in a new family with a new spiritual identity. Other practices described in the tantras, ritual or contemplative, imply that the adept, the ideal reader of the text, will be performing them. However, due to secrecy as noted above, the text presumes a lineage connection in order to gain proper understanding of these practices.

2.2 Narrative Structure

2.2.1 Narrative Context

One of the key textual markers of authenticity in Buddhist traditions is the background (*nidāna*) verse or passage that serves as a preface of sorts for most scriptures, giving the time and place of the scripture's production as an oral teaching by an awakened being such as Śākyamuni Buddha. Naturally, the very presence of such a "preface" makes a none too subtle assertion of authority. According to David McMahan:

> The *śrāvakas* (hearers) claimed to have directly heard and reported the words of the Buddha when he taught in India, and elaborate institutional efforts were employed to keep these words alive. The source of authority for the early teachings was in fact that they were heard from the self-authenticating presence of the Buddha. The repetition of these words was itself the Dharma and was the link to the living presence of Gautama [Buddha] who was now gone forever.[11]

The sign of this authenticity was the standard background verse with which Buddhist sutras typically began: "Thus have I heard at one time . . . (*evaṃ mayā śrutaṃ ekaśmin samaye* . . .), followed by information concerning the speaker, setting, and audience of the teaching. This verse represents an attempt to locate the text in the "self-authenticating presence of the Buddha," and it established a lineage of hearers that extended from the original audience until the present day.

This practice continued in Mahāyāna circles during the first half of the first millennium CE, despite that their newly "rediscovered" texts were composed as texts, and the production and preservation of oral texts was overtaken by the production of written texts among Buddhists long before the emergence of tantric traditions. The prestige of authentic origins maintained via a lineage of "hearers" continued to be influential in the context where it developed, the monasteries.

It is probably true that whenever prestige is placed on lineage, lineages are fabricated, and even though Mahāyāna sutras were almost certainly composed in written form, it is not too difficult to simulate the trappings of an authentically transmitted text. Texts produced in or for monastic communities thus continued to maintain that they originated in the presence of the Buddha and were transmitted thence via an unbroken lineage. The tantric texts generally maintained this practice, which probably indicates that most of them, whatever their ultimate origin, achieved the form in which they were preserved in a monastic context. This was a strategy for legitimation, akin to the appeals to Vedic orthodoxy by later Hindu texts that bear little or no similarity to the Vedas themselves.

For the tradents of Mahāyāna sutras or tantras, "history" presented a problem. As their texts were hitherto unknown, it was necessary to create a revised version of Buddhist history, one that would allow the occult transmission of texts, a lineage deriving ultimately from the Buddha or some other awakened being. There were several ways in which such revision was achieved. A typical explanation accounting for the diversity of texts, including both the sutras and tantras, as well as for their frequent divergence from orthodox standards, is that they represent an exercise of skillful means as a result of historical encounters of awakened beings with persons of diverse needs and predilections. This explanation is frequently invoked by tantric Buddhist exegetes, but here they follow a hoary Mahāyāna tradition of legitimation.

The *locus classicus* of this idea is the *Lotus Sūtra,* particularly the "Parable" chapter, in which the reader is told that the teachings of Buddha to the "hearers" or early monastic audience (*śrāvaka*) were merely provisional, given with the intention of guiding them to the more complete and valid path of the Mahāyāna.[12] Zhi-yi (智顗,

538–597 CE) further developed this idea in his doctrinal classification scheme (判教, *pan-jiao*), describing a class of "indeterminate Teachings" (不定教), which were given by the Buddha with a particular individual in mind, with the implication that different members of an audience might receive the teaching in radically different ways, hearing, in effect, totally different teachings.[13]

The idea that multiple witnesses of a scene might perceive the events therein entirely differently[14] opens a pathway for alternative versions of Buddhist textual history. This vision, however, does not correspond well to the idea of history as understood in the West, where it is generally assumed that reality is singular and thus automatically accessible to the perception of all those with normal sensuous and mental faculties. One might even call this a strategy of *dehistoricization,* that is, the adoption of a rhetorical strategy that downplays the "historical" setting of the Buddhist teachings, that is, the life of Śākyamuni and the mundane locales in which he taught, such as Deer Park in Sarnath, and which emphasizes the ahistorical, cosmic universality of the teachings. Or, as David McMahan put it:

> The tendency of Mahāyāna sūtras, then, was to disembed the teachings from Deer Park and re-embed them in a transcendent realm. The Mahāyāna attempted to transfer the basis of legitimacy from the spoken word of Śākyamuni to the vision of the transcendent Buddha, which rendered the specificity of the places that the Buddha spoke during his lifetime less relevant.[15]

Or, we might say that having dis-embedded the teachings from their spatial and temporal context, Mahāyāna Buddhists steadfastly refused to re-embed them, maintaining instead a stance of ultimacy by insisting on their non-locality; the pure vision of the Buddha is not contingent on the outside world, but on the purity of one's own mind. As the "Concentration for Face-to-Face Encounters with the Buddhas of the Present" *Pratyutpannabuddha-saṃmukhāvasthita-samādhi-sūtra* relates:

> Just as, for example, space is formless, incommunicable, unlocalised (*aniketa*), utterly pure, and undefiled, so the bodhisattva regards all dharmas, and with regard to dharmas conditioned and unconditioned (*saṃskṛtāsaṃskṛtadharma*) his eye becomes unobstructed. To the unobstructed eye of the bodhisattva dharmas are manifested, and if he concentrates, he sees . . . the Tathāgatas, Arhats, Samyaksaṃbuddhas.[16]

For the Mahāyāna adept, the awakened worlds of the Buddhas are always accessible, provided that one has the wisdom and merit to apprehend them.

While Buddhists may have concocted lineage claims, it may be more enlightening to dwell not on the verity of such claims but on their creative consequences. Buddhist tradents were constrained here by convention, a convention that considered the background verse to be of central, definitive importance, a sign not only of scriptural *authenticity* but also of scriptural *identity.* According to the "Ornament of Mahāyāna Sūtras" *Mahāyānasūtrālaṃkāra,* one of the defining characteristics of a sutra is its context (*āśraya*).[17] The Mahāyāna philosopher-saint Asaṅga[18] defines the "context" of the sutra as the place where and the persons by whom and for whom the discourse was taught.[19] Another Mahāyāna philosopher, Sthiramati, defined a sutra's context in terms of the background verse.[20] It appears that the background verse had become so strongly accepted as a sign for scriptural authenticity that it was not lightly abandoned by later tradents, lest they risk obscurity or ignominy for their revelations.

It is not necessary or even advisable, however, to assume that the authors of Mahāyāna or tantric texts were conscious producers of apocryphal texts. For the ideology and practice of revelation may have led their authors to sincerely believe that the texts they produced were in fact the results of genuine revelations deriving from authoritative sources. Of central importance here is not only the *idea* that such revelation is possible, or its *ideological* appropriation as a tool for legitimation, but also the development of specific *practices* or meditative techniques that were believed to achieve such revelation. In other words, the visionary contemplative practices undertaken by Mahāyāna Buddhists may often lead to revelatory experiences that result in the production of new scriptures. I would go so far to suggest that actual attempts to deceive others by self-consciously forging spurious scriptures have probably been very rare. Given the rich contemplative resources of the tantric traditions, it is far more likely that the discovery of newly revealed scriptures are the products of subjectively "genuine" visionary experiences on the part of the discoverers.[21] Needless to say, convincing others of their authenticity is the greatest challenge faced by would-be visionaries, as Gananath Obeyesekere (2012) has argued.[22]

Given the challenge of convincing others of a new scripture's authenticity, it should not be surprising that the discoverers of new Buddhist scriptures adhered to the textual conventions for works deemed to be the speech of the Buddha. However, over time, these new productions tended to stray from the fourth-century BCE Northeast Indian milieu of Śākyamuni. While the sutras of the older, more conservative schools like the Theravāda are always set in this context, some Mahāyāna sutras were contextualized in more visionary settings, a tendency that reaches a peak in works such as the *Avataṃsaka Sūtra*, which contains an extensive and miraculous background text that extends far beyond a verse—many pages in English translation, in fact.[23]

While the Buddhist tantras seem to have originated as extra-canonical collections of magical rituals drawn from diverse sources, by the seventh century the idea developed that these works were the textual basis for a distinct tradition that claimed to have preserved special teachings for rapidly achieving awakening. Once this idea had developed, it became necessary to present these works in a manner that could be deemed authoritative bases for such claims. Since the sutra genre was the model for authoritative texts in Buddhist circles, the early tantras generally followed the sutra model, so much that some of these texts were initially identified as sutras. Consequently, they opened with background passages to assert their status as the speech of an awakened being.

Given that the tantras were not clearly linked to any one buddha, there was naturally a great deal of diversity with respect to how their authors or compilers chose to contextualize them. Some linked the teaching to Śākyamuni. An example of an early tantric text that does this is the "The Noble Sovereign Ritual of Amoghapāśa" (*Āryā moghapāśakalparāja*), a text in two sections, the first part of which likely dates to the sixth century, while the second part dates to the seventh century.[24]

> Thus did I hear at one time. The Blessed One stayed on Potala Mountain, in the palace of Avalokiteśvara adorned with various trees such as sal, tamāla, campaka, aśoka, and atimuktaka. He stayed there together with the congregation of eight thousand monks, surrounded and attended upon by nine hundred and ninety quadrillion crores of bodhisattvas and many hundreds of thousands of gods of the Pure Abode. He was explaining the Dharma, chiefly to the gods such as Īśvara, Maheśvara, and Brahmā.[25]

The setting for this work, Potala Mountain, is likely supranormal, the Pure Land of Avalokiteśvara, although it has been variously linked to actual mountains that are then treated as pilgrimage sites, including Pothigai Malai in Tamil Nadu in South India.[26] It features a large, but not impossibly large, audience of monks, as well as an inconceivably vast audience of bodhisattvas and deities. While the text is linked to Śākyamuni, the setting is somewhat fantastical as might seem fitting for a text rediscovered by supernatural means.

Another early tantric text, the eighth-century "Compendium of the Realities of All Tathāgatas" *Sarvatathāgata-tattvasaṃgraha-nāma-Mahayana-Sūtra,* for example, begins with a lengthy background passage, which can be seen as a subdued version of the massive background passages found in some of the Mahāyāna sutras. It occurs as follows:

> Thus have I heard at one time: the greatly compassionate Blessed Lord Mahāvairocana, who is endowed with the various qualities of the gnosis of the adamantine blessings and commitments of all Tathāgatas, and who has been consecrated as the righteous king (*dharmarāja*) of the three realms with the jeweled crown of all Tathāgatas, and who is the lord of the great yogins of the omniscience of all Tathāgatas, and who fulfills all of the hopes of all beings without exception by doing whatever needs to be done and the equal mastery of all of the mudrā of all Tathāgatas, and who always abides in the three times and who has the vajra of the body, speech and mind of all Tathāgatas, resided in the palace of the divine king of Akaniṣṭha in which dwell, and which is praised by all Tathāgatas, which is studded with great precious jewels, and which is decorated with lovely colors, wind chimes, silk, flower wreaths, yak tail fans, garlands and half garlands and moons, along with twice times nine hundred and ninety million bodhisattvas, including Vajrapāṇi, Avalokiteśvara, Ākāśagarbha, Vajramuṣṭi, Mañjuśrī, Sahacittotpādadharmacakrapravart inā, Gaganagañja, Sarvamārabalapramardinā, and as many Tathāgatas as there are grains of sand in the Gaṅgā.[27]

The context set here is transhistorical. The text begins in Mahāvairocana's palace in the Akaniṣṭha heaven and does not purport to describe events in the life of Śākyamuni or any other historical figure. The audience too is exclusively awakened (buddhas) or awakening beings (bodhisattvas). The text thus portrays a rarified discourse, from Mahāvairocana to an awakened audience.

Tantric texts are traditional in the sense of being prefaced by a background verse or passage, but they diverge from the tradition of the earlier sutras insofar as they do not place their text in the "historical" context of Śākyamuni Buddha. Some diverged even further. Such was the case with the background verse of the "Esoteric Community" *Guhyasamāja Tantra,* another eighth-century text that was included in the Adamantine Pinnacle collection. This verse was infamous for its strong erotic savor. It occurs as follows: "Thus have I heard: at one time the Lord was residing in the vulvae of the Adamantine Ladies, the essence of the Body, Speech and Mind of all Tathāgatas."[28] This verse or its variants occur in many other tantras, reflecting its popularity in tantric Buddhist circles.[29]

There appears to have been a major shift in the significance of the background verse in Tantric traditions. No longer a statement of the context in which the teaching occurred, it came to be glorified in its own right. There is even a tantra dedicated to the glorification of the background verse. "The Light on Reality" *Tattvapradīpa Tantra* claims that "the expression 'Thus have I . . . ' (*evaṃ mayā*), etc., seals everything animate and inanimate in the three worlds without exception, since its nature is wisdom and skillful means. It is famed as the light on reality, and its form is the stainless, perfected fruit."[30] While these background verses no longer make a claim to legitimacy via Śākyamuni Buddha, they reflect an effort to claim that the background verses are legitimating insofar as they encapsulate profound truths concerning ultimate reality. No doubt this claim was needed to justify the more fantastical among them.

For those who were unimpressed by the literal meaning of these passages, many commentators began pointing out their esoteric significance. A trend that developed in tantric circles is a style of analysis I term "atomic analysis," in which the passage is reduced to the smallest possible lexical or sublexical unit, and esoteric meanings are ascribed to either the words, syllables, or letters, and in some cases even the component portions of the letters.[31] This exegetical strategy was particularly applied to the tantric background verses. The "Vajra Rosary" *Vajramālā Tantra* is well known for its elucidation of the hidden significance of the *Guhyasamāja* background verse through forty stanzas of verse, each of which begins with one of the forty syllables that constitute that textual passage.[32]

The *Hevajra Tantra* begins with a slightly shortened, thirty-seven syllable version of the *Guhyasamāja* background verse.[33] The esoteric significance of the verses' syllables is the subject of the third chapter of one of its explanatory tantras, the "Kiss" *Sampuṭa Tantra*.[34] They are also discussed at length by Vajragarbha in his commentary on the *Hevajra Tantra,* where they are correlated to the thirty-seven deities of the *Hevajra* mandala and the thirty-seven aids to awakening.[35] Each syllable is therefore invested with tremendous esoteric significance.

Most Buddhist tantric texts, whatever their origins, reached their final form and were preserved in a monastic context. The background verse, regardless of its form, seems to represent for tantric texts the monastic "seal of approval," a sign of its authentic status as authentic speech of a buddha. That this was the case is suggested by the exegetical kerfuffle caused by the existence of tantras that conspicuously lacked the typical background beginning with "Thus have I heard." Tantras in this category include the "Supreme Bliss of the Wheels" *Cakrasaṃvara,* the "Ḍākinīs' Network That Unites All Buddhas" *Sarvabuddhasamāyoga-ḍākinījālasaṃvara,* the "Litany of the Names of Mañjuśrī" *Mañjuśrīnāmasaṃgīti,* and several others.[36] Most of these texts begin laconically with the word *atha,* "and then," which is quite atypical for Buddhist scriptures, but which was understood by these traditions to point toward the larger legendary texts from which they are believed to derive. For example, the "Supreme Bliss of the Wheels" *Cakrasaṃvara Tantra* opens as follows: "And now I will explain the secret, concisely, not extensively."[37] The late ninth-century commentator Jayabhadra[38] commented on this opening line as follows:

> The [text] "and [now]" etc., through its irregular form, demonstrates that [this text] is an appendix tantra (*uttaratantra*). "I will explain" should be taken to mean that "I will state" this

> [text] now, that is, immediately after having explained the "Sky-like" *Khasama Tantra*.[39]

That is, this concise work was originally revealed by the Vajradhara Buddha immediately after teaching the massive 100,000 (or more) stanza text when both texts were revealed. In other words, a background verse is not needed for a tantra that is an appendix to a larger work, which does presumably contain this essential text.

Shortly after making this comment, Jayabhadra explains the term "secret," *rahasya*. He explains: "The secret is that which must be concealed, that is, not disclosed to the 'hearers' (*śrāvaka*) and so forth. Moreover, the secret is that which is accomplished by uniting wisdom and skillful means."[40] This suggests that the advocates of the tantras were experiencing resistance from members of more conservative Buddhist communities, particularly the monks that adhered to those traditions, as that is the primary meaning of the term *śrāvaka* in this literature. Moreover, the "secret" that must be concealed concerns union; the meaning of this union will be explored further in section 2.3.1.

Ultimately, a background verse could be discerned even for texts that seem to lack them. The "Ḍākinīs' Network That Unites All Buddhas" *Sarvabuddhasamāyoga-ḍākinījālasaṃvara Tantra,* for example, opens with the following text:

> The Hero that is made of all buddhas,
> Vajrasattva, the bliss that is supreme,
> Always abides in the nature of all,
> The secret that's supreme and delightful.[41]

This verse came to be understood as alternative background verse. A close variant of it occurs in the opening chapter of the "Supreme Bliss of the Wheels" *Cakrasaṃvara Tantra* as follows:

The Hero that's made of all ḍākinīs,
Vajrasattva, the bliss that is supreme,
Always abides in the nature of all,
The secret that's supreme and delightful.[42]

Like the "Esoteric Community" *Guhyasamāja Tantra*'s background verse, this verse too was subjected to atomic analysis in a *Cakrasaṃvara* explanatory tantra, with each syllable invested with esoteric significance and connected with the conventional background verse.[43]

Insofar as the context reveals a discrete teacher and audience, we would expect that the text would exhibit a dialogical structure, consisting of questions and answers between the awakened being and his or her interlocutor(s). Some tantras do exhibit such structure throughout their length to varying degrees. For example, the "Wheel of Time" *Kālacakra Tantra* is presented as a teaching by Śākyamuni Buddha to Sucandra,[44] the "Vajra Rosary" *Vajramāla Tantra* as a teaching from Vajradhara to Vajrapāṇi,[45] while the "Ocean of Warlocks" *Ḍākārṇava Tantra* as a teaching from Vajraḍāka Buddha, who is identified with Vajrasattva in the final verse of each chapter,[46] to the female buddha Vajravārāhī. However, there is very little dialogue in most of these works; relatively few chapters contain actual dialogue, mainly in the early chapters when it does occur at all. Generally, most of the chapters are typically portrayed as exposition from the text's authoritative source and hence are not dialogically structured.

2.2.2 The Language of the Tantras

The "first language" of Buddhism was the Middle Indo-European language Māgadhī, spoken in Magadha, North Central India where the Buddha lived circa 400 BCE. While there are no records of this language, it a precursor to later languages from this region that have been preserved, such as the Ardhamāgadhī Prākṛt in which early Jain scriptures were recorded, as well as the later Māgadhī Prākṛt found in some Sanskrit dramas.[47] The earliest surviving Buddhist scriptures, discovered in eastern Afghanistan and Northwest Pakistan, are recorded in the Gāndhārī language, another Middle Indo-European language, and date to a period ranging from first century BCE through the third century CE.[48] The scriptures of the Theravāda tradition are preserved in yet another Middle Indo-European literary language, Pāli. While this tradition, like most Buddhist traditions, claims to preserve the original teachings of Śākyamuni, these scriptures were put into writing somewhat later, during the first half of the first millennium CE.[49]

The Mahāyāna traditions used Sanskrit as its canonical language, and since the tantric Buddhist traditions emerged in a largely Mahāyāna religious context, they followed this precedent and composed their scriptures in Sanskrit, which by the early medieval period was the language of scholarship in India. The Sanskrit found in Buddhist texts, however, often differs considerably from classical Sanskrit. It contains loan words from Middle Indo-Aryan and Prakrit languages, as well as idiosyncratic usages of terms, and often betray influence from these languages. It is distinct enough that Franklin Edgerton labeled it "Buddhist hybrid Sanskrit."[50]

The vast majority of tantras were composed in South Asia and as a result followed the Mahāyāna tradition by composing their scriptures in Sanskrit language.[51] Some contain terminology coming from other languages, usually Middle Indic languages. A particularly common example, found in many of the tantras, is the term *chomā* (variant *chomakā*) meaning "sign." It is a late Middle Indic word derived from the Sanskrit term *chadman,* meaning "disguise" or "deceit."[52] Tantras also contain some terms derived from non-Indic languages. The *Gathering of Intentions Sutra* (*dgongs pa 'dus pa'i mdo*), a tantric work preserved by the Nyingma tradition, was translated from Burushaski, a language isolate spoken in the

Hunza Valley in what is now Pakistan, rather than Sanskrit, and the text preserves a number of untranslated Burushaski words.[53] Another interesting example is the term *prasenā* or *pratisenā,* which means "divinatory image." It refers to a divination ritual in which either the adept or a consecrated virgin gazes into a mirror to see divinatory visions, a ritual described briefly in the "Great Bliss of the Wheels" *Cakrasaṃvara Tantra* as well as the literature associated with the "Wheel of Time" *Kālacakra Tantra.* It turns out that this ritual almost certainly derives from a Tibetan pre-Buddhist divinatory ritual, and the terms *prasenā* and *pratisenā* are Sanskritized loan words derived from the Tibetan term *pra,* which likewise means a divinatory image.[54]

As was typical of the early medieval period, they also exhibit the general tendency toward simplification, such as avoiding more complicated verb forms and using a smaller number of declensions for nominal forms. For example, it is common to find nouns ending in consonants declined as *–a* stem nouns. The nouns *rājan* and *karman,* for example, are often declined as if their stem forms were *rāja* and *karma,* resulting in incorrect declensions such as *vidyārājasya, karmasya,* and *karmeṣu,* in place of the expected *vidyārājñaḥ, karmaṇaḥ* and *karmasu.*

It appears that many of the tantras were composed by authors who either had a loose grasp of the rules of Sanskrit grammar or had no interest in following these. While some of these problems may be due to scribal errors, many were present very early in these texts' histories. Some of these problems are noted, for example, by Jayabhadra, the earliest known commentator on the "Supreme Bliss of the Wheels" *Cakrasaṃvara Tantra,* who wrote within decades of the text's composition, circa the ninth century. For example, regarding the incorrectly declined *caturo ratnā,* which occurs at the end of chapter eight, he commented as follows: "In the Tantra the grammatical cases are shown haphazardly to bewilder everyone. They must be inferred through reference to their meaning."[55] Apparently bewildered himself by the text's ungrammaticality, yet unable to accept the possibility that this text was not awakened speech, Jayabhadra interpreted it as intentional, as a manifestation of the text's deliberate esotericism, composed in this fashion to bewilder the uninitiated.

Perhaps not surprisingly, Buddhist tantras are not alone in exhibiting nonstandard Sanskrit. A similar language is used in the older Śaiva tantras. This language was given the designation *aiśa* in Śaiva tradition, designating its divine origin. The Kaula texts, datable perhaps to the seventh century, typically exhibit "the elliptical Sanskrit liberally sprinkled with non-Pāṇinean forms, archaic styles, and Prākṛt derivations, in the style that in the tradition was called *Aiśa* Sanskrit, because it emanates from *Īśa*, the Lord, enacting his freedom to break the rules of conventional grammar."[56]

The Buddhist commentators explained the imperfect Sanskrit in their tantras via recourse to the concept commonly deployed to explain anomalies, "skillful means" (*upāya*). It was implied by Jayabhadra in his explanation of the incorrectly declined *caturo ratnā,* quoted above. By stating that "the grammatical cases are shown haphazardly in order to bewilder everyone," he implies that the text was *intentionally* taught in this fashion. This idea was expressed even more clearly in the "Stainless Light" *Vimalaprabhā,* a commentary on the "Wheel of Time" *Kālacakra Tantra.* The author of this text, Puṇḍarīka, gives a rather exhaustive list of the sorts of mistakes one finds in the Buddhist tantras, as well as an interesting justification for this, as follows:

> In order to destroy attachment to correct language of those (brahman sages who) advocated correct language (Kalkī Yaśas) relied on the meaning. In some verses (of the *Śrī Kālacakra*) there are ungrammatical words. In some verses the caesuras are lacking. Some have words without case endings. In some, letters and vowels are elided. In some verses, long vowels are short, and short vowels are long. In some the locative case is used for the ablative case, and the genitive case is used for the dative case. In

> some a middle voice is attributed to a root that possesses an active voice, and an active voice is attributed to one that possesses a middle voice. In some the plural number is used for the singular number, and the singular number is used for the plural number. The neuter gender is used for the masculine gender, and the masculine gender is used for the neuter. In some the dental (*sa*) and cerebral (*ṣa*) are used for the palatal letter *śa*; in some the dental and palatal are used for the cerebral; in some the palatal and cerebral are used for the dental. . . .
>
> A yogi should understand ungrammatical words like these, and others too, by reading the sacred texts. Likewise, I (Kalkī Puṇḍarīka) must write the (*Vimalaprabhā*) commentary relying on the meaning, in order to destroy conceit in the correct language. Thus, Buddha and bodhisattvas teach the Dharma for the sake of liberation—relying on the meaning, they use the different vernaculars and the different languages of the grammatical treatises, whichever eliminate the conceit in family, learning, and correct language.[57]

The author of this text understood the tantras' ungrammaticality as intended by their speakers, awakened Buddhas, for the purpose of overcoming brahmanic pride in correct language. This explains why later Buddhists generally did not correct their scriptures' grammatical errors. For if one believed that these mistakes were intended by the buddhas, one would not seek to correct them. It should be noted that the *Vimalaprabhā* was composed within decades of the composition of the *Kālacakra Tantra*,[58] just as Jayabhadra's Cakrasaṃvara commentary was composed shortly after the composition of the *Cakrasamvara Tantra*. These mistakes are thus not solely the result of scribal errors but also reflect the milieu in which these texts were composed, which was not one that highly valued proper Pāṇinian Sanskrit.[59]

Sanskrit is not the only language found in the tantras. Several tantras of the Yoginītantra class, which focus on female deities, feature songs composed in a late Middle Indo-Aryan literary language, Apabraṃśa, which was used from about the sixth through twelfth centuries,[60] during the period when these tantric works were composed. In Buddhist tantras, Apabraṃśa is exclusively used in verse passages and mainly for songs, such as the songs sung at the tantric feast (*gaṇacakra*), which entailed offerings of food and drink, typically meat and alcohol, as well as song and dance. They were known as "adamantine songs" (*vajragīti*). Since they are literary representations of oral song compositions contemporaneous with the composition of the tantras, they may approximate the colloquial language of the communities who produced them, rather than Sanskrit, which was a scholastic language by this time. The "Ocean of Warlocks" *Ḍākārṇava Tantra* contains the following example:

> All beings who have the nature of supreme bliss
> Reside within the circle of the yoginīs.
>
> It's a wonder the deluded beasts don't know this.
> Take the natural beauty and receive great bliss!
>
> All beings of the three worlds have buddha nature;
> Play together with the compassionate young girl!
>
> Those who don't meditate on the ultimate truth
> Will never attain the complete awakening. What a wonder!
>
> Knowing that the inward and outward aren't distinct,
> Your aim will be to liberate the entire world. What a wonder![61]

Another nice example of this sort of colloquial song is found in *Hevajra Tantra*, which describes a tantric feast as follows:

> The *yogin* stays at Kollagiri, the *yoginī* at Mummuṇi.
> Loudly the drum sounds forth. Love is our business and not dissension.
> There we eat meat and drink wine in great quantity.
> Hey there, the true followers are come together, but the frauds are kept far away.
> We take the fourfold preparation and musk and frankincense and camphor,
> Herbs and special meat we eat with relish.
> Going this way and that in the dance, we give no thought to what is chaste or unchaste,
> Adorning our limbs with bone ornaments, we place the corpse in position.
> Union takes place at that meeting, for Ḍombī is not there rejected.[62]

The latter example contains examples of "coded language" (*sandhyābhāṣa*), verbal codes found in many of the tantras, often for some of the more transgressive elements of tantric ritual practice. These include the relatively well-known euphemism for elements of human anatomy, such as *vajra* "diamond" or "ritual scepter" for the penis, *padma* or "lotus" for the vulva, and *bodhicitta* "spirit of awakening" for sexual fluids. As Ronald Davidson has discussed, this coded language is found in many of the tantras, particularly the Yoginītantras, dating back to at least the eighth-century "Ḍākinīs' Network That Unites All Buddhas" *Sarvabuddhasamāyogaḍākinījālasaṃvara Tantra*.[63] They include not only verbal codes but also physical gestures.

These passages typically are embedded in long sections dealing the *yoginī*s, female practitioners of the tantras who appear like ordinary women, but who can be recognized by the knowledgeable adept yogi. The "Supreme Bliss of the Wheels" *Cakrasaṃvara Tantra* likewise contains a long series of chapters (15–24) dealing with the clans of the yoginīs, which Alexis Sanderson has shown derive from earlier Śaiva tantric sources.[64] They describe the physical characteristics of the yoginīs of the various clans, the coded language that can be used to communicate with them, and secret gestures that the knowledgeable yogi can display to communicate his insider status, and the yoginī's gestural response. The nineteenth chapter, for example, relates the following:

> She is short with thick calves, always prefers yellow garments, and drapes cloth over her shoulders. Seeing such a wanton one, display the wheel gesture. Then the second gesture, that of the conch, should be eagerly presented. It is held that turning to the left is her counter gesture. The fourteenth is her day, and a vajra is drawn in her house. This is characteristic of the Śrī Herukī lāmās.[65]

The term *lāmā,* used in tantras such as this one to describe a class of female divinities akin to ḍākinīs, is not a Sanskrit term, and it may possibly be another loan word from Tibetan, namely the Tibetan term *lha mo,* "goddess."[66] The *Hevajra Tantra* indicates the fruits of successfully identifying and communicating with the yoginīs as follows:

> Then the yoginīs say: "Well done, O Son, thou of great compassion." If they show wreaths in their hands, they are signifying that you should come together in that place; motioning forward with their wreaths (they mean to say) "O True One, stay at this ceremony and take part." So there at the meeting-place, abiding within that sacred orbit, he should do whatever the yoginīs say.[67]

These texts describe a secretive religious subculture that was, given the antinomian practices it featured, subject to persecution. The esotericism that is a key textual feature of the tantras may have originally been a survival mechanism, to thwart attempts at persecution by weaving an aura of secrecy around communities of tantric practitioners.

2.3 The Contents of the Tantras

2.3.1 Philosophical View

The Buddhist tantras do not contain a great deal of philosophical argumentation, which is one of the reasons they were neglected by past generations of Western scholars, as noted in the previous chapter. That said, there are some philosophical passages in the Buddhist tantras, enough for us to get a sense of the philosophical worldview that underlies the practices that properly speaking are the focus of this literature. However, one must be careful when reviewing the philosophical content in the tantras. Ron Davidson has argued that the philosophical nomenclature found in many of the tantras served as coded language or even a disguise, *chadman,* deployed with the ulterior motive of facilitating the acceptance of the tantras in Buddhist monastic institutions. He argued that

> the image of a masquerade might be an appropriate metaphor for the Vajrayāna *pramāṇa* statements. A masquerade requires a costume, in this case philosophical nomenclature. It needs actors, here the Vajrācāryas. An occasion is necessary, such as the increased authority of the philosophical systems during the early medieval period. The purpose of the event was clearly the movement for the institutionalization of esoteric Buddhism, a purpose well served by this language.[68]

Philosophical language was often deployed in tantric commentaries, sometimes to explain and arguably render less offensive transgressive passages. Philosophical language qua masquerade is a feature of many of the tantras. As I have argued, the "Supreme Bliss of the Wheels" *Cakrasaṃvara Tantra* was composed over a period of at least a few decades, most likely in the ninth century. There is very little Buddhist terminology in the text, and a good deal of Śaiva terminology due to the relatively slight revisions made by the tradents when compiling much of it from Śaiva sources. There are three sections of the text that exhibit Buddhist philosophical terminology, a section in the tenth chapter dealing with the theory of a buddha's three levels of embodiment (*trikāya*), another section at the end of chapter 50 that correlates the pilgrimage sacred sites to the ten bodhisattva stages or "grounds" (*bhūmi*), and the final chapter, 51, which is replete with Buddhist terminology. All three of these sections were added to the work later,[69] perhaps to facilitate its acceptance at Buddhist monastic institutions such as Nālandā and, particularly, Vikramaśīla, since many of the Indian commentators on this work were abbots at this institution, which was renowned as a center of tantric Buddhist studies.[70]

If we discount the passages that appear to be gratuitous, we still find many passages that discuss key Buddhist teachings, most notably selflessness (*anatmān*) and emptiness (*śūnyatā*). This is because the nature of the self and the nature of reality were central concerns to the tantric adept, who aimed to transform her or his understanding of both to achieve complete awakening. The passages that address these issues often do so in the context of discussing contemplative practices, which points to the connection between these practices and notions of the self and the cosmos that underlie them.

This content is rich enough that Tibetans, from about the thirteenth century onward, debated the underlying philosophical view of the tantras. They tried to correlate the tantras to one of the mainstream Mahāyāna philosophical schools, either the Yogācāra or "Mind Only" school, or the Madhyamaka "Middle Way" school of Nāgārjuna, often differentiating the latter into the "autonomist" (*svatantrika*) approach to Middle Way reasoning, using autonomous syllogisms, advanced by the Indian scholar Bhāvaviveka (c. seventh century CE) and the "consequentialist" (*prāsaṅgika*) approach, which used *reductio ad absurdum* reasoning, advocated by Buddhapālita (c. fifth to sixth century CE) and Candrakīrti (c. seventh century CE). Tibetans also advanced some new positions, including the "other empty" (Tib. *gzhan gtong*) position advanced by the Tibetan scholar Dölpopa Sherap Gyeltsen (*dol po pa shes rab rgyal mtshan,* 1292–1361 CE), who, in a vision inspired by his study of the "Wheel of Time" *Kālacakra Tantra,* developed a substantialist theory of awakening, concluding that buddha nature, rather than being empty of intrinsic reality as conventionally viewed by most Mahāyāna Buddhists, was intrinsically real, drawing on an older Mahāyāna theory that awakening depends on an embryonic buddha essence (*tathāgatagarbha*) that all beings possess.[71]

While these debates motivated interesting scholarship in Tibet, they are beyond the scope of this work, since the tantras generally give little indication of affiliation with any particular school of Mahāyāna philosophy.[72] Here instead we find passages that bolster the claim made by the Buddhist tantric traditions, namely that by secret techniques taught by the buddhas and then transmitted to the world when the time was right, it is possible to achieve the full awakening of a buddha in as little as one lifetime, shortening one's spiritual evolution as an awakening being (*bodhisattva*), which according to traditional Mahāyāna sources could take an inconceivably long amount of time. It thus claims to possess a fast-track to enlightenment, much like the Chan/Zen traditions of East Asia, which likewise claimed that this is possible through secret teachings about the nature of mind passed mind to mind through a lineage of masters, which permitted one to realize the awakened mind that is in fact the true nature of one's mind.[73]

The Mahāyāna theory of emptiness—understood as the ultimate truth or true nature of all things, including the mind and also the awakened mind—makes the shortcut possible. Ordinary beings imagine that the persons and things that they perceive and the abstract concepts they conceive really exist, that they have some intrinsic reality such that they exist independently, as things in themselves. Mahāyāna Buddhists counter with the theory of the two truths, the conventional and ultimate truths. While it is true that things exist conventionally as conditioned, interdependent entities, they have no intrinsic, independent existence, they are *empty* of this. Emptiness is simply a negation of the presumed intrinsic reality of things. This is significant because, in the Buddhist view, emptiness makes awakening possible. Imagine, for example, that the author of this book desires to become a buddha yet imagines himself a deluded fool. If his conception of himself as a deluded fool is intrinsically real, his desire to become a buddha would be nonsensical. However, since this conception is empty of intrinsic reality, the outlook looks brighter. One is a deluded fool, or anything else for that matter, insofar as the collective impact of one's past conditioning, one's cognitive and behavioral habits, led to this condition. Changing one's modes of thinking and action and one will transform oneself accordingly. While the idea of "emptiness" sounds negative—which it is, being simply a negation—its consequence is infinite potentiality.[74] Emptiness, the thinking goes, makes possible awakening for all beings, and the only limitation is one's willingness to transform oneself.

It turns out that there is no fundamental difference between the ordinary mind of deluded beings and the awakened mind of a buddha. Just realizing this, deeply and profoundly, one can liberate oneself from the cycle of suffering. This can be achieved by transforming one's self-understanding, through tantric visualization practices. Accordingly, realizing the nature of mind, as well as its central role in the creation of one's sense of reality, is of utmost importance. Thus the "Esoteric Community" *Guhyasamāja Tantra* describes the mind as follows: "Devoid of all existents, free of the aggregates, the sense objects and media, and subject and object, one's mind, being identical to the selflessness of dharmas, is originally unarisen and has emptiness as its nature."[75]

If this is the case, then there is no need to spend years arduously purifying one through asceticism or difficult religious exercises designed to transform one into something else. Awakening simply entails recognition of one's actual true nature, which is emptiness, which means that we are not "locked in" to any conventional way of conceiving ourselves, since these conceptions lack any underlying reality. Supposedly, one of the distinguishing features of the tantric Buddhist approach is its direct facilitation of realization of ultimate reality via its contemplative practices. This point was made by the twelfth-century pundits, Raviśrījñāna, who wrote a commentary on the "Wheel of Time" *Kālacakra Tantra,* and Vibhūticandra, who wrote a sub-commentary on the former's work. According to Vesna Wallace:

> Raviśrījñāna . . . alludes to the integrative character of the Mantra-Mahāyāna by distinguishing Mahāyāna from Vajrayāna in terms of their respective domains of inquiry and realizations. He does so by asserting the following: "Mahāyāna pertains to conventional (*saṃvṛti*) reality, while Vajrayāna refers to the ultimate reality (*paramārtha*)." Vibhūticandra further explains this statement, commenting that Vajrayāna practice (*caryā*) utilizes the ultimate reality, which is luminosity (*prabhāsvara*), and the Mahāyāna practice utilizes conventional reality, which is generosity (*dāna*) and so on. He asserts these two types of practices as compatible.[76]

Given the importance of these ideas, they are highlighted in some tantras. For example, the "A Noble Noose of Methods, the Lotus Garland Synopsis" (*'Phags pa Thabs kyi zhags pa padma 'phreng gi don bsdus pa*), an early tantra preserved in Tibet that is included in the Tibetan lists of eighteen "Great Yoga" (*mahāyoga*) tantras, dedicates its first chapter to the subject of the two truths.[77]

Rongzom Chökyi Zangbo (Rong-zom Chos-kyi bZang-po), a Nyingma scholar who lived in Tibet during the eleventh century, discusses the importance of this realization in his work *The Attainment of Divine Vision in the Mantra-Vajrayāna*. He explains:

> In the mantric method, the two truths are inseparable. . . . Furthermore, there is no production of non-delusion by means of removing delusion, and awakening occurs through purification by means of the very actuality of delusion. Therefore, all things

> are completely awakened from the beginning, and things which appear in diverse states are the mandala of the adamantine body, speech and mind itself; they are similar to the Buddhas of the three times who have not passed beyond the actuality of purity. The characteristics of sentient beings and Buddhas are not different from the very actuality of things. The mind attributes to them distinct appearances through the power of imagination, in the same way that things appear distinct and caused in a dream.[78]

Accordingly, purity, understood as a positive description of the way things exist on the basis of their ultimate lack of intrinsic reality, permits the equation of the path with the goal. Achieving awakening thus entails identifying one's "body, speech and mind" with awakened state itself, here represented by the mandala. The appearance of self and environment as impure and bewilderingly diverse is a product of ignorance manifesting as discursive thought. The cure for this is precisely the knowledge that things are otherwise, understood not discursively and intellectually but realized through a special means of knowing, variously termed the nondual gnosis (*advayajñāna*) or transcendent gnosis (*lokottarajñāna*) of reality. According to Francesco Sferra:

> This knowledge constitutes the purifying element *par excellence* and represents, in the final analysis, the very nature of reality, transfigured and shining. It is not by chance that, according to some texts, the last phase of yoga, in which transformation of the physical and psychical elements of the *yogin* into pure elements actually occurs is, indeed, nothing but the attainment of a body of gnosis (*jñānadeha*).[79]

Rongzom, following the classical Vajrayāna formulation, understands this transformation as occurring through the medium of the mandala:

> Since all things are pure through their reality, their reality is not even slightly impure. Body, speech and mind also have purity as their reality. Purity is awakening, and through purity body, speech and mind which are differentiated become inseparable and unelaborated, and thus should be understood to be the mandala of the adamantine body, speech and mind, since it is completely pervasive.[80]

Purity is redefined as awakening, making "actual" physical purity or impurity irrelevant. In tantric practice, it is characterized by visualization of oneself as a deity in the awakened environment of the mandala. In this arena, conventional distinctions such as self and other collapse and give way to the bliss of nondual union. As the "Glorious Sky-like Great Bliss" *Śrīsaṃvarakhasama Tantra* put it, "the path of great bliss is the supreme nonduality of skillful means and wisdom, achieved through the power of joy which arises from great compassion."[81]

Since one takes the "goal" of being awakened buddha as one's path, the object of one's contemplative focus, the identification in Mahāyāna Buddhism of the aspiration for awakening with awakening itself conceptually pioneered the course of development that would lead to the techniques of self-identification with an awakened deity that is a central feature of tantric Buddhism. We find this idea expressed in the chapter on the contemplative process in the "Wheel of Time" *Kālacakra Tantra.* Just after calling on the practitioner to generate the aspiration to awakening, the text provides the following instructions:

> The entire world is empty, devoid of reality, and is of the nature of material form. Therefore, there is neither buddha nor spiritual awakening nor compassion beneficial to others, nor is there a vow with a sign [pointing toward future attainment]. O king, knowing all this in this way, bodhisattvas should contemplate the

> vajras of body, speech, and mind in the *mandala* as the lord of the *mandala*, whose virtues are immeasurable.[82]

In other words, to achieve the goal one must first realize the emptiness of all things, including the very goal one is trying to achieve, as an essential step in the realization process. Unifying oneself with the mandala deity is only possible if one has broken down the tendency toward reification and the consequent attachment to the self-other distinction. As we learn in the in the first chapter of the eight-century "Ḍākinīs' Network That Unites All Buddhas" *Sarvab uddhasamāyogaḍākinījālasaṃvara Tantra*, the spirit of awakening is the *vajra*, here the essence of mind from which one generates oneself as a deity. The passage occurs as follows:

> Union (*yoga*) does not arise in reflections, cast images, and so forth. Through the great yoga of the spirit of awakening, yogis become deities. This spirit of awakening is the vajra, the nature of all buddhas. Thus, through the union of the self with all one attains the nature of all buddhas. One is all buddhas, and all heroes are oneself. Therefore, through the union of oneself as the deity, one will be accomplished. Through this will accomplish all buddhas and also all heroes and all Vajradharas in this very life.[83]

Awakening depends on the realization that distinctions between oneself and others illusory; one's nature is equal to the buddhas' nature, as are the natures of all sentient beings. The claim that the impure, benighted sphere of existence, namely cyclic existence or *saṃsāra*, and the sphere of liberation, cessation or nirvana, are nondual and differ only cognitively, via the distinction between ignorance and correct knowledge of reality, is a powerful claim, which opened the way for the development of tantric Buddhist contemplative techniques. This claim was in fact made by Tripiṭakamāla, who wrote the following in his "Light on the Three Methods" *Nayatrayapradīpa:*

> It is said in both the sutras and the sovereign tantras that nondual gnosis (*advayajñāna*) alone is the cause of perfections, that is, the stages (*bhūmi*), concentrations (*samādhi*), spells (*dhāranī*), perfections (*pāramitā*), supernormal cognitions (*abhijñā*), and the infinite doors of liberation which were proclaimed with the very ambrosial voice of great compassion.[84]

"Nondual gnosis" is the goal of the practice of "deity" or buddha-yoga.[85] Deity yoga is the meditative practice of visualizing oneself as a deity, the term "yoga" here translatable as "union." The "Discourse Appendix Tantra" *Abhidhānottaratantra* succinctly links nondual gnosis with deity yoga, as follows:

> Supreme and complete awakening is
> Instantly and permanently attained
> Through awareness of the nondual gnosis,
> And through the divine yoginīs' yoga.[86]

The identity of the potential for awakening with awakening itself is made possible through this special, nondual gnosis of reality, an understanding of the emptiness that permits one not so much to understand but to *tolerate* the inconceivable manner in which phenomena are deeply interrelated. This view of reality is described in Mahāyāna sūtras such as the *Vimalakīrti* and the *Avataṃsaka*.[87] The Avataṃsaka school in East Asia, the Huayan or Kegon (華嚴) school, developed intricate meditative practices for the cultivation of this vision of reality, characterized by the interpenetration of the ultimate and the conventional,[88] so it is not surprising that Kūkai placed this school just below the Esoteric (*Mikkyō*) form of Buddhism in the hierarchy presented in his essay "Jeweled Key to the Secret Treasury" (秘藏寶鑰, *Hizō hōyaku*).[89] In another essay, "Attaining Enlightenment in This Very Existence" (即身成佛義, *Sokushin jōbutsugi*), Kūkai described the tantric vision of reality drawing on the imagery typical to this school, as follows:

> "Endlessly reverberating like Indra's net is that which is called the body": this is a metaphor for the compete interpenetration without obstruction of the three mysteries, the atoms of which are luminous Buddhalands. "Indra's net" is the jeweled net of Indra which is also called the "body," which designates one's own body, the Buddha's body and the bodies of sentient beings. The "body" also has four types, such as the Truth (*svabhāvika*, 自性), Beatific (*saṃbhoga*, 受用), and Emanation (*nirmāṇa*, 變化) [bodies], etc. The body also can be thrice characterized as word, gesture and image, which are also like those [above types]. The body is vertically and horizontally vibrant like an image in a mirror or rays of lamplight. Interpenetrating, that body is this body, and this body the bodies of sentient beings, whose bodies are the Buddha's body: [these] are not the same yet similar, not different yet differentiated.[90]

Tantric visualization implies at least an understanding of reality as not "solid" and unpliable but rather transformable and deeply interrelated to one's own body, mind, and imaginative powers, which from a certain perspective create one's perception of it. It thus involves a process of active imagination (*dhyāna*) coupled with the discipline of meditative concentration (*samādhi*), without which the visualization has no power, and yogic techniques such as breath control that enrich and empower the meditative experience. It is based upon the assumption of a fundamental link between cause and effect, such that the attainment of the latter requires a similar cause; buddhahood is thus attained through a process of identifying oneself, mentally, verbally, and physically, with a buddha.

This process is typically called "deity yoga" or, in the case of texts such as the "Universal Secret Sovereign Tantra" *Sarvarahasya-nāma-tantrarāja*, "buddhayoga," which is described as follows:

> If one meditates upon uniting with the buddha (*buddhayoga*), one by that means becomes identical to the buddhas. All Buddhas are

> alike in nature in that they arise from concentration (*samādhi*) and gnosis (*jñāna*). Without the practice of Buddhayoga, the yogin will not attain Buddhahood.[91]

According to some Tibetan commentators, the meditations that might be characterized as "buddhayoga" have two aspects: the cultivation of both the "divine pride" of oneself as a deity and the "vision" or vivid appearance of one's environment as a divine environment. The current Dalai Lama, Tenzin Gyatso (*bstan 'dzin rgya mtsho*), has described them as follows:

> Divine pride protects one from the ordinary [conception], and divine vivid appearance protects one from ordinary appearances. Whatever appears to the senses is viewed as the sport of a deity; for instance, whatever forms are seen are viewed as emanations of a deity and whatever sounds are heard are viewed as the mantras of a deity. One is thereby protected from ordinary appearances, and through this transformation of attitude, the pride of being a deity emerges. Such protection of mind together with its attendant pledges and vows is called the practice of mantra.[92]

The "divine pride" of tantric practice differs from ordinary pride in that, unlike the latter, it does not imagine a false distinction between subject and object, self and other, glorifying the former at the expense of the latter. Instead, it involves the reimagination of both self and other as deities, and one's environment as a divine deity palace that is schematically represented by the mandala. This practice is necessarily built upon the foundation of an awareness of both subjective and objective emptiness, for if one still imagines that there is an intrinsically real self, it is impossible to rise beyond the level of ordinary, gross perceptions of reality.[93]

This point is made in the "Universal Secret" *Sarvarahasya-nāma-tantrarāja,* which begins with what we might term as a statement of the tantric ethos:

> If one does not regard sentient beings as having definite bodies, produced as they are from the five elements,[94] and if one also does not ascertain a definite mind, then meditate on the buddhas in this way also. If a great being desires to bow down to the buddha, one should bow down to one's own gnosis.[95] The Buddha's gnosis and one's own have the same original source. Their secret nature is that they exist in a nondual fashion. If one understands that all things arise selflessly, then that which arises is nondual gnosis. As liberation is attained amidst both the desirable and the undesirable, there is nothing to which one should not bow down. Things have neither arisen nor will they arise. That which has been born and that which has died do not abide. Contemplating the buddhas thus, bow down to one's own true gnosis.[96]

Similar passages occur in other tantras. The "Revelation of the Intention" *Sandhivyākaraṇa Tantra,* for example, recommends that "through the union of oneself and one's deity, worship oneself and others."[97] While "buddhayoga" so conceived implies a previous or concurrent realization of emptiness, the tantric tradition portrays itself as superior to the Mahāyāna in its method. A classic textual example of this claim occurs at the end of the first chapter of the "Noble Ḍākinīs' Adamantine Cage" *Āryāḍākinīvajrapañjara Tantra,* as follows:

> If emptiness is taken as skillful means, then there is no buddhahood, since the effect is none other than the cause. Skillful means thus is not emptiness. The victors taught emptiness to counteract selfish conceptions for the sake of those who have wrong views and those who seek a view with regard to the self. Therefore, skillful are "the mandala wheels," the binding of bliss. Through the yoga of buddha pride buddhahood is rapidly attained. As for the Teacher who has the thirty-two signs and who has the eighty marks, his or her skillful form is that which is attained through skillful means.[98]

Tsongkhapa (*tsong kha pa*, 1357–1419), in his *Great Mantric Process*, argued that the Mantrayāna assumes the emptiness taught by the Mahāyāna, but goes beyond it, teaching meditative arts that enable one to rapidly achieve the mental and physical state of an awakened buddha.[99] Hence we see that the tantras, building on Mahāyāna theory, claim to possess secret teachings for rapidly attaining awakening.

2.3.2 Contemplative Ritual Practices

2.3.2.1 Mandala Creation and Initiation Therein

This section surveys major ritual practices addressed in the Buddhist tantras. These are ritual practices qualified as contemplative because in most tantric traditions outer ritual practices also have an inner contemplative dimension, namely, the practice of visualization. Most tantric rituals also entail a contemplative practice, usually a visualization, that either the master of ceremonies, the "Adamantine Master," is to perform while engaged in the outer ritual practices for public ceremonies or the individual adept for private practice. Moreover, tantric contemplative practices are not necessarily conducted silently, "in one's head," although they can be when circumstances dictate this. Instead, they employ the "three mysteries" of body, speech, and mind, with the body employed to make ritual gestures (*mudrā*) and the speech faculty occupied with mantra recitation, either out loud or inaudibly, as circumstances dictate. Moreover, while the outer rituals are usually described in a cryptic fashion, the contemplative dimensions are typically even more obscure and are often seen as the secrets to be conveyed to the adept following initiation.

A central feature of tantric Buddhist ritual is the mandala. It is the focus of many rituals and features prominently in tantric visualization practices. The Sanskrit term *maṇḍala* literally means a "circle," and in the Buddhist context it is indeed a magical circle, a consecrated space where rituals are performed. But in political discourse it also designated both the physical and conceptual circular space surrounding a king, and the subsidiary figures surrounding him were called *maṇḍalin*, or courtiers, from which the English word "mandarin" derives.[100] Hence a mandala is a representation of the court of a king, a palace as typically depicted in three-dimensional sculptural images, although the mandala is best known in terms of the two-dimensional paintings or drawings representing this court. The three-dimensional structure to be visualized is illustrated by a short description of the Great Wrath (*mahākrodha*) mandala in the eighth-century "Great Sovereign Lord of Spirits" *Bhūtaḍāmara Tantra,* as follows:

> It is four-sided and has four doors
> Surmounted by four portals.
> It has sixteen divisions and is adorned
> With a perimeter wall of vajras.
> In its center one should place Great Wrath;
> Fierce, he is surrounded by a halo of flames.
> He has four arms and shines with light
> The color of collyrium.[101]

The focus of the mandala is its palace, which is depicted as sitting atop the cosmos. The palace, a symbol of royalty, is also typically the central feature of the buddha lands as depicted in Mahāyāna texts. Therein, the Mahāyāna scholar Asaṅga wrote, "the Blessed Lord's magnificent palace is radiantly arrayed with the seven types of precious things,[102] from which arise light rays which completely fill immeasurable worlds."[103] In the "Root Precept of Mañjuśrī" *Mañjuśrīmūlakalpa,* a tantric text that mainly dates to the eight century,[104] the Buddha Ratnaketu in his mandala palace is compared to the ideal "wheel turning" king, the *cakravartin.* "[Ratnaketu] the great *cakravartin*-chief is to be placed at the centre. He has the colour of saffron and is like the rising-sun. He holds a great wheel which is turning. Thus painstakingly should one draw him. He is like a great king with his palace."[105]

The palace occupies a central position in the mandala, which itself occupies a dominant position in the cosmic hierarchy, as is clear in Nāgabuddhi's description in his "Established Arrangement of the [Esoteric] Community Meditation Manual" *Samājasādha navyavasthāna,* which begins not with the creation of the cosmos from the bottom up, but with the creation of the mandala at its peak in Akaniṣṭha, the highest heaven:

> Then, in the midst of space . . . generate the palace from [the syllable] *bhuṃ,* and with reverence place there all of the deity wheels such as Akṣobhya's. After that, Mahāvajradhara is generated by means of the process of union (*yoga*), subsequent union (*anuyoga*), utmost union (*atiyoga*), and great union (*mahāyoga*). The deities of the mandala arise through the union of the two organs. It is said that this is the invitation [for them] to come through visualization and recitation, or, in short, [just] visualization.[106]

Only after one has generated oneself as the deity in the mandala does the generation of the cosmos below it commence, first with the elemental disks:

> Then, through the power of adhesion, winds gradually begin to move, and these winds increase, to a depth of 1.6 million leagues. This wind disk, which is measureless in extent, sits atop space. From this wind disk falls streams of rain as wide as a wagon wheel, which forms a disk of water. Regarding its size, it is 1,120,000 leagues deep. Moreover, the wind churns the water, forming golden earth atop the water, 320,000 leagues in size. A disk of fire also exists within these.[107]

Buddhists drew upon the imagery of royalty as well as Hindu theism in portraying the buddhas as sovereign figures, with mastery over the cosmos, which one emulates in visualizing oneself as these majestic deities.

Externally, mandalas were traditionally made on consecrated ground using colored powders, a practice maintained by Tibetan Buddhists, who have popularized the "sand mandalas" by performatively constructing them publicly at large-scale ritual events, such as the teachings and initiation ceremonies performed by regularly by teachers such as the Dalai Lama.[108] Traditionally, mandalas were using naturally available colored pigments. The "Supreme Bliss of the Wheels" *Cakrasaṃvara Tantra* contains a succinct description of this ritual as follows:

> The mandala ground should be anointed there with unfallen cow dung, with charnel ground ash together with the five ambrosias. Anointing thus the ground, there the maṇḍala should be undertaken, and truly accomplished [as] a charnel ground. The master who has all good qualities should draw the divine mandala with powdered funeral pyre char together with charnel ground brick.[109]

After a digression on the master's good qualities, the text continues as follows:

> Having taken oneself to be Śrī Heruka with a skull staff placed in one's hand, think of Śrī Heruka, and place him in the center of the wheel. Having thus armored oneself, place the fences in the directions. Having thus armored oneself, place as well the weapon below. Oneself being equivalent to the wheel, and having made above for oneself a net of arrows and a floating enclosure, one is well-positioned. Thus armed, one who has this armor is unbreakable even by the Thirty-three deities.

> Well-protecting oneself thus, ornamented with insignia and mantras, draw the terrifying mandala that bestows great power. Then, with a corpse thread, or one colored with the great blood, lay out the terrifying mandala, Heruka's supreme mansion. [It is of] a single cubit, four or eight, [with] four corners all around, bedecked with four doors, adorned with four arches. The one who has the mantra (*mantrin*) should double [the thread].[110]

This text makes it clear that visualization is an essential part of the ritual. Having consecrated the space, the master is to both visualize himself or herself as the chief deity, Śrī Heruka, and to visualize him in the center of the to be created mandala wheel. Additional preparation includes armoring oneself with the protective armor mantras by imaginatively placing them on various points of the body and visualizing that the consecrated space is protected by weapons set below, a fence consisting of a row of vajra scepters around the periphery, and a net of arrows and a cage above; these visualizations are accompanied by mantra recitations that are not listed in the root text but are given in explanatory tantras or ritual manuals. Within this purified and ritually protected space, one can commence to draw the mandala, using cords and colored powders to lay out the mandala structure, with details filled in once the basic outline is established.

The "Discourse Appendix Tantra" *Abhidhānottaratantra* contains within its fourth chapter a meditation manual for this practice that nicely illustrates the contemplative dimensions of the mandala creation process. The passage occurs as follows:

> Inwardly and outwardly, one
> Should see that all things are empty.
> Place oneself with just one's own mind
> In awakenings' supreme requisites.
>
> Visualize a solar mandala
> Positioned amidst the space of one's heart.

Seeing this, there's reality supreme,
As well as the five auspicious gnoses.[111]

Then various divine light rays,
Radiating thus all around,
Summon the saints of previous
Times, and inspire their resolve.

Seeing the supreme mandala,
In the pleasing palace in space,
See the fierce goddesses everywhere
In a sesame seed-like shape.

Seeing the buddhas and bodhisattvas,
Awakening spirit, the guru who's chief,
As well as the various goddesses,
The worshipper should worship all of them.

Radiating emanations,
Of buddhas, fierce kings, and yoginīs,
All beings of the six realms
Are established in Buddhahood.

See them abiding there in the
Space realm, amidst which is the wheel
Of awakening, to which they
All go for the three refuges.

All beings will be established
In that very position there.
The adept, wishing this, always
Should himself go for refuge there.

The fortunate one should generate a
Self-conception in terms of five heaps,

> And so forth, thus form, feeling, cognition,
> Conditioning and also consciousness. . . .

Thus the yogī should purify his nature with respect to heaps, elements and sensory spheres, saying:

prakṛtipariśuddhāḥ sarvadharmāḥ prakṛtipariśuddho 'ham

"All things are naturally pure, naturally pure am I"

Afterward go for the triple refuge, and then assume a mantric body. Thinking "I become Śrī Heruka in order to achieve all beings' aims. I am thus established." One should obtain Heruka's state of all joys. One will be established if one says:

oṃ svabhāvaśuddhāḥ sarvadharmmāḥ svabhāvaśuddho 'haṃ

"Oṃ all things are essentially pure, essentially pure am I"

One should radiate a light ray garland going to the end of the ten directions, the limit of the universe. Seeing thus the light rays, there is the fence and cage, as follows:

> The adamantine ground is established,
> As well as the arrow net canopy,
> Outside one should lay down from a distance,
> The adamantine fence of blazing fire.[112]

The text then digresses, briefly discussing the creation of magical blessing pills, and then it relates at some length the visualization of oneself as the chief deity of the mandala, "Adamantine Syllable Hūṃ" Vajrahūṃkara, as well as the remaining mandala deities, whom he emanates. Then one visualizes oneself as Vajrahūṃkara in the center of the mandala. Having done this, one reflects as follows:

> Reflect upon the mind alone, the wisdom of mere appearances. This is sky-like, with no entities and also no lack of entities. It is like space, not besmirched, lacking essence, and undefiled. All of the three realms are non-dually present in the turning of the mind through generation and destruction, in the subtle perspective, illuminating that which abides in the hollow of the heart. I bow down to the supreme and clear realm of reality. It is a stainless and sky-like glory that is present as the cause of tranquility, the three realms that serve as the receptacle gathering all of the victors, who have knowledge about all of the sense powers movement when impelled by objects. Through the yoga of recollecting the Buddha there is meditation on the recollection of reality (*dharma*). Become oneself the body of reality (*dharmakāya*) through the yoga of recollecting reality.
>
> Have no doubt that consciousness
> Illuminating the middle,
> The supreme wisdom, blazes
> Through intensive meditation.
>
> If a person meditates on
> The very single soundless drop
> That always exists in the heart,
> Gnosis will thereupon arise.[113]

This passage relates an interesting contemplation that one would do at the conclusion of the visualization. It also illustrates the two main modes of tantric contemplative practice, the "creation" or "generation" stage (*utpattikrama*), in which the meditator visualizes himself or herself as the deity surrounded by a court of awakened beings. This visualization should be firm and vivid, which requires tremendous mental stability, and is traditionally mastered in the Tibetan context through three-year meditation retreats.

The last two verses also hint at practices that involve yogic exercises focusing on the subtle body. This is the final stage of contemplative practice called the "perfection" or "completion" stage (*niṣpannakrama*). The creation stage, with its intense training of the mind's internal focus, provides the "subtle perspective" enabling one to see the subtle internal workings of one's psycho-physical matrix, the body and mind inseparably intertwined. This stage involves the contemplations and yogic exercises relating to the subtle body, *sukṣmakāya,* which consists of channels (*nāḍi*) through which flows vital energy (*prāṇa*) as well as "drops" of subtle consciousness. The framework for this body is the central channel (*avadhūti*) that is surrounded by two subsidiary channels, the left and right *lalanā* and *rasanā* channels, which intertwine around it. The points where they intersect are known as "wheels," or *cakra*s, from which emanate smaller subsidiary channels. One of the goals of this practice is to open the orifice of the central channel in the genital or navel area and force the vital energy from the subsidiary channels into it. This unification gives rise to the "supreme wisdom" that is the nondual gnosis, which is engendered when the vital energy is unified in the central channel. This is because the bifurcation of vital energy, which happens shortly after conception when the channels emerge from the heart center, gives rise to dualistic thinking, manifesting in the apparent bifurcation of things into dualistic categories, such as self and other, and so on.

Entering the central channel, it "blazes," which is a reference to the subtle "fury fire" (*caṇḍālī, gtum mo*) that travels up the channel and melts the subtle "drop" of the brain center, whose molten descent down the channel awakens increasingly intense levels of bliss.[114] The "very single soundless drop" is reference to the very subtle drop, the most primal manifestation of consciousness, which is embedded in the heart center. Subtle body yogic practices, associated with the "unexcelled yoga tantras" (*niruttarayogatantra*) composed from the eighth century onward, are considered by many to be the highest secret of the tantras, and they are generally only elliptically referred to in the tantras, as they are in the above quoted passage from the "Discourse Appendix Tantra" *Abhidhāno ttaratantra*.[115]

Returning to the tantric rituals and their relation to contemplative practices, Richard Kohn noted, "a general pattern in tantric ritual is for the meditator to first create a visualization discursively described by the text and then to recite a mantra that actualizes the imagined scenario." He argues that mantra practice "limns a portrait of a Buddha and Buddha activity. The portrait is prescriptive rather than descriptive; it aims not so much at defining a Buddha as at creating one. A Buddha, a *sūtra* tells us, does not act in a sequential premeditated way, but rather directly and spontaneously."[116] Commenting on the ubiquity of mantra recitation in tantric rituals, he continues, noting that "the curiously quiescent activity that we see in mantra recitation does at the very least resonate with the canonical descriptions. After all, what could be closer to spontaneous effortless action than the works of a radiant heart?"[117]

Once the mandala is drawn, it is the site for initiating students into the tradition since revelation of the image of the mandala is one of the features of the tantric initiation ceremony. As is now well known, the tantric Buddhist initiation rite of *abhiṣeka*, literally "consecration," was modelled on the older Vedic rites of coronation (*rājasūya*).[118] In other words, the adept, who will be initiated into the contemplative practice of visualizing him- or herself as an awakened sovereign, is ritually coronated in preparation for this. Buddhists were aware of both the similarities and differences between their rite of consecration and that used in the royal consecration ceremony. Śubhakarasiṃha, in his "Running Commentary on the Awakening of Mahāvairocana Sutra" explicitly compared them. After describing the Indian rite of coronation, which involves consecrating the crown prince seated on a lion throne with water from a jeweled vase, he describes the Buddhist rite as follows:

> In this abhiṣeka, the prince of the Dharma sits on a miraculous lion throne adorned with the lotus blossoms of the subtle Dharma, the throne being placed before the great map [mandala] of the secretly glorified universe, the Dharmakāya's domain. Then the water of wisdom and compassion, impregnated with goodness, is poured on the Dharma prince's mind. . . . Thereupon the master, following tradition of the ancient kings of the Dharma [Buddhas], announces, "From now on, this prince of the Dharma will attain birth in the family of the Tathāgatas and succeed to the throne of the Buddhas."[119]

Drawing upon the older Vedic rite of coronation, in the early Buddhist tantras there was a focus on consecration with specially blessed water contained within a ritual jar or pot (*kalaśa*). Known as the jar consecration (*kalaśābhiṣeka*), it traditionally divided into six distinct consecrations. The first five, the water, crown, vajra, bell, and name consecration, were known as the "wisdom" or "spell" (*vidyā*) consecrations, so called because they are connected with the female goddesses associated with the five buddhas who are associated with the five gnoses. The final consecration, the "master" *ācārya* consecration, sanctions one to fully participate in the practices associated with the tantra and to eventually serve as a master oneself.[120] At the conclusion of the ritual, the mandala is revealed to the newly initiated adepts, who are, in many traditions, blindfolded during earlier phases of the ceremony, which are removed when they are properly initiated. They are also taught the mantras of the mandala deities and given instructions on the contemplative practices related to them.

There was another influence on tantric Buddhist initiation rituals in connection with the mandala, and these are rituals involving possession by deities as well as sexual union with a consort. These elements are found in many of the early tantras, and thus seem to be an important part of the early tantric Buddhist traditions. We can see this, for example, in a mandala ritual described in the in the "Mantric Precept Division of the Glorious Supreme Prime" *Śrīparamādya-mantrakalpakhaṇḍa,* a text that may date to the eighth century.[121] The passage reads as follows:

> He who undertakes the worship of the mandala attains all powers. He should worship with dance, displaying the gestures. He should always worship the mandala by means of the five sense pleasures. Then his own *mudrā*[122] will be presented by the secret goddesses. *Hrīḥ hūṃ śrī bhyo.* As for the complete production of the mandala, it is square with four gates, and has four lines and four great pillars. It is adorned with four corners. In the center of that one should thus draw the four mandalas. Place at the gate the four-faced Nanda bearing a sword in his hand, endowed with the Essence [mantra], the proud power producer. Now, in the primal mandala one should thus be immersed. One should be possessed by the sisters (*sring mo, *bhaginī*) in due order. Engaged, worship in accordance with the procedure with incense and so forth. One accomplished in secret bliss will perform the summoning. *Oṃ kā li ma ni ra de pro ta la me bhū rāksha si pa rastā ma ya he ba ho ba, ba ra he bi dye tī ma ya svā hā, sid dhi ke sid dhi stā ma a he.* With the gestures, *hrīḥ hūṃ śrī bhyo.* Then all are possessed. Being possessed, [they] should enter.[123]

There are many interesting features of this text. It prescribes worshipping the mandala with dance, ritual gestures, and the five sense pleasures for the purpose of attracting goddesses to possess the officiant. Alexis Sanderson has argued that this was a feature drawn from Śaiva sources, dating back to the Kāpālikas, whose practices were advanced by the Śākta Śaivas, that is, Śaivas who focused on goddess worship.[124] The goddesses to be invoked in this case, the "sisters," are a class of goddesses similar to the ḍākinis or yoginīs. We may recall that Dharmakīrti mentioned not only heretical *ḍākinītantra*s but also *bhaginītantra*s, which Sanderson has identified with the Śaiva works focusing on the "four sisters" goddesses of the "left-handed stream" (*vāmasrotaḥ*) of the goddess-oriented Vidyāpīṭha tantras.[125]

Another eighth-century text, the "Ḍākinīs' Network That Unites All Buddhas" *Sarvabuddhasamāyoga-ḍākinījālasaṃvara Tantra*, the earliest Buddhist ḍākinī tantra, preserves a great deal of lore concerning the worship of goddesses for the purpose of attracting them for the purpose of possession (*āveśa*). For example, it includes the following passage that relates in more detail exactly how this worship with dance and gestures should be conducted:

> With song, cymbals, and dance, with gestures and with the sentiments—namely eroticism, heroism, compassion, humor, ferocity, terror, disgust, wonder, and tranquillity—one's aim will be achieved. By being endowed with the sentiments of eroticism, etc., dancing with the various gestures, and by uniting oneself with all, one will achieve all states of possession (*āveśa*). Eroticism (*śṛṅgāra*) corresponds to Vajrasattva, heroism (*vīra*) to the Hero Tathāgata, compassion (*karuṇa*) to Vajradhara, humor (*hāsya*) to the supreme Lokeśvara, ferocity (*raudra*) to Vajrasūrya, terror (*bhayānaka*) to Vajrarudra, disgust (*bībhatsa*) to Śākyamuni, wonder (*adbhuta*) to Ārali, and tranquility (*śānta*) always corresponds to the Buddha, since it pacifies all suffering.[126]

This is a fascinating text on several points. It evokes nine sentiments (*navarasa*) that were associated with classical Indian dance. It calls for dance as a form of worship as well as the elements that would normally accompany it in the South Asian context, namely music and symbolic gestures or *mudrā*. The association of the dramatic gestures with Tantric deities points to the ritual nature of this dance practice, which apparently had the aim of invoking trance-like states of possession, *āveśa*, a term that literally means "entering."[127] Here it refers to the employment of dance to invoke the deities, with the implication that different styles of dance, employing one of the nine sentiments, could invoke the deity correlated to that sentiment. The text is following what is evidently an ancient pattern in India. As Dale Saunders and others have pointed out, the use of gestures in dance probably derives from their use in ancient Indian religious ritual.[128] Their deployment in tantric ritual seems to be a reappearance of what Louis Renou termed "immemorial magical ritual language."[129]

By the eighth century the term for ritual gesture, *mudrā,* also came to signify female "consort" participants in tantric rituals, particularly those with an erotic nature. The idea here is that *mudrā* came to mean not only the gestures used to summon goddesses but also, by extension, the goddesses themselves, as well as female practitioners who were thought to embody them, either through possession or by visualized self-identification.[130]

Another eighth-century tantra, the "Compendium of the Realities of All Tathāgatas" *Sarvtathāgatatattvasaṃgraha-nāma-Mahāyāna-Sūtra*, portrays the initiation process as entailing erotic practices with (presumably) human females. An example occurs as follows:

> One should make a mandala that is like the wheel of truth (*dharmacakra*),[131] surrounded by consort wives (*mudrābhāryā*); the Buddha should be inserted there. As soon as he enters one should speak the secret to the Buddha: "All-bestowing Lord, give me your wife!" Speaking thus, one obtains the secret accomplishment, unequalled splendors of the buddhas in all of the methods of the clan consort.[132]

Another passage in the *Sarvtathāgatatattvasaṃgrah-nāma-Mahāyāna-Sūtra* sheds further light on the initiatory nature of these practices. The passage opens with the step in the initiation sequence when the adept's blindfold is removed, and one is introduced to the mandala and the tradition's secrets. It occurs as follows:

> Then, one should release the blindfold, duly display the mandala, and declare the secret of the commitment consorts

> (*samayamudrā*): "These commitment consorts are good, and will serve you in everything. The mother, sister, wife, and daughter [are] the servants." Then the essence mantra is: *oṃ sarvavajragāmini sarvabhakṣe sādhaya guhyavajriṇi hūṃ phaṭ*. By repeating this once, all women are subjugated and can be enjoyed, and there is no immorality (*adharma*) [in so doing].[133]

The Buddhist system of consecrations were influenced by older and almost certainly Śaiva practices involving the invocation of deities for the purpose of consecration at the time of initiation. The text maintains a sense of both coercion and transgression, as indicated by the above passage's assertion that "all women are subjugated and can be enjoyed," and the assurance that doing so is not immoral. In another closely related text, the "Sovereign Mahāyāna Precept Called the Glorious Supreme Prime" *Śrīparamādya-nāma-mahāyānakalparāja,* the practitioner is again assured of this, as follows: "The Master of Mudrā practices the dharma, is pure and wears clean clothes. In eating everything and doing everything he is beyond reproach. He is attended by the consorts who are messengers of Śiva and he repeats the essence [mantra]."[134] The text perpetuates the equation between ritual transgression and magical power made in earlier Śaiva tantric texts and discredits the idea that such transgressions might have negative consequences.

The above quotation from the *Śrīparamādya-nāma-mahāyānakalparāja* occurs at the beginning of a passage describing an initiation ritual that takes place in the "consort mandala known as the commitment of all powers."[135] The rite is described as follows:

> Then the great [syllable] *bhyo* is heard within the mandala. Then, aside from the master, how should all of the other enter? This excepts [those who have] the commitment of the evil ones.[136] The disciple holds a flower in his hands and is blindfolded. He is admitted with the hand gesture of Mahākāla, and the great oath (*mahāsamaya*) [syllable] *bhyo* should be applied to his ear. Then, being terrified, he should cast the flower. He will attain as his

> chosen deity that on which it falls. If it does not fall [on a deity] he should enter to cast again. Then he will attain the ability to terrify as well as each and every yoga. Then he should be released from the blindfold and the mandala shown [to him]. Worshipping with the gestures of the evil ones, etc., the essence mantras and their respective signs should be given [to him].
>
> Then the commitment is taught. All sentient beings being sealed, the commitment is that one should eat despised [substances]. Mantras should not be taught. [This] commitment will grant the achievement of yoga. The fierce commitment[137] is marked by the lance and seal of the mothers. If transgressed, one's essence is permanently destroyed. Now, undertaking this, one who eats human flesh one will attain yoga before long. One who does not eat will have no success (*siddhi*). If one does not transgress the oath, one will not be killed by any host,[138] and one will learn the gnosis of the consort (*phyag rgya'i ye shes*). These aims will be fulfilled by worshipping with gestural dance, offering sacrifice (*bali, gtor ma*), and satiating oneself with food and drink and pleasure. This is the consort mandala called "the commitment of all powers."[139]

This passage appears to describe an initiation rite empowering one to participate in tantric feast ceremonies, involving the consumption of "despised [substances]," with human flesh (*sha chen po,*mahāmāṃsa*) specifically mentioned, which implies a charnel ground locale for the practice. The presence of deities strongly associated with Śaiva traditions, originally at least, is also notable.[140]

An important event in the history of tantric Buddhism, well documented in the early eighth-century Buddhist tantras, was the development of rites of consecration in partial dependence upon Śaiva ritual precedents, involving sexual activity as well as other forms of sensual stimulation, such as dance, music, the consumption of meat and intoxicants, and, originally at least, entry into an altered state of consciousness for the purpose of "bringing down" the deities into the participants. A further passage from the *Sarvatathāgatatattvasaṃgraha-nāma-Mahāyāna-Sūtra* illustrates this nicely:

> One should exhibit the adamantine erotic dance and fasten the adamantine garland. One should compose the adamantine song and worship with adamantine dance. The consecration through sexual pleasure is supreme. Aside from the bliss of dance and song there is no other. Thus the secret worship is unexcelled.[141]

This "consecration through sexual pleasure" (*kāmaratyābhiṣeka*) may be an early designation for the rites that came to be known as the "secret" and "consort gnosis" consecrations. This consecration was seen as essential for the cultivation of magical power, the *siddhi*s. The same scripture reports that "The Lord Vajraratna said: 'Having become a holder of the actual consort (*karmamudrā*), and endowed with all ornaments, embracing a woman magical power (*vibhūti*) is delivered in worship, and one will succeed.' "[142]

Developing through these precedents, tantric Buddhists eventually settled on a group of three "higher consecrations" or initiation rites that were introduced in the eighth and ninth centuries, in the "Ḍākinīs' Network That Unites All Buddhas" *Sarvabuddhas amāyogaḍākinījālasaṃvara,* "Esoteric Community" *Guhyasamāja*, and "Supreme Bliss of the Wheels" *Cakrasaṃvara* tantras. This set up was adopted in the class of works that came to be classified as the highest "unexcelled yoga tantras." Grouping the consecrations described earlier into one, the "jar" or "master" series of consecrations, three additional consecrations were added. The first, which is second in the sequence of four, was called the "secret consecration" (*guhyābhiṣeka*). It entailed the master entering sexual union with a female consort, apparently one provided by the initiate, and the master consecrating the disciple with the mixed sexual fluids produced through this union. Interestingly, this ritual uses the imagery and substances of lineage transmission via sexual reproduction in a ceremony for the transmission of a spiritual lineage. It was followed by the "consort gnosis" (*prajñābhiṣeka*) consecration, in which the adept was instructed in sexual union with the same consort. The "Supreme Bliss of the Wheels" *Cakrasaṃvara Tantra* describes these rites very succinctly as follows:

> Then the well-equipoised master
> Should indeed worship the consort.
> One the second day he should make the drop
> For the students with blood thrice-enchanted.
>
> Having unveiled the student's face,
> He should show him the mandala,
> It's there that he should reveal her
> In whom is the deity's place.[143]

Most of the tantras are very unclear about these two stages of the initiation process, given its transgressive nature. But the commentator Jayabhadra describes it in more detail as follows:

> On the second day, once again one worships the mandala and produces the blessing, and so forth, sets up an abode of bliss, such as a mat, couch, and so forth, either in or near the mandala, and commences with the secret consecration. Regarding "he should make the drop with blood thrice enchanted," together with an outer woman who has the previously explained characteristics and who is menstruating, he gives rise to sexual joy by means of the process of drinking *soma*,[144] and so forth. Then, through the practice of rubbing the vajra and lotus, and so forth, when the [sexual fluids] are flowing, the essence, quintessence, and garland mantras are recited over the blindfolded disciple. Bestow the consecration with the vajra and lotus upon the [disciple's] seven spots—the crown, forehead, both eyes, mouth, throat, and heart. The disciple should consume it as if it were bliss-bestowing ambrosia. Immediately after that, his "face should be unveiled"

> and he "should be shown the mandala. He should be shown her in whom" is "the deity's place" of the lotus, the place of the secret consecration. This means that he should be shown the outer woman who has the power to bestow consecration.[145]

For this system, the initiation is a two-day process, with the first initiation, the "master" or "jar" series of rites, with the final three continuing on the second day. Jayabhadra here only describes the secret consecration, alluding to the gnosis of the consort consecration when he briefly notes that the initiate is shown the consort's lotus. Another great Indian master, Atiśa Dīpaṅkaraśrījñāna (982–1054 CE), who played a major role in the dissemination of tantric Buddhism to Tibet as will be discussed in chapter 3, sheds further light on these consecrations by describing a visualization, in which the adept reimagines being initiated by the mandala deities. It occurs as follows in his "Analysis of The Realization" commentary:

> Imagine that the five, the four mothers and Vārāhī, [descend] from the sky holding the "jar" filled with the ambrosia of gnosis, and that they bestow "consecration" with their hands. Then, the four mothers dissolve into [Vajra]vārāhī, and bestow the "secret consecration" with the spirit of awakening (*bodhicitta*) of equipoise with Śrī Heruka. Then, Heruka takes Vārāhī as his consort (*mudrā*), and through being equipoised their winds dissolve. Relying on that, contemplate the experience of the natural (*sahaja*). Then you, a child of the clan, unite with the consort (*mudrā*) as Heruka, and, depending on that, meditate on clear light, that wisdom which is attained in visionary experience. This is the very essence of the Transcendence of Wisdom (*prajñāpāramitā*) which is the purity of the three consciousnesses,[146] and which is liberation from birth due to the non-existence of body, speech, and mind. This is the ultimate truth that has the characteristic of always appearing completely luminous like the moon, sun, fire, and jewels. Regard [everything] with the eye of the "consort gnosis" [consecration],

> the vision that is beyond the objectification of the other. In this way, do not see anything in and of itself, but *see* the clear light. And while there is no sort of causation at work with this sort of clear light, conventionally, see the thirty-seven deities from mere wind-mind clear and complete like a reflected image, colored like a rainbow, and distorted like [the image of] the moon in water. Regard them as caused, and since they arise, they are conventional. The integration that does not divide the two truths, the great spirit of awakening, is "the fourth" [consecration].[147]

Here Atiśa was commenting on a famous *Cakrasaṃvara* meditation manual, the "Realization the Supreme Bliss of the Wheels" *Cakrasaṃvarābhisamaya,* attributed to the great adept Lūipa. The adept, who would already have received initiation from his or her guru, imagines re-experiencing the consecrations as a deity at the hands of the other deities. Atiśa describes the initiation process to be visualized and also its significance in his understanding. Although the final three consecrations are rarely clearly disclosed, the "gnosis of the consort" consecration is an introduction to subtle body yogic practices via union with a consort. The final consecration, "the fourth," is a disclosure of secret teachings concerning the nature of the self and reality. Here Atiśa intimates what these teachings entail, namely details concerning perfection stage contemplations that map the mandala deities onto the network of channels constituting the subtle body, with the ultimate aim of realizing the nature of mind as "clear light," which emerges as the nondual gnosis when vital energy is unified in the central channel and the very subtle mind in the heart wheel is released from the knotted channels that secure it.

2.3.2.2 Other Ritual Practices

Once one has been initiated as a master in a tradition, one is qualified to perform the various rituals described in the tradition's tantra and other associated ritual texts. And with most traditions, these rituals are very numerous. These ritual practices described in the tantras are often categorized in terms of the goal of the practice. The first is the ultimate accomplishment (*lokottarasiddhi*), which refers to those practices believed to help one achieve the ultimate goal of awakening. Included here would be the contemplative practices and their ritual supports, such as the consecrations, that are thought to lead to awakening. But there are also practices categorized as "worldly accomplishments" that are thought to achieve various mundane ends. These are typically what we would term magical powers, designed to give one supernormal powers of perception or abilities affecting oneself, such as flight and invisibility, or the ability to control natural forces, such as the weather, or to control or affect in various ways other people.

Now, the distinction between ultimate and mundane implies a hierarchy, with the former privileged. We might be inclined to value the former and discount the latter. This approach, however, would be misguided. As Charles Orzech argued:

> When *siddhi* is considered from the perspective of ultimate enlightenment, *anuttarasaṃyaksambodhi,* then one refers to it simply as *siddhi* or more specifically as *lokottara siddhi* (出世成就, or 出世悉地). When this attainment is channeled toward action in the conditioned universe through images, maṇḍalas, and mantras it is referred to as mundane *siddhi* (*laukika siddhi,* 世間成就) and is manifested through application of supernormal powers used to aid in the salvation of beings. Though the purpose of any given ritual might be predominantly *lokottara* or *laukika,* all rites assume both goals.[148]

This is the case since the ultimate accomplishment of awakening is a requirement for success in the mundane rituals. Try as one might, a neophyte with a modicum of realization is unlikely to succeed, regardless of how many times he or she attempts to perform the rituals described in the tantras. Yet some esoteric works demand very little of the practitioner and promise great results. For example, the "Great Amulet Spell" *Mahāpratisarā-dhāraṇī*, a text translated into Chinese by Baosiwei (寶思惟, d. 721) in 712 CE, promises the following if one merely inscribes the spell on a sash and wears it as an amulet:

> Noxious poisons (厭蠱) and curses (呪詛) will not be able to harm you. [The karmic retribution coming from] sins that you previously committed will all be eradicated. Poison will not be able to harm you and fire will not be able to burn you. Blades will not be able to cut you and water will not be able to drown you. You will not be diminished or injured by thunder and lightning, thunderbolts, and unseasonable storms and tempests.[149]

Such protection has long been one of the main appeals of Buddhist ritual practices, going back to the protective spell (*rakṣā*) literature preserved by early Buddhist traditions.

Tantric ritual draws upon prior Indian ritual practices. Most prominent among these are the rituals of Vedic Hinduism, which centered on sacrificial offerings made to the gods, undertaken by a priestly class, the Brahmins. Their ritual focused on the construction of often elaborate altars in which were kindled sacred fire, in which oblations would be made, in conjunction with recitations of passages from the *Veda*s, the sacred scriptures of ancient Hinduism. The core ritual, *homa* fire sacrifice, was appropriated wholesale by Buddhists. This appropriation happened long before the rise of tantra,[150] but this and other ritual practices were adopted by tantric Buddhists, drawing again on the repertoire of rituals already in use among Mahāyāna Buddhists as well as those practiced by rival groups such as the Śaivas.

Tantric Buddhists also drew on the established Indian practice of sorcery, a pan-traditional practice of magic that drew upon the Vedic rites while adding post-Vedic innovations. This tradition of sorcery was usually referred to by the title "the six magical rites" (*ṣaṭkarmāṇi*), although the various accounts of this list amount to far more than six. Included in the list are usually the following: pacifying (*śāntika*)—that is, the pacification of hostile influences; enriching (*pauṣṭika*)—enriching oneself or others; controlling (*vaśya*)—causing others to do one's bidding; and destroying (*abhicāraka*)—killing or seriously harming enemies. Each type of ritual has its own requisites. For example, for pacifying rites, the ritual would be performed at an auspicious time using auspicious requisites, usually white colored, such as milk and white sesame seeds, while destroying rites would be performed at midnight using inauspicious, black colored requisites, such as black sesame seeds.[151] This is a type of sympathetic magic, using like materials to ritually achieve a like end. In some rituals this is obvious. For example, the "Supreme Bliss of the Wheels" *Cakrasamvara Tantra* describes the following ritual for driving one's enemy or enemies insane: "Binding the conjoined skull seals, repeat [the quintessence mantra] without breathing. He whose name the fierce one [utters] will instantly become mad. As many as one thousand people will be maddened. One can mentally release them."[152] While this very brief account is unclear, the sympathetic magical approach becomes clear in the commentaries, where we learn that to accomplish this rite one needs the powerful intoxicant datura as well as the skull of a rabid dog. The fifteenth-century Tibetan commentator Tsongkhapa describes the rite in his *Illumination of the Hidden Meaning* commentary, as follows:

> Draw a wheel augmented with the victim's name. Prepare the seeds, roots, stalk, leaves, and branches of the datura plant, and put it in the closed mouth of a rabid dog's "skull." "Bind" its fissures with mud [made of] charnel ground ash, and repeat the augmented quintessence mantra seven times "without breathing." If you put it in a charnel ground, "he whose name one" [utters] "will become mad. As many as one thousand people will be maddened." If one bathes [the skull] with milk reciting with a peaceful mind, they will be "released."[153]

The highly intoxicating plant datura and the skull of a rabid dog are ideal accoutrements for a spell causing madness. Many of the harmful rituals described in the tantras are accompanied by counter-rituals that reverse them. In this case, bathing the enchanted skull in milk would be the pacifying ritual antidote.

Another interesting example is found in the "The Practice Manual of Noble Tārā Kurukullā" *Āryatārākurukullākalpa*, a tantra focusing on the Kurukullā form of the Mahāyāna deity Tārā. An enriching rite, it focuses on the color yellow as well as the precious items that the ritual is seeking to attract to the practitioner. The ritual occurs as follows:

> If one desires the attainment of a lord, one should draw a citron and, in its center, a bow. Inside the bow, one should draw a jewel-shaped lotus-bud. In the center of the lotus-bud is the syllable *jrūṃ*, surrounded by the seven syllables. One should draw this on a golden tablet and keep it in the upper part of the house. One should surround it with an outer garland of lotuses, and, on the eighth or twelfth day of the month, using a jar containing five types of jewels, one should take it down. Having washed and worshiped it, one should recite the mantra one hundred and eight times. Within a year, one will become the equal of Kubera.[154] Such a charm should be worn correctly.[155]

The tantras offer a great wealth of magical ritual practices for those inclined toward such. Belief in their efficacy played a huge role in the dissemination of the tantras within India and throughout Asia, as will be discussed in the next chapter.

3

Dissemination and Reception of the Tantras

The newly emergent Buddhist tantras were quickly disseminated in Asia during the seventh and eighth centuries. The promise of the efficacy of these new Buddhist traditions via their ritual practices ensured that there was serious interest in them throughout Asia. However, the antinomian practices found in many of the tantras gave rise to resistance to their dissemination in these new cultural settings. This section will introduce the dissemination of Buddhist tantric traditions to East and Southeast Asia, Tibet, and Central Asia during the medieval period and finally to the West during the modern era.

3.1 Tantric Buddhism in Asia in the Seventh Through Ninth Centuries CE

Maritime trade among India, Southeast Asia, and China was pivotal for the rapid transmission of the newly established tantric Buddhist traditions in the seventh and eighth centuries. When tantric traditions first developed in the mid-seventh century, there were already well-established maritime trade routes linking East India with Southeast Asia and China. Buddhist monks, nuns, and pilgrims traveled on merchant ships, thereby disseminating new texts and traditions The Chinese pilgrim Yijing, for example, traveled by sea from the southern Chinese port of Guangzhou to Śrīvijaya on Sumatra Island in the Indonesian archipelago. There he

The Buddhist Tantras. David B. Gray, Oxford University Press. © Oxford University Press 2023.
DOI: 10.1093/oso/9780197623831.003.0004

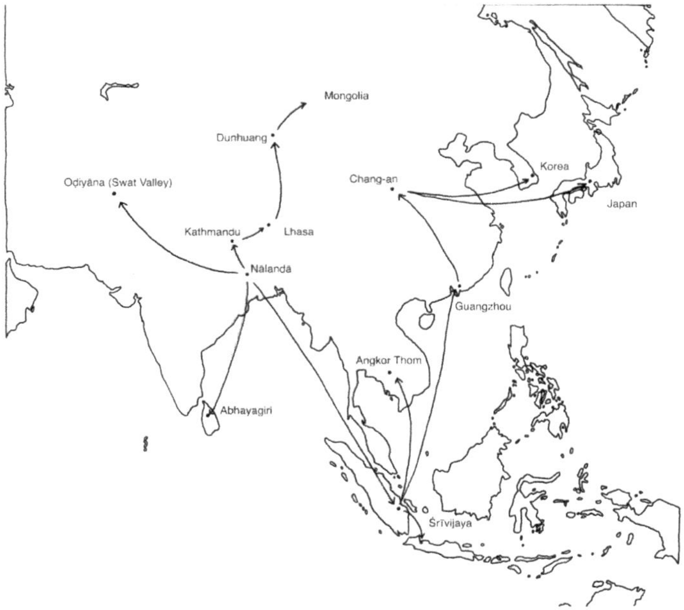

Map 3.1 The Spread of Tantric Buddhism, Seventh Through Sixteenth Centuries.
Map by Karuna Gray.

discovered a vibrant Buddhist community with more than a thousand monks; he studied Sanskrit there before continuing to the port of Tāmralipti in Northeast India.[1]

Buddhist institutions took advantage of trade networks to spread Buddhist teachings. Nālandā Monastery, as noted in chapter 1, played a major role in the dissemination of the new tantric Buddhist teachings. Vajrabuddhi, one of the Indian monks who brought tantric Buddhism to China, began his career as a novice monk there.[2] Nālandā's oversized role was facilitated by its international reach, attracting pilgrims from across Asia such as Xuanzang and Yijing. As Tansen Sen has argued:

> By the seventh century, this institution was not only attracting students from across Asia, it was also actively sending monks to propagate the doctrine. The monastery also received donations from local and foreign rulers. Indeed, the establishment of Nālandā seems to have had significant impact on cross-regional Buddhist exchanges during the second half of the first millennium.[3]

Nālandā was not the only monastery to play such an important role at that time. Another important monastery that played a significant role in the spread of tantric Buddhism was the Abhayagiri Monastery in Sri Lanka, a Mahāyāna monastery that also was a center of tantric Buddhism in South Asia by at least the early eighth century. The tantric master Vajrabuddhi traveled there enroute to China in the early eighth century, and his disciple Amogavajra also traveled there in 741 to acquire tantric texts that were not yet available in China. Monks from Abhayagiri were also instrumental in the dissemination of Buddhism to Java and played a role in the establishment of the monastery at Ratu Boko in Java in the late eighth century. As Jeffrey Sundberg has argued, there is archeological evidence of tantric practice at this site.[4] The Śrīvijaya kingdom in Southeast Asia played an important role as a regional center for tantric Buddhism, as was the related Śailendra kingdom in Java. There is evidence that the Sarvadurgatipariśodhana and Trilokavijaya mandalas, and, presumably, their associated practice and textual traditions, were introduced to Java circa 700, which would mean that they were rapidly transmitted there, with decades of their compilation in India.[5]

Tantric Buddhism was introduced to China in the early eighth century by Śubhakarasiṁha and Vajrabuddhi, both of whom traveled to China along the sea route,[6] with Śubhakarasiṃha arriving at Chang-an, the capital of China in 716, and Vajrabuddhi and his disciple Amoghavajra arriving five years later, in 721.[7] Amoghavajra, in particular played a central role in the establishment of esoteric

Buddhism in China. A monk of Indian and Sogdian descent, he departed Central Asia for China and beyond with his maternal uncle on a trading expedition in 714, and met Vajrabuddhi in Southeast Asia in 717, becoming his disciple.[8]

Śubhakarasiṃha and Vajrabuddhi were hosted and patronized by the Chinese imperial government. However, their teachings were not enthusiastically received by the Xuanzong emperor (玄宗, r. 712–756) of the Tang Dynasty (618–690, 705–907), who was a devoted Daoist. It was Amoghavajra, fully fluent in Chinese, who managed to secure sufficient patronage to establish a distinctly tantric Buddhist school in China. He gained prominence during the An Lu Shan rebellion in 756, during which time he remained in the capital, which was under rebel control. He assisted the new emperor Suzong (肅宗, r. 756–762), sending secret messages to him and performed rites invoking the fierce protector deity Acala to defeat the rebels. Amoghavajra developed a close relationship with the next emperor, Daizong (代宗, r. 762–779). He provided ritual support for the emperor, whose reign was very precarious in the political chaos that followed the An Lu Shan rebellion. In 765, the capital was again threatened by an invasion of a 200,000-strong army, a coalition of Tibetans and Uighurs, led by the general Pugu Huai'en (僕固懷恩). On behalf of the emperor, he performed an elaborate ritual to protect the state, again invoking the protector Acala, based on *The Scripture for Humane Kings,* a Chinese Buddhist apocryphal scripture that Amoghavajra "retranslated" or revised.[9] Following his completion of the ritual, Pugu Huai'en suddenly died, and the invading forces retreated. This success led to the emperor's faith in esoteric Buddhism, leading him to receive tantric initiation from Amoghavajra in 765. The emperor granted him imperial titles and patronized his projects to build new monasteries.[10] With the emperor's support, he was able to establish the "Mantra" (Zhenyan, 真言) School as a viable tradition in China, one that had a reputation for its ability to provide ritual support for the ruler and the state.

Chang-an was a regional center for tantric Buddhism in the eighth century. Amoghavajra and his Chinese successors attracted students not only from within China but also from neighboring regions, including the Korean monk Hye-il (惠日) who arrived in 781 to study with Amoghavajra's disciple Huiguo (惠果, 746–805); the Japanese monk Kūkai, who arrived for the same reason in 804; and the Indonesian monk Bianhong (辯弘/*Ājñāgarbha), who arrived from the kingdom of Kəliṅ on northern Java around 780 and remained in China until 806.[11]

Amoghavajra successfully implemented what is portrayed as a natural alliance in Buddhist tantras. One may recall that the mandala is a representation of a divine palace, inhabited by an awakened buddha qua king. When one is initiated, one undergoes a ritual coronation modeled in part on the ancient Indian coronation ceremony. The ideal "Adamantine Master" is also a spiritual advisor to a king, a *purohita,* and a king is the ideal disciple, as King Indrabhūti was according the Jñānamitra. However, even the ideal student cannot evidently make sense of the tantras without professional guidance. Jñānamitra's narrative, introduced in section 1.5.1, continues with Indrabhūti examining the new tantric scriptures that were revealed to him as follows:

> King Indrabhūti examined the scriptures but could not make sense of them. Through the force of his previous actions, however, he saw by means of extra-sensory perception that in Mālava in the land of Madhyadeśa there lived the Master Kukkura. He was called the "Dog Master" since by day he taught the dharma to just one thousand dogs, and by night he bestowed the enjoyment of the sacraments to those dogs.[12] [Realizing] that he was a suitable vessel for this vehicle, and that [the king] himself might be

destined to be his disciple, the king sent a messenger beseeching the master to come.

This master also, through the force of his past karma, was endowed with the five extra-sensory cognitions,[13] and ascertained whether the king was destined to be his disciple and whether he himself was a suitable vessel for these scriptures. He gave to the messenger his reply, that while the king was destined to be his disciple, he himself was a suitable vessel for the scriptures, and the king's doubts would be resolved, however it would be very bad if he were not able to dispel the king's doubts on account of not having previously seen the scriptures. The king replied, "Send those scriptures that I previously asked to see!"

The scriptures arrived and he read them, but from beginning to end they were unlike anything he had ever read, on account of which he collapsed, without recourse. Exclaiming "I am without refuge," Śrī Vajrasattva appeared and asked him what he desired. He asked, "I wish that I could understand these scriptures just by reading them." [Vajrasattva] said, "Thus shall it be granted," whereupon the meanings of these unopened texts of the "Union of All Buddhas" *Sarvabuddhasamāyoga,* etc. became directly apparent in his mind.

The master then went to Zahor and taught these teachings to the king and his retinue. Having received the instructions of Vajrasattva, the king and his retinue were commanded to meditate in the manner of the Adamantine Realm (*vajradhātu*) mandala, with the king himself in the center, his four holy queens positioned as his consorts, his four ministers positioned as the four clans, his four daughters positioned as the inner goddesses, his four concubines positioned as the outer goddesses, and the lesser officers positioned as the four gate keepers and the virtuous bodhisattvas. As a result, the king thought that he along with his

> retinue had achieved the state of a wizard (*vidyādhara*), and in order that this holy teaching would not decline, the consecration was bestowed on his son, Śakraputi, and the Master Kukkura taught the prince, investing him with the scriptural and oral transmissions, [teaching him the practice whereby] a king and his retinue can attain [the state of a] bodhisattva-wizard residing in emptiness. His son Śakraputi meditated thus, and through seven hundred meditations on the mandala he attained the state of a wizard.
>
> The prince Śakraputi, for his younger sister Govadevī, arranged and withdrew the *Naya-śatapañcāśatikā* from within the *Śrīparamādya*,[14] and the king commanded her to teach it in the countries and lands held by him. She also meditated on the mandala one hundred times and attained [the state of a] wizard. Then the princess entrusted the scriptural and oral transmissions to the prince and propagated it, which is now this very [tradition].[15]

This text relates an ideal paradigm in portraying the king and his family, under the guidance of a tantric master qua royal preceptor, constituting the mandala in court, and assuming the roles of the deities of the Adamantine Realm mandala, which is the mandala of the "Compendium of the Realities of All Tathāgatas" *Sarvatathāgata-tattvasaṃgraha Sūtra.* Just as Amoghavajra performed rituals in the royal palace for the Daizong emperor, so too were tantric masters portrayed as doing so in the Indian context.

Jñānamitra's commentary is not the only Indian text to portray this ideal master-disciple relationship. The "Tantra on the Adamantine Womb King of Wealth" **Vajragarbharatnarāja Tantra*/最上大乘金剛大教寶王經, a text preserved only in the Chinese translation made during the Northern Song Dynasty (960–1127) in the tenth century,[16] depicts an Adamantine Master, in this case the premier tantric master Vajrapāṇi, consecrating a king, as follows:

> When the Bodhisattva arrived at the palace, King *Vīryadatta (精進授王) offered the seven-jeweled Lion Throne. He bade the Bodhisattva to sit upon it and reverentially offered up to him all sorts of gold, silver, and precious gems, as well as offering vessels filled to the brim with sublimely scented water. He made five kinds of offerings to the Bodhisattva. In addition, a large monastic community came to listen to the Dharma bearing incense and flowers to present to the Bodhisattva. Then Vajrapāṇi Bodhisattva, in accordance with the method he learned from the Buddha, entered the great mandala and consecrated (灌頂) the King with vajra-purified water. King Vīryadatta thus attained consecration. Thereupon the monastic community, the warriors, brahmin priests, commoners, servants,[17] and so forth all arrived at the royal palace and came before the Bodhisattva, desiring to listen to the Dharma. Giving rise to the Spirit of Awakening, they entered the Mahāyāna.[18]

This text portrays a clear hierarchy of participants that is, as in the royal court qua mandala, articulated via proximity to the center, with the center assumed by the guru, who is then served by the king, the most privileged of disciples, who is followed in the hierarchy by the monks, and last of all by the laity, which is hierarchically arranged via the social classes.

The guru here is depicted as assuming the position of a brahmin priest,[19] the *purohita*, or royal preceptor, likely reflecting the social reality in India in regions where Buddhism was patronized by the ruling class, which certainly would have included, for example, Northeast India under the Pāla Dynasty, whose patronage of Buddhist institutions such as Nālandā and Vikramaśīla is well known.[20] And this was also the case in the one region of South Asia where tantric Buddhism survived, namely the Kathmandu Valley of Nepal. The *vajrācārya* in the Newāri context is understood to be exactly that: "family priests (*purohita*) for hereditary patrons (*jajmān, jaymā*)."[21] This synthesis was achieved perhaps even more smoothly than in the brahmanical tradition itself, which, because of its intense concern with purity and pollution, could not help but see the assumption of mundane power as a compromise, and thus came to view the role of the *purohita* with ambivalence.[22] The nondualistic tantric perspective, however, rejects the relevance of the purity-pollution distinction, opening the way for the spiritually realized guru to assume power as well as authority.

While the tantric master assumes, in the ritual context at least, the central and most authoritative role, the king becomes, by virtue of his submission, the disciple par excellence. The tantric master, in the mandala, assumes the king's central position, receiving the treatment due to a king of kings from the king himself, who is privileged in receiving greatest access to the figure of the guru. In some tantric texts the figures of the king and the guru are assimilated. Indrabhūti himself was included in the list of the eighty-four great adepts (*mahāsiddha*),[23] without losing his role of king. A later text, the "Glorious Light on Reality" *Śrī-Tattvapradīpa*, reconciles these roles by depicting King Indrabhūti as an incarnation of Vajrapāṇi, the tantric master extraordinaire, and Vajrapāṇi as a king. The text describes its origin as follows:

> The Goddess asked, "Who brought to light and explained this extremely secret Tantra?"
>
> The Lord replied, "In the north, at the adamantine seat (*vajrapīṭha*)[24] of Oḍiyāna, the king called Indrabhūti brought it to light, and explained and clarified it for sentient beings."
>
> The Goddess asked, "Hey Lord, tell me, how many [bodhisattva] stages (*bhūmi*) has this 'Great King' Indrabhūti mastered?"
>
> The Lord answered, "That very King is Vajrapāṇi, about whom I spoke in the 'Gnostic Drop Sovereign Tantra' (*Jñānatilaka-tantrarāja*),[25] and he has mastered the tenth stage with his

> emanation body (*nirmāṇakāya*) as Indrabhūti, and has mastered the fourteenth stage with his gnostic body form (*jñānakāya*)."[26]

The king, as the ideal disciple, naturally often appears to be the assumed recipient of tantric discourse. For example, a king is the presumed candidate for initiation in the "Supreme Bliss of the Wheels" *Cakrasaṃvara Tantra*, as indicated by the fee (*dakṣiṇā*) required of initiation. The relevant verses occur in chapter 3 as follows:

> [10] Saluting the mandala and guru,
> In accordance with the rite, then make an
> Offering to the guru, presenting
> The fee declared by the Tathāgata:
>
> [11] A hundred thousand gold [pieces],
> A variety of treasures,
> One hundred pairs of clothing, and even
> Elephants, horses, and a realm;
> [12] Earrings, bracelets, necklaces, an
> Excellent ring, and a golden
> Sacrificial thread, and also
> One's very own wife and daughters,
> [13] Servants and maids and one's sister too;
> Should all be offered, bowing down.
> The wise one should offer himself
> With all his things to the guru,
> [Saying:]
> [14] "Henceforward I am entrusted
> Over to you as a servant."
> Having thus completed the rite,
> [All's] well settled by the adept.[27]

Descriptions of the initiatory fees are often quite elaborate, and one would obviously need to be very wealthy to qualify. The inclusion of items such as elephants, horses, and especially a "realm" or territory (*rāṣṭra*) indicates that kings are the ideal recipients of tantric initiation.

Amoghavajra, in assuming the role of royal preceptor for the Daizong emperor, was not improvising but was fulfilling the *vajrācārya* role as presented in the tantras. During the medieval period, successful transmission of tantric Buddhism necessitated winning over the ruling class in a new region to secure the patronage necessary to establish the tradition. This is because tantric Buddhist practice is somewhat resource intensive, requiring a fair amount of material wealth to perform the mandala rituals and so forth. While many tantras can in theory be practiced entirely with materials scavenged, for example, from a charnel ground, for larger public rites patronage would be required. Wealth too would be needed to provide food and shelter to an elite group of meditators who would need to spend years of training to master both the external rituals as well as the internal meditations. Hence tantric Buddhists appear to have always sought out patrons when making inroads into new cultural worlds.

While traditions can experience dramatic growth when the search for a powerful patron is successful, as it was in China in the eighth century, reliance on patronage is also a potential weakness. The institutionalized "Mantra" (真言) school founded by Amoghavajra, centered in large monasteries in and near the capital Chang-an, did not survive the Wuzong emperor's (武宗; r. 840–846) infamous persecution of Buddhism in the 840s.[28] Despite the relatively short lifespan for the school, its impact was considerable both within China and beyond.

This is illustrated by the transmission of esoteric Buddhism to Japan. Japan during the Nara era (710–794) had close cultural and trade ties to China, and Japanese Buddhists looked to China as a source of knowledge about Buddhism. Hence, it is not surprising that a copy of Śubhakarasiṃha's translation of the *Awakening of Mahāvairocana Tantra*, which was completed in 726, made its way to Japan by 737.[29] This and other esoteric works slowly made their way to Japan through the remainder of the eighth century. However, the transmission of the practices and the commentaries that would enable one to make sense of these works had not yet reached Japan.

This would change in the early ninth century. In 804, a diplomatic fleet of four ships departed for China. On one of the ships was Kūkai, a young monk who was interested in traveling to China to learn more about the esoteric Buddhist texts, including the *Awakening of Mahāvairocana Tantra*, which he had encountered in his studies in Japan. On board another ship in the fleet was Saichō (最澄, 767–822), a more senior monk who received permission from the Kanmu Emperor (桓武, r. 781–806) to travel to China to study the teachings of the Tiantai (天台) school, a Chinese Mahāyāna tradition founded in the sixth century that emphasized the teachings of the *Lotus Sūtra*.

The ships were separated in a storm; Saichō's ship landed at the port of Ningbo, from where he secured permission to journey to Mount Tiantai, where he met and studied with the seventh Tiantai patriarch, Daosui (道邃). While Saichō was not seeking and apparently unaware of esoteric Buddhism, he was introduced to it during his nine-month sojourn in China. It turns out that Amoghavajra's fame and imperial patronage led to increasing interest in esoteric Buddhism in China. During Saichō's last month in China, while he was awaiting a boat to return to Japan, he met the monk Shunxiao (順曉), who both instructed him and granted him a tantric initiation. After that he received three additional consecrations from different teachers. He returned to Japan bringing with him not only new Tiantai works but also esoteric Buddhist texts, illustrations of deities to be visualized, and ritual implements.[30]

Upon his return to Japan, Saichō established the Tendai school,[31] integrating exoteric Mahāyāna and esoteric tantric teachings as he learned in China. Emperor Kanmu recognized the significance of this in an 805 edict, and later that year, "Saichō, at Kanmu's command, performed a state-sponsored *abhiṣeka* ["coronation" initiation rite] at Takaosan-ji. Eminent priests from the Nara Buddhist community were invited to participate in this, the first Mikkyō [esoteric Buddhism] initiatory ritual performed in Japan, and Saichō became renowned as a teacher of esoteric Buddhism."[32] However, Saichō had very little training in esoteric Buddhism. He later received teachings and initiations from Kūkai. However, they later parted ways, because Kūkai objected to Saichō disseminating teachings the latter received from him, which Kūkai considered a violation of the traditional commitment to secrecy that Saichō assumed when Kūkai initiated him.[33] Moreover, Saichō did not compose any works on tantric topics, and "hardly any of his writings elaborate on tantric doctrines or rituals."[34] While there is a tradition of tantric teachings in the Tendai school, known as the Taimitsu (台密), or Tendai, esotericism, they were actually mainly brought to Japan by the Tendai monks Ennin (圓仁, 794–864) and Enchin (円珍, 814–891), both of whom traveled to China for extensive studies during the ninth and tenth centuries, respectively.[35]

Kūkai, meanwhile, enjoyed a more extended period of study in China. His boat went astray in the storm, ending up in Fujian Province, far to the south of the mission's intended destination. Despite this obstacle he eventually made his way to Chang-an, where he was able to study with masters of the "Mantra" (真言) school established by Amoghavajra. He was granted permission to stay at Ximing Monastery (西明寺), and he soon met and began studying Sanskrit with Prajñā, an Indian monk from Nālandā Monastery then teaching and translating in Chang-an. He also soon met one of Amoghavajra's disciples and successors Master Huiguo. Kūkai studied intensively with Huiguo for six months, during which time Huiguo initiated him and conferred the lineage transmissions to him. He also provided him with paintings and ritual implements. Prior to Huiguo's death in late 805, he instructed Kūkai to return to Japan and teach.[36]

Kūkai did so, returning to Japan in 806. Upon his return to Japan, he remained in isolation for four years, evidently because the new Heizei emperor (平城, r. 806–809) had little interest in new forms of Buddhism.[37] Kūkai emerged from obscurity after the coronation of the Saga emperor (嵯峨, r. 809–823), who supported Kūkai, appointing him administrator of Tōdaiji Temple (東大寺) in Nara in 810. He also granted Kūkai's request for a land grant at Mt. Kōya (高野山) to build a new monastery there in 816, although it was not completed until after Kūkai's death in 835. He constructed an *abhiṣeka* hall at Tōdaiji Temple and conducted many consecrations there, including a consecration of the Emperor Saga following his retirement in 823.[38] The Buddhist rite of *abhiṣeka* was, as Ryūichi Abé has shown, eventually adapted and incorporated within the Japanese imperial coronation ceremony.[39] As Abé argued, tantric discourse, in the East Asian context,

> legitimized the emperor's authority by characterizing him as the ideal Buddhist ruler, the cakravartin, while the emperor affirmed the authenticity of the Eight Schools of exoteric and esoteric disciplines as the orthodoxy of the state. . . . This state of affairs suggests that the symbiosis between emperor and clergy . . . was in fact constructed in the language of Esoteric Buddhism.[40]

His Shingon "Mantra" School (真言宗) was finally recognized in 835, shortly before his death, and it became one of the most important schools of Buddhism in Japan during the Heian era (794–1185), and it was a significant influence on other traditions, including not only the Tendai tradition, which was directly impacted by Kūkai's teachings, but also many other traditions as will be addressed below.

Esoteric Buddhism was also transmitted to Tibet around this same time, circa the late eighth and early ninth centuries. Tibetan Buddhist traditional histories view the seventh century as the time when Buddhism first reached Tibet, during the reign of the great king Songtsen Gampo (*srong bstan sgam po,* r. 618–650), who unified the Tibetan plateau, and then entered a series of conflicts with his neighbors to the east and south, the Chinese Tang Dynasty and the Licchavi Nepalis. These were resolved with marriage alliances with two princesses, the Chinese princess Wencheng (文成) and the Licchavi Princess Bṛkuṭī, both of whom were Buddhist and brought Buddhist images as part of their dowries, for which the king erected the famous Jokhang Temple in Lhasa.[41] He also reportedly sent the scholar Thon mi Saṃbhoṭa to India to develop a script for the Tibetan language and who undertook the first Tibetan translations of Buddhist scriptures.[42] Early Tibetan historical documents also claim that King Songtsen Gampo was visited by monks from Khotan, who expressed the view that he was an incarnation of the Buddhist deity Avalokiteśvara, making the link between kingship and awakening that was a hallmark of tantric political theory.[43]

Although the earliest tantric scriptures were being composed in India toward the end of Songtsen Gampo's life, it took over 100 years for the tantras to reach Tibet. This happened during King Tri Songdetsen (*khri srong lde btsan,* r. 755–794), who was renowned as one of the three great "Dharma Kings" (*chos rgyal, dharmarāja*) of Tibet, along with his ancestor Songtsen Gampo and his grandson, Ralpacan. He reputedly was devoted to Buddhism and desired to bolster the religion in Tibet, which at the time had apparently not yet made much of an impact there.[44] He was responsible for the construction of Samye (bSam yas), the first monastery in Tibet. To assist with this, he invited to Tibet first the great Mahāyāna scholar Śāntarakṣita (c. 725–788), who at the time was the abbot of Nālandā Monastery, which once again plays a central role in the dissemination of tantric Buddhism.[45]

According to traditional accounts, attempts to build the new monastery were obstructed by the gods and spirits of Tibet. To remedy this problem, Śāntarakṣita recommended that the great tantric adept Padmasambhava be invited to assist with this problem. Padmasambhava, who in his hagiography is portrayed as the miraculously born son of King Indrabhūti,[46] became a tantric adept renowned for his ability to subdue obstructing spirits. He journeyed to Tibet from the Kathmandu Valley in Nepal, subduing the gods and spirits along the way, binding them to oaths to protect Buddhism. Eventually he reached Central Tibet, where he aided the effort to build Samye Monastery and instructed the king and other Tibetans in Buddhist teachings. Tibetan histories and hagiographies depict Padmasambhava as giving consecrations to King Tri Songdetsen and his court.[47] He is also believed to have hidden Buddhist teachings—physically in various sites in Tibet and within the minds of his disciples—to be rediscovered at later, preordained times as "treasure texts" (*gter ma*). His teachings, along with Buddhist texts translated during the imperial period, became the core teachings of the Nyingma school of Tibetan Buddhism.[48]

King Tri Songdetsen successfully established a monastic order in Tibet and supported large-scale translations of Buddhist texts. He invited several scholars, foreign and Tibetan, to begin the work of translating Buddhist scriptures into Tibetan. He ushered in what came to be known as the "early dissemination" (*snga dar*) of Buddhism in Tibet; most of the translations made during the imperial period were made with imperial support and oversight between 779 and 838.[49] As evidenced by imperial catalogs compiled during this period, as well as tantric manuscripts preserved at Dunhuang (敦煌),[50] which were assembled around the mid-tenth through early eleventh centuries,[51] a significant number of tantric scriptures and ritual texts were translated into Tibetan during the imperial period, including the eighteen Mahāyoga tantras that represented the eighth-century cutting edge of Indian tantric Buddhist traditions.

Imperial-sponsored translation activity ended in Tibet with the collapse of the Tibetan Empire following the death of the King Tri Ui Dumtsen (*khri u'i dum btsan*, r. 838–842), who is better known as Lang Darma (*glang dar ma*). Traditional sources indicate that he, around the same time as his Chinese counterpart the Wuzong emperor, launched a persecution of Buddhism in 840, which ended when he was assassinated by the Buddhist monk Lhalung Pelgyi Dorje (*lha lung dpal gyi rdo rje*).[52] The Tibetan Empire, which was already in decline, soon collapsed. While official support ended around in 842, translation activity did not cease, with translations continuing to be made throughout the ninth and into the tenth centuries.[53]

3.2 Tantric Buddhism in Asia in the Tenth Through Nineteenth Centuries CE

Official support of Buddhism ended in China and Tibet at virtually the same time, in what Matthew Kapstein has termed "one more synchronicity between events in Tibet and Tang China."[54] While the institutionalized esoteric Buddhist school founded by Amoghavajra did not survive the Wuzong emperor's infamous persecution of Buddhism in the mid-ninth century, esoteric Buddhist traditions have survived in China in many forms. Not only did the lineages descending from Amoghavajra's three disciples persist,[55] but also new teachers and teaching arrived, most notably during the Northern Song Dynasty during the tenth and eleventh centuries, when there was renewed transmission of tantric texts to China as well as imperial sponsorship of their translation. Tantric rituals became incorporated into mainstream Chinese Buddhism, particularly in the well-known ghost-feeding rituals,[56] and there also was an impact on esoteric Buddhism on Daoism.[57]

In yet another synchronicity, state-supported translation activity resumed in both China and Tibet during the late tenth century. Over a period of about 140 years between the cessation and resumption of translation work in both China and Tibet, from about 840–980, there was a tremendous amount of tantric Buddhist textual production in India. The cutting edge of new tantric texts produced during this period were the texts that came to be called "unexcelled yoga tantras" (*niruttarayogatantra*), which were notable for their transgressive content.

Official Chinese sponsorship of the translation of Buddhist scriptures resumed with the establishment during the Northern Song Dynasty of the Institute of Canonical Translation (譯經 院) in 982, which was later renamed the Institute for the Propagation of the Teaching (傳法院). It hosted considerable translation activity for 100 years, until it was disbanded in 1082.[58] Some of the more popular "new" tantras were translated by this institute, although the effort was generally considered to be a failure insofar as the translation work does not appear to have been accompanied by the successful transmission of the associated practice traditions to East Asia.[59]

The Chinese "Mantra" school was transmitted to Korea and had some success there during the eighth and ninth centuries. Both Śubhākarasiṃha and Vajrabuddhi each had a Korean disciple, Pulga Saui (不可思義; fl. eighth century) and Hyech'o (慧超; fl. eighth century), respectively, each of whom composed works on tantric subjects.[60] During the Goryeo Dynasty (918–1392), a "golden age" of Buddhism in Korea, there were two additional esoteric schools established there, the "Mudrā" Sinin school and the "Dhāraṇī" Ch'ongji school; unfortunately, little is known about either of these schools.[61]

Some sporadic translation activity appears to have continued in Tibet over the century and a half, from about 840–990, but not much is known about it, for which reason it was traditionally called the "time of fragments" (*sil bu'i dus*), a term reflecting the cessation of state oversight and recordkeeping following the collapse of the Tibetan Empire.[62] The most important Buddhist activity during this time was on the periphery of the Tibetan cultural world, in the West and in the Northeast. Textual production continued in the Northeast for at least two centuries, as evinced by the texts collected at Dunhuang. And Tri Kyidé Nyimagön (*khri skyi sde nyi ma mgon*, c. 911–950), the grandson of the Tri Ösung (*khri 'od srungs*, d. ca. 905), one of the contenders for the succession following Lang Darma's assassination, fled to Purang in western Tibet, where he founded the dynasty that would govern western Tibet for the next several centuries.[63]

It was in the stable region of western Tibet that the officially sponsored translation of Buddhist texts, including the tantras, resumed. The grandson of Tri Kyidé Nyimagön, Lha-lama Yéshé-ö (*lha bla ma ye shes 'od*, 959–1024), led this effort. It appears he was motivated by the unauthorized spread of "new" tantras into Tibet from India. He was also a deeply religious figure, as his name indicates; it translates into English as "Divine Guru, Gnostic Light." He appears to have integrated secular and spiritual authority in an attempt to fulfill the tantric Buddhist ideal. He would not be the last Tibetan to attempt this integration.

The transgressive new "unexcelled yoga tantras" gradually made their way into Tibet. These new teachings greatly concerned Lha-lama Yéshé-ö, who in 985 wrote an ordinance criticizing these practices, characterizing them as non-Buddhist, as follows:

> Heretical tantras, pretending to be Buddhist, are spread in Tibet. These have brought harm to the kingdom in the following ways:
>
> As "deliverance" has become popular goat and sheep are afflicted. As "sexual rite" has become popular the different classes of people are mixed. . . . As the ritual of sacrifice has become popular it happens that people get delivered alive. As demons who eat flesh are worshipped there is plague among men and animals.[64]

The practices of sexual rites and "deliverance" and violent sacrifice are among the transgressive practices described in many of the tantras. Due to doubt about whether the suspect works that describe these practices were genuinely Buddhist, Lha-lama Yéshé-ö is reported to have sent the Tibetan translator-monk Rinchen Zangpo (*rin chen bzang po*, 958–1055) to India precisely "to find out whether these practices were correct at all."[65]

When Rinchen Zangpo arrived in Kashmir circa 975, he soon discovered that these scriptures were not deemed heretical by the Buddhists that he met there, rather they were deemed to be among the "highest" teachings. He would thus, with the help of several Kashmiri Buddhist scholars, translate several tantras and tantric works into Tibetan, including the "Supreme Bliss of the Wheels" *Cakrasaṃvara Tantra,* which is probably one of the Buddhist tantras most open to the charge of being a "heretical tantra, pretending to be Buddhist."[66]

The orthodoxy of the Buddhist tantras, as understood by Indian advocates of tantric Buddhist traditions, was confirmed by the famous Indian Buddhist master Atiśa Dīpaṃkaraśrījñāna, a Buddhist monk and scholar who spent twelve years studying with the Buddhist master Dharmakīrtiśrī in Sumatra,[67] before returning to India where he served as the abbot of the Vikramaśīla Monastery in Northeast India, an important site for tantric studies. According to Tibetan histories, King Lha-lama Yéshé-ö's dying wish was that the great Indian scholar Atiśa be invited to Tibet, a wish that the king's nephew, Jangchup-ö (*byang-chub-'od*), attempted to fulfill. Atiśa acceded to the request, arrived in Tibet in 1042, and spent the rest of his life there, translating Buddhist tantric works and writing commentaries.[68]

Over the next 450 years thousands of new texts from India, most of which were tantric in nature, were translated into Tibetan. This exchange was facilitated by Tibetans like Rinchen Zangpo who traveled to India and Nepal, as well as Indian and Nepali masters, like Atiśa, who journeyed to Tibet. This activity was most prominent from the eleventh through thirteenth centuries; the thirteenth century saw that destruction of great Indian monastic centers in Northeast India such as Nālandā and Vikramaśīla, and a migration of Buddhist masters north to Nepal and Tibet to escape the chaos. Relatively few teachers went to Tibet during the fourteenth and fifteenth centuries, and the era of large-scale translation activity ended by 1500.[69]

This second wave of translation activity in Tibet, which occurred from about 1000–1500 CE, came to be known as the "later dissemination" (*phyi dar*) of Buddhism to Tibet. During this time, the Buddhist tradition that adhered to the texts and traditions transmitted to Tibet was known as the "Ancient" Nyingma (*rnying ma*) school,[70] while the schools that were established based on the new teachings were designated as "New" Sarma (*gsar ma*). The four main Sarma schools, the Sakya (*sa skya*), Kagyü (*bka' brgyud*), Jonang (*jo nang*) and Geluk (*dge lugs*), all practice tantric traditions transmitted to Tibet during the later dissemination period. All Tibetan schools, Ancient and New, are tantric in character, and preserve texts and practice traditions that are reputed to have been transmitted from India by masters such as Padmasambhava and Atiśa Dīpaṅkaraśrījñāna.

During the period of the later transmission of the Dharma there was an increasing tendency in Tibet to attempt to combine political power and spiritual authority, perhaps under the influence of tantric ideology. Patrons of Buddhism, like Lha-lama Yéshé-ö, often attempted to combine the secular and spiritual lineages within their clans, no doubt to bolster their authority, if not their power. A famous latter example of this phenomenon is the formation of the Sakya school, one of the new schools that developed during this period, from within the 'Khon family of gTsang, who themselves "claimed genealogies stretching back to the times of the early kings and to mountain-god ancestors,"[71] the major sources of legitimation during the imperial and post-imperial periods. Cassinelli and Ekvall argued that "the history of the Sa sKya is in effect the history of the 'Khon,"[72] but this is just one side of the story. While one can trace the lineage of the Sakya abbots (literally great throne [holders], *khri chen*) back through the 'Khon family lineage into the hoary realm of Tibetan legend, one could also trace their spiritual lineage back to the great adepts of India. For the Sakyas combined within one descent group both types of lineage, the secular and the spiritual.

Lineage claims thus can have tremendous power and consequences, which are not dependent upon the verity of those claims, and require only a certain amount of verisimilitude. And their power can be subtle. That it was the renowned scholar Sakya Paṇḍita Kunga Gyaltsen (*sa skya paṇ ḍi ta kun dga' rgyal mtshan*, 1182–1251) whom Godan, second son of Ögödei Khan, summoned in 1244 to instruct him in Buddhism, rather than any other Tibetan lama, shows that the position of authority in which his lineage placed him was taken seriously, either accepted or contested, by a significant number of Tibetans.[73] And it was his high standing among Tibetans that interested the Mongols, for whom the subtle details of authenticity were probably irrelevant.[74]

Interestingly, Sakya Paṇḍita, in a letter to the Tibetans following his meeting with Godan Khan, articulated his newly forged relationship with the Mongolian leader as that between what has usually been termed a "priest" and a "patron."[75] The terms he used, however, indicate that he conceived of their relationship in terms of the *guru*-centric ideology of the tantras. "Priest" is a loose translation of *yon-gnas*, that is, the recipient of the fee to be given at tantric initiation. The "patron" is the one who bestows this fee in exchange for instruction, the *yon-bdag*.[76] Here patronage took on institutional forms as well; Godan built Buddhist monasteries at his capital near Lanzhou.[77] And it was from among his Sa-skya successors that new "priests" were selected by the Mongols. His nephew, Drogön Chogyal Phakpa (*'gro mgon chos rgyal 'phags pa*, 1235–1280), learned fluent Mongol and served as the religious instructor of Khubilai Khan (r. 1260–1294), who established the Yuan Dynasty (1271–1368) and granted Phakpa the title of National Preceptor (國師). Phakpa also played an important role in the Mongol administration of Tibet.[78] Evidently, Phakpa bestowed Khubilai Khan with the Hevajra initiation and performed war magic for him, invoking the fierce deity Mahākāla to aid his military endeavors. As Herbert Franke argued:

> All known sources, Chinese, Mongol, and Tibetan, agree that Khubilai was given a consecration (*abhiṣeka*) in 1253. It was an initiation to the rites of dGes-pa rdo-rje (Sans. Hevajra), a tutelary deity specially worshipped in the Sa-skya monasteries and whose cult is closely linked with that of Mahākāla, a protector and defender of the faith who is, like Hevajra, represented in terrifying aspect. It seems that the rites of Hevajra and Mahākāla became customary for every enthronement of a Yüan emperor, a fact which is also mentioned in Chinese sources. The terrible Mahākāla was invoked when the Sino-Mongol armies went into battle.[79]

Buddhism became the state religion under the Yuan, and various Yuan emperors patronized Tibetan lamas from across the various traditions. As Franke noted, the Mongol adoption of Tibetan Buddhism was apparently motivated, in part, by their favorable impression of Tibetan magic, war magic in particular.[80] This impression was confirmed by Marco Polo.[81]

The *History of the Yuan Dynasty* relates that rites involving a large group of participants, apparently rituals involving Buddhist mandalas, were enacted in the court of Yuan Emperor Toghon Temür, also known as Huizong (r. 1333–1368), who patronized the Karma Kagyü tradition of Tibetan Buddhism under the instruction of a Tibetan master named "Ka Linchen," *Karma Rinchen. They may have entailed sexual rituals, perhaps the "secret consecration" initiatory rite.[82] It appears that the conversion of the Mongols to esoteric Buddhism had a significant impact, given the vast size and prestige of their empire. Tantric court rituals were performed during the thirteenth and fourteenth centuries elsewhere in Asia, in Korea, Cambodia and Indonesia, evidently due to Mongol influence, as will be discussed below.

The collapse of the Yuan Dynasty did not end Mongol interest in tantric Buddhism. There continued to be interactions between Tibetan lamas and Mongols interested in receiving instruction from them. Of note was Altan Khan (1507–1582), the leader of the Tümed Mongols, who was interested in the Geluk school of Tibetan Buddhism, and invited the third Dalai Lama, Sonam Gyatso (bSod nams rgya mtsho, 1543–1588), to teach him. Sonam Gyatso accepted the invitation and journeyed to Kökenuur, where he gave teachings in 1578. The association with the Geluk school was secured when the son of a Tümed prince was recognized as the fourth Dalai Lama.[83] This association strengthened with the rise of the Oirat confederation, an alliance of four western Mongol tribes, which developed in the Altai Mountain region during the sixteenth century. They rose to prominence during the seventeenth century, converting to Buddhism in 1616 and expressing a preference for the Geluk school of Tibetan Buddhism, sending young men to study as monks at Geluk monasteries in Tibet. They eventually gained control over a vast span of territory in the seventeenth century that spanned from the Volga steppes in Russia through Central Asia, including the Xinjiang and Qinghai regions of modern China, as well as most of Tibet, south to the border with Nepal.[84]

The Oirats intervened in the conflict that developed between the Geluk school and Karma Kagyü school, which was supported by Karma Tenkyong (Kar ma bstan skyong, 1606–1642), the Tsangpa hierarch (*sde pa*) who ruled most of central Tibet. In 1635, the army of the Oirat Mongol ruler Gushri Khan (1582–1655) invaded Tibet in support of the young fifth Dalai Lama Ngawang Lobsang Gyatso (Ngag dbang blo bzang rgya mtsho, 1617–1682), and succeeded in overthrowing Karma Tenkyong and his allies by 1642. This resulted in the enthronement of the fifth Dalai Lama as the political and spiritual leader of Tibet,[85] which cemented strong bonds between the Geluk school and the Mongols, who continued to journey to Tibet for further study up until the twentieth century.

The Mongols launched a series of invasions of Korea starting in 1231, and the Korean Goryeo Dynasty eventually capitulated and sued for peace, becoming a client state of the Yuan Dynasty from 1270 until 1356. During this time the Mongol adoption of Tibetan tantric Buddhism as their official state religion had some impact in Korea as well. Henrik Sørensen relates that one historical source, the *Koryŏ sa*, "dating from the reign of King Chŭngyŏl (r. 1275–1308), tells about a Tibetan lama who practiced sexual rites, although covertly, and who later organized a large-scale tantric ritual in the royal palace in which a special three-dimensional mandala with numerous deities made of dough was used."[86] However, the impact of these practices appears to have been limited to the court, and they do not appear to have continued after the fall of the Yuan Dynasty. During the Joseon Dynasty (1392–1897), Buddhism fell out of favor and went into decline, being deprived of royal patronage and eventually shut out of the capital. During this era the Sŏn (the Korean pronunciation of the Chinese term Chan/禅, better known through its Japanese pronunciation "Zen") school rose to prominence, and other schools were merged into it by royal decree in the fifteenth century. Esoteric texts focusing on mantras and *dhāraṇī* spells circulated in Korea during this time,[87] some of which were taken up by Sŏn practitioners. As a result, numerous esoteric practices were preserved by the Sŏn school, including the use of mantras in both ritual and meditative practices.[88]

In Japan, the tenth through twelfth centuries saw what might be termed the "golden age" of tantric Buddhism there, with the Shingon and Tendai schools enjoying widespread popularity and prestige. However, during the Kamakura period (1185–1333), these schools were somewhat eclipsed by the rise of "new Buddhist teachings" (*shin bukkyō*, 新仏教). These included the Pure Land and Zen traditions, which rose in popularity in China during the Song Dynasty and were transmitted to Japan, as well as the Nichiren school, founded by the former Tendai monk Nichiren (日蓮, 1222–1282). Although the popularity of the Shingon and Tendai schools waned, they remained influential. The Shingon monk Kakuban (覺鑁, 1095–1143) developed an esoteric version of the Pure Land practice of *nembutsu* (念仏), involving recitation of the name of Amitābha Buddha, a practice that in pre-tantric, exoteric

Mahāyāna Buddhist traditions often entailed visualization as well. Kakuban developed and popularized a practice called "esoteric nembutsu" (秘密念仏). It is a contemplative practice involving the visualization of the seed syllable *a* on a lunar disk in the heart, which is linked to all living beings via the circulation of in and out breaths as one repeats the Buddha's name. This practice was not restricted to the Shingon school but spread to other traditions as the popularity of Pure Land devotional practices grew.[89] There was also limited influence on Zen traditions; Zen traditions in Japan, following precedents in Chinese and Korean Zen, incorporated some elements of esoteric Buddhism into their practice, most notably rituals incorporating the recitation of dhāraṇī spells.[90] Esoteric Buddhist rituals, such as the *homa* (Japanese *goma*) fire sacrifice were also borrowed by other religious traditions in Japan, including Shintō[91] and folk religious traditions such as Shugendō.[92]

Transgressive tantric practices made an appearance in twelfth-century Japan, when a Shingon sub-lineage arose known as the Tachikawa-ryū (立川流), supposedly founded by a monk named Ninkan (仁寛, d. 1114). It evidently became very popular during the thirteenth century and influenced both the mainstream Shingon and Tendai traditions. However, in 1375 the Shingon monk Yūkai (宥快, 1345–1416) launched a rhetorical attack on the tradition, portraying it as a heretical teaching that involved sexual practices. The tradition was suppressed in the fifteenth century, and very little documentation about it remains. One surviving document, however, describes a "skull ritual" that entails repeatedly applying secretions from heterosexual union onto a skull, which must also be painted to resemble a living head, and kept warm. After seven or eight years it would reportedly come to life and give oracles.[93] Since the ritual employs both a human skull and sexual practices, it bears some resemblance to the yoginītantras, which were never formally transmitted to Japan, although several were translated into Chinese during the Northern Song Dynasty. It is possible that this ritual was inspired by circulation of *yoginītantric* texts in Japan during the twelfth century.[94] However, there is no evidence that this was indeed the case, and the ritual may have developed within the context of Japanese esoteric Buddhism without the input of new texts or practice traditions.[95]

There were also transmissions of tantric works to Southeast Asia during this period. Burmese historical records claim that the founder of the Pagan Empire, Anawrahta Minsaw (r. 1044–1077), embraced Theravāda Buddhism and suppressed a community of Buddhist monks known as the Ari, "who are vilified in these accounts as heretics guilty of unpardonable violations of the monastic code (*vinaya*) who officiated at animal sacrifices, were addicted to magic and sorcery, and who worshipped a pantheon of spirits and gods."[96] While these texts do not identify them as such, they may very well have been tantric practitioners. Despite the Theravāda identity of Burma, esoteric literature from India continued to trickle into Burma. One of the consequences of this is the survival in Burma up to the contemporary period of a tradition known as the *weikza-lan*, or "path of the occult knowledge," which if practiced successfully can lead to the state of the *twet-ya-pauk*, "a kind of Buddhist wizard who prolongs his life for eons."[97] The term *weikza*, or *weizzā*, is actually an abbreviation of the term *weizzādhour*, the Burmese equivalent to the Sanskrit term *vidyādhara*, "the wizards" of the tantric Buddhist traditions.[98] Adherents of this tradition are "organized into semi-secret associations called *gaing* that function to dispense esoteric knowledge to initiates under the guidance of a charismatic teacher-adept (*saya* or *gaing-saya*)."[99] The practices advocated by this tradition include visualization practices, including a tantric version of the Buddha meditations. In it the practitioner visualizes him- or herself seated before the Buddha on a throne below the tree of awakening, with a beam of light connecting the Buddha's eyebrow tuft with the practitioner's. She or he then invites the Buddha to take a seat on his or her head. Having done so, one then visualizes the Buddha sinking down and pervading one's body and transforming oneself. At this point, the practitioner should reflect as follows: "The bodily factors are not the yogi's anymore; the yogi's body has disappeared and the yogi should think thus: 'I am the Buddha, the Buddha is me.' The yogi's own body and he or she has transformed into a living Buddha."[100] This meditation system is very close to creation stage visualization practices in the classical Indian Buddhist tantric traditions.

As Peter Sharrock has argued, there was a revival of Buddhism in Cambodia during the tenth century, under King Rājendravarman, and it was primarily tantric Buddhism that was introduced at this time.[101] Tantric Buddhism persisted in Cambodia until at least the thirteenth century, when a Yoginī temple was constructed in Bayon, based on the iconography of the *Hevajra Tantra*.[102] The Khmer King Jayavarna VII (1181–1219), a Mahāyāna Buddhist, also reportedly received the Hevajra initiation.[103] David Bade likewise argues, following a century of Dutch scholarship, that King Kṛtanagara (r. 1268–1292) of the Siṅghasari state in Java likewise received and practiced the Hevajra tradition. He was a contemporary and rival of Khubilai Khan and rebuffed the latter's demand for tribute and submission in 1289.[104] Tantric Buddhism may have had an indirect impact on statecraft during this period, with political leaders drawing on tantric rituals to augment their spiritual and worldly powers.

3.3 Tantric Buddhism in the Contemporary World

At the dawn of the twentieth century, tantric Buddhism hit a relatively low point. It had largely disappeared from most of South and Southeast Asia, with the exception of the Kathmandu Valley and the ethnic Tibetan regions of India, as well as some remnant traditions, such as the "Path of Occult Knowledge" *Weikza lan* in Burma. It remained the dominant tradition in the Tibetan and Mongolian cultural worlds, although both regions were ill-equipped for the

Map 3.2 Tantric Buddhism Circa 1900.
Map by Karuna Gray.

upheavals of the twentieth century; Tibet was functionally independent in 1900 but relied on the Qing Dynasty (1636–1912) for protection, while the Mongolian cultural world was divided between imperial Russia and Qing China, both of which would collapse early in the century. In Japan, the Shingon and Tendai traditions remained, although they were somewhat constrained by the anti-Buddhist policies instituted by the imperial government during in the late nineteenth century. In China and Korea, esoteric Buddhism no longer remained as distinct traditions (aside from Tibetan Buddhism in China), although some tantric practices were maintained by other traditions as noted above.

The twentieth century would bring more challenges. These included the Russian Revolution and the founding of the Soviet Union, which resulted in much of the Mongolian cultural world under communist control. The Qing Dynasty collapsed in China in 1911, leading to a period of instability characterized by civil war and eventually war with Japan. One of the interesting features of the Republican period in China was a growth of interest by Han Chinese in Tibetan Buddhism.[105] Han Chinese interest in Tibetan Buddhism appears to have been motivated in part by the perception that it is a "powerful" tradition, a perception that may go back to the Mongol patronage of Tibetan Buddhism during the Yuan Dynasty. Tibetan lamas were employed by Chinese rulers during the Republican period for their services as war magicians, much as they were by Mongol leaders such as Khubilai Khan.[106]

The growth of interest in Tibetan Buddhism among the Han Chinese during the Republican period was likely stimulated by the collapse of the political barriers to movement between Tibetan and China that were in place during the Qing. From the 1890s, when Qing power was in serious decline, up until the victory of the communists in 1949, increasing numbers of Tibetan lamas traveled to China to teach, and a number of Chinese monks traveled to Tibet to study, most notably the influential monks Nenghai Lama (能海剌麻, 1886–1967) and Fazun (法尊, 1902–1980), who facilitated the spread of Tibetan Buddhism among Han Chinese communities.[107] Nenghai Lama and Fazun were principle figures in the modern Chinese "Tantric Buddhist Revival Movement" (密教復興運動). Both were members of the Geluk school of Buddhism, played major roles in the establishment of Tibetan Buddhism in Han Chinese communities, and were involved with serious efforts to translate the major texts of Tibetan Buddhism into Chinese. This was the first major attempt to translate Buddhist works directly from Tibetan to Chinese since the Yuan Dynasty.[108] Nenghai Lama and a group of disciples translated the *Kālacakra Tantra,* several of the *Yamāntaka* and *Vajrabhairava Tantras*, and numerous meditation manuals.[109] Fazun translated a biography of Tsongkhapa, the founder of the Geluk school, as well as his magisterial *Detailed Exegesis of the Graduated Mantric Path.*[110] There were also a number of other works translated by other Tibetan masters and their Chinese disciples during this period.[111] Their legacy is ongoing; students of Fazun recently published Chinese translations of the *Cakrasaṃvara* and *Guhyasamāja Tantras*.[112]

Following the defeat of Japan in 1945, the Chinese Communist Party quickly gained the upper hand over their Nationalist opponents and took control of mainland China in 1949, and then invaded Tibet, which the Chinese government claimed, citing Qing dynastic involvement in Tibet's defense and foreign policy. By this point, almost all the Tibetan and Mongolian cultural worlds were under communist control, exempting only Bhutan and ethic Tibetan regions in India and Nepal. Buddhists in both the Soviet Union and China faced severe persecution, with monks and nuns killed or laicized and temples destroyed or converted to secular uses.[113]

These events had a dire effect on tantric Buddhism in what had become its most important heartland. However, it also had the consequence of a diaspora of hundreds of thousands of Tibetans and Mongolians, with many lamas (*bla ma*, the Tibetan term for guru), monks and nuns fleeing in exile. The flight of Tibetan refugees in the late 1950s and early 1960s led to revivals of Buddhism in India and Nepal, where many of the refugees resettled, and stimulated a growth of interest in Tibetan and tantric Buddhism.[114]

Many Tibetan lamas have served as spiritual teachers in ethnic Chinese communities in regions subject to less government oversight and control, such as Taiwan, Hong Kong, Macau, Malaysia, and Singapore.[115] The generosity of Chinese Buddhist communities has enabled these lamas to rebuild their institutions in exile.[116] Moreover, the relaxation of controls on religion in mainland China in the 1980s and 1990s led to a revival of Tibetan Buddhism there, which has involved not only Tibetan lamas but also their Han Chinese students.[117] However, Tibetan Buddhist institutions remain under serious government surveillance and control, and they continue to be subject to crackdowns. The fate of tantric Buddhism in China is still unclear. In contrast to the situation in Chinese-controlled Tibet, in Mongolia there has been a revival of Buddhism over the past thirty-five years following the fall of the Soviet Union. Buddhist temples and monuments have been rebuilt, and the monastic community and traditional Buddhist system of education reestablished. The religion once again enjoys state support, as the government has tended to view Buddhism as central to Mongolian identity.[118]

There has also been several Chinese new religious movements inspired by Tibetan Buddhist traditions. They have been founded by contemporary masters who claim lineage descent through the Tibetan Buddhist traditions but are not directly associated with any of the mainstream Tibetan schools. One of the most successful self-proclaimed Chinese masters is Lu Sheng-yen (盧勝彥, 1945–present), who refers to himself as the "Living Buddha Lotus-Born" (蓮生活佛), most likely in reference to the great founder of the Nyingma school of Tibetan Buddhism, Padmasambhava. He founded in Taiwan a new religious movement called the True Buddha School (真佛宗), which identifies itself as a Vajrayāna Buddhist tradition, although it also draws heavily from traditional Chinese popular religion, both Buddhist and Daoist. The school now has numerous temples throughout the world, with the majority founded in areas where there is a sizable Chinese community, such as Taiwan, Malaysia, Singapore, Indonesia, Australia, and North America. Lu Sheng-yen currently lives in Redmond, Washington, where the main temple of this school is based. He is a prolific author and has written, according to one source, 110 works in Chinese, several of which have been translated into English.[119]

Another Chinese master, Yee Wan Ko (Yi Yungao, 義雲高, b. 1951), claims to be the third incarnation of Vajradhara Buddha, as indicated by the title he has assumed, H. H. Dorje Chang Buddha III, as well as the second incarnation of Vimalakīrti, a famous bodhisattva who is the central figure in one of the most popular Mahāyāna sutras in China, the "Teaching of Vimalakīrti"

Vimalakīrtinirdeśa Sūtra.[120] These claims are made in his widely distributed book *H. H. Dorje Chang Buddha III: A Treasury of True Buddha Dharma*.[121] He currently resides in the United States and evidently has established a considerable following. While the claims of figures such as Lu Sheng-yen and Yi Yungao are by no means universally accepted and are doubted by many Tibetan and Han Chinese Buddhists, their success in attracting disciples and establishing what are almost certainly new Chinese religious traditions is a testament to considerable prestige of Tibetan Buddhism among Han Chinese Buddhist communities.

There have also been several new religions that arose in Japan during the twentieth century that have been inspired or directly influenced by tantric Buddhist traditions. These include Gedatsu-kai (解脱会, Gedatsu-kai), founded in 1929, drawing on both Shintō and Shingon teachings and practices; Bentenshū (辯天宗), a lay missionary movement of the Shingon tradition; Agonshū, or "Āgama Tradition," which purports to be based on early Buddhist teachings but was also influenced by Shingon Buddhism, which its founder practiced; and the Shinnyoen (真如苑), founded in 1936 by Shinjō Itō (真乗伊藤, 1906–1989), who was ordained as a Shingon high priest.[122]

The diaspora of Tibetan lamas in the 1960s also coincided with the coming of age of the postwar baby boom generation; the 1960s could be characterized by a growth of interest in Asian religions in Europe and North America. Several Tibetan and Mongolian lamas were well placed to stimulate interest in Tibetan Buddhism in the West, such as the Tibetan lama Chögyam Trungpa[123] and the Kalmyk Mongolian lama Geshe Wangyal.[124] This ushered in several decades of spectacular growth of Tibetan Buddhist institutions in the West, with hundreds of new Buddhist centers founded, as well as a dramatic rise in the serious study of tantric traditions, which hitherto were largely ignored by the academy. As Tibetan Buddhism has become established in the West, there has also been a growing number of reincarnated Tibetan lamas identified abroad, among nonethnic Tibetans, pointing toward the growing globalization of the tradition.[125]

Tantric Buddhism has been quite successful in the West thus far, although primarily via the Tibetan Buddhist tradition, which has long had the most active missionary activity of any of the tantric Buddhist traditions. While there have been some attempts to transmit the Japanese Shingon tradition to North America, these efforts have not been as successful, evidently because their focus has been on Japanese communities living in diaspora, not on a broader dissemination of the tradition in a new cultural context.[126] As a new religion in most of its current global contexts, its long-term staying power remains an open question. It faces some challenges in the contemporary world, most notably scandals arising from accusations of sexual abuse leveled at a number of prominent lamas. These often entail lamas allegedly and secretly enacting what they claim to be tantric sexual rituals with female disciples. The repeated attempts by tantric masters to engage in tantric "secret consort" (*gsang yum*) practices are controversial and may prove to be a serious obstacle to the successful transmission of these traditions.[127]

4

Canonical Status of the Tantras

4.1 The Varieties of Buddhist Tantric Literature

The Buddhist tantras are not stand-alone works, rather they are textual manifestations of a practice tradition. As such, they cannot be understood on their own but need to be studied contextually, with understanding of the practice traditions connected with them and the modes of commentary with which they are traditionally understood. To advance this goal, this chapter will begin with an outline of the major types of tantric literature and then explore how they have traditionally been categorized and understood by the tantric Buddhist traditions.

The Buddhist tantras, like all Buddhist scriptures, are revelations ultimately originating in the inspired speech of an awakened being, as discussed in chapter 2. A tantra, if popular and successful, may constitute a core or axle for a tradition, from which radiates a body of literature that collectively constitutes its textual embodiment. As such, they are "primary revelations," insofar as they are the first stage of a tradition's growth, like the core of a tree ring. The textual "wheels" of a tradition may be very large or very small, depending on the popularity of that tradition. The central works are called "root tantras" (*mūlatantra*) since they are understood to be the tradition's basis. More popular traditions received considerable commentarial attention and would often also inspire secondary revelations, resulting in new works that might eclipse in practice the older *mūlatantra*, and which would in turn be commented upon. An examination of these bodies of literature, which due to

The Buddhist Tantras. David B. Gray, Oxford University Press. © Oxford University Press 2023.
DOI: 10.1093/oso/9780197623831.003.0005

their concentric or polycentric structures were labeled "cycles" (*skor ba*) by Tibetans,

> reveals that successive textual layers exist, amongst which we can often recognize a text or texts that seem to be intended to represent the revelatory teachings as such. We may consider these texts as the "visionary core" of the cycle. They are similar to the *mūla* or *kārikā* genres of Indic literature in that they are the referents of the commentaries and subsidiary rituals in the visionary system. Such visionary core texts are almost always anonymous.[1]

Generally, the root tantras can be identified by the large amount of literature, commentaries, ritual texts, and so forth that surrounds them. They are typically identified as such in the commentaries. Important root tantras for major tantric Buddhist traditions include the "Awakening of Mahāvairoca" *Mahāvairoca nābhisaṃbodhi,* "Compendium of the Realities of All Tathāgatas" *Sarvatathāgatatattvasaṃgraha,* "Glorious Supreme Prime" *Śrīparamādya,* "Esoteric Community" *Guhyasamāja,* "Supreme Bliss of the Wheels" *Cakrasaṃvara, Hevajra,* and "Wheel of Time" *Kālacakra* tantras, although this is by no means an exhaustive list.

As anyone who has ever tried reading a tantra knows, understanding a tantra requires commentary. While this ideally would be the oral commentary of one's guru, such exegesis was quickly set down in writing by Buddhists as commentary. There are many types of exegetical works produced by Buddhists, so here one might distinguish the "primary exegesis," the commentaries on the *root tantras* that typically hold important places in their traditions. Major works that remained popular for long periods of time will have many commentaries, as practice traditions, building on the work of their predecessors and refining understanding of these works to reflect new developments in practice, which in turn leads practitioners to see their root texts in a new light. The Tibetan canon, for example, preserves eleven commentaries for the

"Supreme Bliss of the Wheels" *Cakrasaṃvara Tantra*,[2] ten for the *Hevajra Tantra*,[3] eight for the "Wheel of Time" *Kālacakra Tantra*,[4] and four each for the "Great Magic" *Mahāmāyā Tantra*[5] and "Esoteric Community" *Guhyasamāja Tantra*,[6] with each of these traditions having many more ritual texts and commentaries thereupon. And the Tibetans built on this foundation, composing many more modular commentaries and ritual texts of their own, drawing heavily upon the works of their predecessors as faithful tradents are wont to do.

The more popular traditions also gave rise to new revelations, which might be termed "secondary revelations." There are two main types of revelation connected to a tradition that are linked by the tradition to the earlier root tantra. The first and somewhat complex type is the genre of what were "explanatory tantras" (*vyākhyātantra*). These tantras are closely intertextually linked with the older root tantra with which they are associated. They likely originated in another, older category of tantra termed an "appendix tantra," *uttaratantra*. The oldest example of this is almost certainly the addendum to the "Esoteric Community" *Guhyasamāja Tantra* that was simply titled *Uttaratantra*. It is a short work about the length of the chapter in the root tantra, for which reason it is sometimes considered to be the *Guhyasamāja Tantra*'s eighteenth chapter. It contains descriptions for many magical ritual practices, such as to deprive others of their wealth and of mantras, to attract divine and human females, and so forth. It certainly *could have served* as a chapter in the root tantra itself, but it appears that it did not, probably because it was compiled well after the root tantra was established. It was thus given a generic name and likely circulated along with the root tantra.[7]

Given the influence of the Guhyasamāja tradition, the generic name given to its addendum, *uttaratantra*, facilitated its use by other tradents in other traditions. For example, the oldest explanatory tantra for the "Supreme Bliss of the Wheels" *Cakrasaṃvara Tantra* is almost certainly the "Discourse Appendix Tantra"

Abhidhānottaratantra. It was given this name because it was understood by its tradents to be the appendix tantra to the legendary hundred-thousand-plus verse *Abhidhāna Tantra*. It eventually came to be considered an appendix or explanatory tantra for the *Cakrasaṃvara* root tantra, which names itself, at the end of each chapter and in its colophon, the "Discourse of Śrī Heruka" (*śrīherukābhidhāna*).

Explanatory tantras are often intertextually related not only to the root tantras that are the presumed source text for the tradition but also to other explanatory tantras, as well as meditation manuals and commentaries. For example, Yukei Matsunaga has shown how the explanatory tantras of the Guhyasamāja tradition are interrelated in a very complex fashion with each other as well as with Nāgārjuna's "Globule Stage Meditation Manual" *Piṇḍīkramasādhana* and his "Five Stages" *Pañcakrama* commentary on perfection stage contemplative practice, as well as Candrakīrti's "Illuminating Lamp" *Pradīpoddyotana* commentary, showing the iterative process by which tantric texts were compiled by their tradents, drawing on the current cutting edge of tantric practice.[8] The "Esoteric Community" *Guhyasamāja Tantra* has four explanatory tantras, two of which, according to Christian Wedemeyer, have an "exegetical/hermeneutical" focus, thus attempting to outline proper approaches to understanding the root tantra, while two others have a yogic focus, explaining in more detail the tradition's yogic and contemplative practices.[9]

The *Cakrasaṃvara Tantra* has a considerable number of explanatory tantras, anywhere from five to nine, according to different commentators.[10] Several of the these explanatory tantras, including the "Discourse Appendix Tantra" *Abhidhānottaratantra* and "Adamantine Warlock" *Vajraḍāka Tantra*, are much longer than the *Cakrasaṃvara Tantra*, intertextually incorporating many modules or microforms from the root tantra, while adding new modules to fill in details concerning practices that are omitted in the root text. For example, the fourth chapter of the *Abhidhānottaratantra*, from which a long passage was included in section 2.3.2.1, is basically an extended meditation manual (*sādhana*), and it almost certainly includes microforms and lemmata borrowed from older texts of this genre.

Explanatory tantras can serve multiple roles in a tradition. While they are understood as adding to or aiding the understanding of the root tantra, there are multiple ways that they can serve these roles. The Tibetan scholar Butön Rinchendrup (bu ston rin chen grub, 1290–1364) listed seven types, as follows:

> In regard to [texts] taken to be explanatory tantras, it is claimed that they fall into seven types: those which clarify that which is unclear, those which complete the incomplete, those of different methodology, those which summarize the meaning, those which correspond to a portion [of root text], those which give rise to definitive understanding, and those which discern its word and meaning.[11]

Here Butön Rinchendrup lists different functions of this genre, all members of which would exhibit at least one of these functions, some more, but few if any would exhibit all seven. An examination of explanatory tantras makes it clear that they can be very strongly exegetical in character, as is for example, the "Explanation of the Intention" *Sandhyāvyākaraṇa* explanatory tantra for the Guhyasamāja tradition. It is a relatively straightforward commentary on its root tantra,[12] "clarifying the unclear." The "Discourse Appendix Tantra" *Abhidhānottaratantra* in the Cakrasaṃvara tradition is a work that completes the incomplete," filling in practice details omitted in the root tantra, which it does not directly clarify or explain.

Explanatory tantras, however, are not mere commentaries; they are believed to be textual records of the speech of an awakened being and hence are revealed scripture. The difference between root tantras and explanatory tantras, and hence "primary" or "secondary" status, may be somewhat arbitrary, but this distinction reflects the historical development of the tantric traditions and the ways these texts were understood by Buddhist communities.

The category of "secondary revelations" should also include texts attributed to the great adepts of India. They played key roles in many of the tantric traditions. Nāgārjuna, we may recall, was considered the founder of the Adamantine Pinnacle tradition, having recovered the text hidden within an iron stūpa, as discussed in section 1.5.1. Many tantric traditions credit a great adept for the revelation of their scriptures. Moreover, texts composed by them tend to be particularly valued by traditions, as a secondary revelation of sorts, coming from the mind of a great practitioner who achieved the highest goal of awakening in this very life.

For example, the great adept Nāgārjuna played a major role in the Guhyasamāja tradition, being the reputed author of three texts that are highly valued by the tradition, while his disciple Āryadeva was even more prolific, with six texts in the tradition attributed to him.[13] The most important commentary to the "Wheel of Time" *Kālacakra Tantra,* "The Stainless Light" *Vimalaprabhā* is attributed to an awakened being, King Puṇḍarīka, who is considered an emanation of Avalokiteśvara,[14] and the tradition also has a commentary attributed to a great adept Nāropa.[15] The *Hevajra Tantra* has three commentaries that count as secondary revelation, one attributed to the bodhisattva Vajragarbha, and two attributed to the great adept Kṛṣṇācarya/Kāṇha.[16] There are also a number of Hevajra meditation manuals and ritual texts attributed to great adepts, most noticeably Ḍombipa.[17] Along with Ḍombipa, the great adepts Vīrupa, in particular, and Nāropa and Śāntipa, also known as Ratnākaraśānti, were strongly associated with the transmission of oral instructions that served as the basis of the Sakya tradition's "Path and Result" (*lam 'bras*) system of tantric practice based on the Hevajra tradition.[18] This system is based on texts transmitted to Tibet that were preserved extra-canonically by the Sakya tradition. An example of a text of this type is the *Upadeśanaya* (*man ngag lugs*), a text in this tradition attributed to Virūpa. It is described by Ronald Davidson as follows:

> The text is a concise, systematic presentation of the Guhyamantrayāna ["Secret Mantra Path"], emphasizing the internal yogic dimension. . . . According to the hagiographical accounts, Virūpa received the cryptic program of the text from Vajrayoginī through a mystic process involving the conservation of consecratory power—thus ensuring that the divinity of its origin was maintained.[19]

The Cakrasaṃvara tradition has three main practice traditions, each attributed to a great adept, namely Lūipa,[20] Kṛṣṇācarya/Kāṇha,[21] and Ghaṇṭāpāda, who is also known as Vajraghaṇṭa.[22] The Lūipa tradition is particularly prestigious as he, like Virūpa, is reputed to have received transmission of the Cakrasaṃvara tradition directly from Vajravārāhī. This tradition also has a "bodhisattva commentary" attributed to Vajrapāṇi,[23] as well as two commentaries attributed to great adepts, Kambala and Indrabhūti.[24]

The category of secondary exegesis includes commentaries on the explanatory tantras as well as those on the authoritative works attributed to the great adepts. Some of the more influential works by great adepts have multiple commentaries, so this is not an insubstantial category. There are also many tantric works that are neither deemed to be revelation nor are exegetical in nature. These include the very large number of practice texts, including meditation manuals (*sādhana*) as well as guides for other ritual practices, such as manuals for fire sacrifice (*homavidhi*), mandala creation (*maṇḍalavidhi*) and initiations (*abhiṣekavidhi*). Buddhist communities maintain up-to-date manuals of this sort, and the older text preserved in Buddhist canons are records of how these rites were practiced at various times in the past.

4.2 Classifying the Tantras

4.2.1 Indo-Tibetan Classification Schemas

While we know that Indian Buddhist monasteries contained substantial textual collections,[25] we do not know how they were organized because no catalogues from these institutions survive. We do have records, however, of various Indian attempts to classify the tantras based on an analysis of their content. Given the propensity for classification and love of classificatory schemes in Indian Buddhism, as well as Indian culture in general, Indian Buddhists came up with many different analyses of Buddhist tantras. Probably the best known is the fourfold scheme that was developed and popularized by the Tibetan Sarma schools by the fourteenth century. The classes into which Tibetan scholars divided them were "ritual action tantras" (*kriyātantra, bya rgyud*), "practice tantras" (*caryātantra, spyod rgyud*), "yogatantras" (*yogatantra, rnal 'byor rgyud*) and "unexcelled yoga tantras" (*niruttarayogatantra, bla na med pa'i rnal 'byor gyi rgyud*).[26]

The Nyingma school had an alternative classification of tantras into two broad classes, outer and inner classes, each of which was subdivided into three. The Nyingma "outer tantras" consisted of "ritual action" *kriyā-tantra*s and *upa-tantra*s, or "near tantras"; this category is often equated with both the "practice" *caryā* tantra and "dual" *ubhaya* tantra categories, which will be discussed below, followed by yogatantras. The Sarma "unexcelled yoga tantras" more or less equate to the Nyingma "inner tantras" category, which are subdivided into three types, "great yoga" (*mahāyoga, rnal 'byor chen po*), "subsequent yoga" (*anuyoga, rjes su rnal 'byor*), and "utmost yoga" (*atiyoga, shin tu rnal 'byor*), which derive from Indian analyses of the types of yoga or contemplative exercises found in the tantric traditions, as will be seen below.[27]

At the core of these classificatory schemas is a distinction between "outer" and "inner" practices that appear to have been originally conceived as a distinction between "ritual actions" (*kriyā*) and "contemplative practice" (*yoga*) going back to at least the eighth century. The eighth-century Buddhist scholar Buddhaguhya[28] addresses this distinction in what was one of the early attempts to categorize the tantras, in his *Detailed Commentary on the Awakening of Mahāvairocana Tantra,* as follows:

> The Lord originally discovered the omniscient gnosis, with which He saw that beings who are to be educated are twofold: those who mainly aspire to that which is comprehensible, and those who mainly aspire to the vast and profound. For those two types of students there are two types of practices: practice having entered into the gate of the perfections,[29] and practice having entered into the mantric gate. There are two types of practice connected with the perfections' gate, namely that which primarily aspires to the comprehensible, and that which primarily aspires to the vast and profound. The Vinaya, the sutras, the abhidharma and likewise the Mahāyāna sutras were taught to the householders and heroes and so forth for the sake of those students who practice the perfections and who primarily aspire to the comprehensible. Vast and profound sutras, such as the *Gaṇḍavyūha*, *Daśabhūmika*, and the *Samādhirāja*, were taught for the sake of those students who aspire to the vast and profound.
>
> Furthermore, there are also the same two types for those students who practice entering into the mantric gate. The ritual action tantras (*kriyātantra*) such as the Noble "Excellent Accomplishment" *Susiddhi Tantra* and the "Wizard Collection" *Vidyādharapiṭaka* were taught for the sake of those who aspire primarily to the comprehensible. Likewise, the "Compendium of Tathāgatas" *Tattvasaṃgraha Tantra* was taught for those who train by means of the vast and profound. While it is not the case that those "who primarily aspire to the comprehensible" do not also aspire to and do not practice the vast and profound, the majority do in fact aspire to and practice the comprehensible. And

> while it is not the case that those who mainly aspire to the vast and profound do not also practice the comprehensible, they do largely practice the vast and profound. And while the *Tattvasaṃgraha* and so forth mainly teach inner contemplative practices (*yoga*), they do not lack outer practices. Likewise, while the ritual action tantras mainly teach outer practices, they also do not lack inner practices.
>
> It is said that the *Wizard Collection*, etc. are fixated on the three doors of liberation,[30] and one should understand that this also applies to the practitioners of the gate of the perfections. While the *Awakening of Mahāvairocana Tantra* is a yogatantra which focuses on discerning wisdom and skillful means, it teaches as well practices which accord with the ritual action tantras for the sake of those students who aspire to ritual actions. Or, it is understood that it can be identified as a "dual tantra" (*ubhayatantra*).[31]

This schema is based on an initial distinction between the outer versus the inner. The *kriyā*, or ritual action, tantras are thus those that tend to focus more on outer ritual actions, while the yoga tantras are those that tend to focus more on inner contemplative practices such as visualization. That this distinction is problematic is indicated by Buddhaguhya's insistence that both types of tantras share both types of practice. The difference is one of emphasis, not presence or absence.

That Buddhists were not content with a dichotomous formulation is indicated by their development mediating terms, such as the "dual" *ubhaya* category that shares the qualities of both the *kriyā* and *yogatantras*.[32] The eighth-century commentaries suggest that the earliest classification may have been a distinction between *kriyā* and *yoga* tantras. Buddhaguhya's comments here seem to have been based on the recognition that not all texts fall neatly into either of these binary categories, hence the creation of the category of *ubhayatantras* in which, as Buddhaguhya explains, one can place tantras such as the *Awakening of Mahāvairocana*, which exhibit a roughly equal emphasis on outer and inner procedures. Vilāsavajra, in a commentary also dating to the eighth century, probably a bit later than Buddhaguhya's, likewise attests "practice tantras" *caryātantra* as the mediating term. In another commentary, however, he omits this and instead adds another third category, "skillful means tantras" *upāyatantras*, but not as a mediating term, rather as a higher class above yogatantras.[33]

This points toward a tension within tantric Buddhist traditions. Buddhism has, probably since its inception, exhibited a pronounced fascination with internal processes and the meditative arts that purport to influence them. Yet Buddhists have also practiced rituals of various sorts. Rituals were gradually developed by Buddhist communities, with greatest acceleration during the periods of royal patronage of Buddhism, the classical age of which extended from the Mauryan up to the Gupta dynastic periods. It is during this period when Buddhists developed more elaborate ritual practices drawing on Vedic precedents such as the *homa* fire sacrifice,[34] Buddhist iconography developed,[35] and it is likely that the production of images was, without lengthy delay, accompanied by worship, ranging from consecration ceremonies to public worship of the consecrated images. But images were sometimes linked with internalized visualization practices, such as the pre-tantric Mahāyāna visualizations of the "buddha lands" (*buddhakṣetra*) and the buddhas and bodhisattvas who dwell there.[36]

Tantra arose in a context that was awash in ritual, and the early ritual action tantras were simply ritual texts compiled by Buddhist communities. But tantric Buddhism developed as a self-aware movement when Buddhists saw these rituals as part of a secret path to awakening, which necessitated inner contemplations along with outer rituals, and over time increasing emphasis was placed on the internalized contemplations, although the outer rituals were never jettisoned. Tantric Buddhist traditions, much like the Hindu Vedic tradition about a thousand years earlier, quickly segued toward the internalization of their ritual practices.[37]

The eighth century saw the rise of the *yogatantra*s that moved the focus of practice to one's own self, through the radical equation of oneself with a buddha. No longer was a buddha something external to be worshipped. The secret of practice was that each person was a buddha, and that one should see oneself thus and act accordingly, the subject and object, worshipper and worshipped, seeker and goal conflated and thoroughly unified. This is the practice known as "buddha yoga" or deity yoga, discussed in chapter 2. As Jacob Dalton argued,

> The tantric interiorization of Buddhist ritual was not a rejection of ritual. Nor was it a psychologization; it did not reduce ritual "to the spiritual state of the faithful practioner." This shift took place in the physical realm. Its beginnings can be traced to the first half of the eighth century, and the ritual technologies it spawned continued to develop through the ninth century. By the end of these two crucial centuries, a new ritual discourse of the bodily interior was in place. The tantric subject had become the site for the entire ritual performance; the body's interior provided the devotee, the altar, the oblations, and the buddha to be worshipped.[38]

One of the developments in the eighth-century yogatantras, which was further developed in the "unexcelled yoga tantras," was the focus on the body as the site for practice, with the development of sexual practices, internalized mandala and *homa* fire sacrifice visualizations, and perfection stage yogic practices focusing on the subtle body, namely the *cakra* energy centers and the network of channels that connect them and pervade the physical body.

As new tantras were composed that placed more emphasis on internalized practices, Indian Buddhists felt the need to come up with a new "highest" class of tantras. Initially, the term "great yoga" *mahāyoga* was used as the label for the highest class. Placed into this category were works such as the "Esoteric Community" *Guhyasamāja Tantra*, the *Hevajra Tantra*, and pretty much all tantras revealed from the ninth century onward. Later, even the term "great yoga" was replaced by the superlative "unexcelled yoga" (*niruttarayoga, rnal 'byor bla na med pa*), although this new term appears to have been initially used for a subdivision of the *mahāyoga* class. This classification was proposed by the scholar Śraddhākaravarma, one of the Indian scholars who worked with the Tibetan translator Rinchen Zangpo in the late tenth century, in his *Introductory Summary of the Import of the Unexcelled Yoga Tantras* as follows:

> There are four doors for entering into the Adamantine Path, the fruition of secret mantra. These are generally known as ritual action tantra, practice tantra, yogatantra, and great yoga tantra. They are secret, achieved by that which is hidden, since they are not in the experiential scope of those who are not suitable vessels. It is also called the Mantric Path, since one achieves the accomplishments by way of mantra and gestures (*mudrā*).[39]

He then introduces the classes, connecting them to disciples of varying capabilities and with specific tantras as examples. He goes on to describe the great yoga tantra class as follows:

> The great yoga tantras are taught for the sake of disciples of highest faculties, who mainly practice yoga. In short, there are twelve thousand of them, but expansively, their distinctions are inconceivable. With respect to that, there are two types of great yoga tantra, natural and conceptual.[40] With respect to the natural tantras, in short there are three types, causal tantras, result tantras, and skillful means tantras. Here the [*Esoteric*] *Community Appendix Tantra* states:
>
> > "[34] Were one to state tantra's subject matter,
> > That subject matter should be tripartite,
> > And distinguished as the fundamental,

> The natural and the irresistible.
> [35] Now the natural is that which is the cause,
> The irresistible's the fruition,
> And the fundamental is skillful means.
> These three do summarize tantras' import."

> There are two types of conceptual tantras, yoga-skillful means tantras and yoga-wisdom tantras. These are also called supreme yoga tantras and unexcelled yoga tantras.[41]

Śraddhākaravarma's analysis of the *mahāyoga* class is quite complex and reflects what came to be the common idea that the highest class can be distinguished into two basic types, correlated both to skillful means and wisdom as well as to gender. Śraddhākaravarma makes this point as well, noting that the "[yoga-]expedience tantras have mandalas in which the majority of deities are male gods, since their disciples are men, while the [yoga-]wisdom tantras have mandalas in which the deities are mainly goddesses, which accords with their disciples, who are women and outsider heretics to be disciplined."[42] These categories correspond to what Indians often referred to as *yoga* or *mahāyoga* tantras versus *yoginītantras,* the latter referring to the goddess-oriented traditions like the Hevajra and Cakrasaṃvara, which do indeed feature mandalas primarily populated with goddesses, the *yoginīs* or *ḍākinīs*. These texts are also among the most transgressive, featuring often obvious adaptations of Śaiva textual microforms and iconography, which the origin myth explained via the trope of conversion, and to which Śraddhākaravarma here refers when he suggests that they were taught to convert women and heretics.[43] Tibetans commonly referred to these two subsets of the highest class as "father tantras" (*pha rgyud*) and "mother tantras" (*ma rgyud*).

By the fourteenth century, Tibetan Buddhists who followed the Sarma schools settled on the fourfold classification of the tantras, with the highest class usually subdivided into two further classes.

However, this was by no means a settled issue in India, where there were many different classificatory schemas advanced, including a sevenfold classification proposed by Atiśa Dīpaṅkaraśrījñāna in the eleventh century.[44]

The Nyingma sixfold system, mentioned above, appears to be based on discussions concerning different types of yoga contemplative practices in the eighth-century tantras. Since the practice of yoga was linked to these higher classes, these distinctions seem to have informed the classification efforts as well. Several works list the series "union" *yoga*, "subsequent union" *anuyoga*, "extreme union," "utmost union" *atiyoga*, and "great union" *mahāyoga*. They are listed as four contemplative stages in the "Black Bane of Death, the Body Speech and Mind of All Tathāgatas" *Sarvatathāgatakāyavākcitta-kṛṣṇayamāri Tantra*, as follows:

> The first meditation is *yoga*, the second *anuyoga*, the third *atiyoga*, and the fourth *mahāyoga*. *Yoga* is understood to be the perfection of Vajrasattva, and *anuyoga* is famed as the causally efficacious body of the deity. The perfection of all of the wheels is known to be *atiyoga*. *Mahāyoga* should be taken to be the body, speech and mind [of the deity], the blessing of the divine eye, etc., the entry of the Gnostic Wheel, the experience of ambrosia, worship, and great praise.[45]

This list, with *mahāyoga* omitted, is also found in the "Ḍākinīs' Network That Unites All Buddhas" *Sarvabuddhasamāyogaḍākinīj ālasaṃvara Tantra*, as follows:

> Adhering to bliss through the enjoyment of all yogas, worship oneself through union (*yoga*) with one's own deity. And if, worshipping through subsequent union (*anuyoga*), one tastes everywhere the bliss of all yogas, one will succeed with utmost yoga (*atiyoga*). This bliss which extracts the essence (*rasāyāna*)

> of all Buddhas achieves supreme bliss and the glorious life of Vajrasattva, youthful and free of disease.[46]

A similar, but not identical, description also occurs in Kukurāja's "Explanation of the Secret Meaning of Glorious Vajrasattva," a commentary on the Vajrasattva section of the *Sarvabuddhasamāy ogaḍākinījālasaṃvara Tantra,* as follows:

> The mandala is perfected by means of the four types of yoga, and it is attained by means of the ritual observances. Being equipoised in gnosis alone is called union. Worshipping and summoning by means of the play of feminine blessing is subsequent union. Creating, projecting and recollecting purified, perfected mandalas is utmost union. Perfection in the blessings and consecrations is great union.[47]

A similar but lengthier description is provided by Indranāla in his "Detailed Exegesis of the Import of the Sarvabuddhasamāyogaḍāki nījālasamvara Tantra," as follows:

> First, yoga, is worshipping oneself through union of oneself with the superior deity. The body of Mahāvajradhara produced through the five awakenings[48] is the superior deity, the essence of all buddhas. One unites with the consort (*mudrā*) of his body, speech and mind. One is initiated with the ornaments and costume, and receives the blessings, whereby one worships oneself. Regarding subsequent union, one worships through the further application of the bliss of all yogas, and gives rise to a woman who accords with one's clan. For example, just as a shadow is produced when a shoot is illumined with light, when illumined by gnosis an image which accords with reality is produced. After undergoing the preliminaries of consecration and blessing, she is exhorted with the signs and so forth, and then enjoyed. Abiding in blissful concentration for the sake of all yogas, the victors are delighted

> and beings purified through the worship of subsequent union. Regarding utmost union, when one takes pleasure in all things, then one will succeed by means of it. Having purified the outer sign with luminous bliss, one creates the habitat and inhabitant mandalas within the secret place. Regarding great union, this bliss which extracts the essence (*rasāyāna*) of all buddhas achieves supreme bliss and the glorious life of Vajrasattva, youthful and free of disease. Being initiated with the blessings of the six sense media, the blessings of the four great elements,[49] the symbol of the crown and the vase of the goddess, and being purified, one attains the four glories through the bliss of alchemy (*rasāyana*), which is the flow of the spirit of awakening.[50]

Indranāla's commentary indicates that "union" corresponds to creation stage visualization of oneself as the deity, in this case Vajrasattva, and union with Vajrasattva's consort, through visualization and possibly with an actual partner in the initiation process. "Subsequent union" is a post-initiation practice that evidently involves summoning a magical female partner with whom one practices. While this might sound unusual, this is actually a feature of many Buddhist tantras, in which goddesses are summoned for sex and empowering sexual fluids that were thought to confer magical powers, and it is yet another feature borrowed from Śaiva tantras.[51] In later Buddhist contexts, it appears to have been understood as referring to a visualized partner. "Utmost yoga" here is only barely described but appears to be a sexual yogic practice involving the contemplation of the mandala within the "secret place" or genital area, the site of sexual union, while "great union" appears to be a perfected state in which the practice is fully achieved.

While Indian Buddhist attempts to classify the tantras were quite complex, they seem to have been based on the content of the tantras as well as a basic distinction between outer ritual and inner contemplative practice. While the two are ideally integrated, emphasis was placed on the latter as sign of a more definitive presentation of the adamantine path to awakening. The main contribution of the Tibetans in this arena was making sense of the complex intellectual tradition inherited from India, and simplifying it, coming up with the settled Sarma fourfold classification and the Nyingma sixfold system.

4.2.2 East Asian Classification Schemas

A smaller number of tantras and associated tantric literature was successfully transmitted and translated to East Asia. As a result, the Indian concern with categorizing the tantras was not particularly relevant there. That said, East Asian advocates of the tantric traditions developed their own system for understanding the tantras, and they generally paid greater attention to the question of the relation of the tantras to the larger Mahāyāna tradition from which they emerged.

The differentiation of "esoteric" tantric forms of Buddhism from the previous "exoteric" Buddhist traditions was a major concern of Kūkai, as Ryūichi Abé has demonstrated. Kūkai used several names for the new teachings he learned in China. These include the names "Adamantine Path" (*vajrayāna, kongōjō,* 金剛乗) and "secret treasury" (*guhyapiṭaka, mitsuzō,* 密藏), terms which he learned from his Chinese master, Huiguo.[52] He distinguishes the esoteric teachings of tantra from the exoteric mainstream Mahāyana teachings in two basic ways. In a letter that he sent to Tokuitsu (徳一), a prominent Japanese Buddhist, in 815, he wrote the following:

> The Exoteric Teaching (*kengyō*) and the Esoteric Teaching (*mikkyō*) are distinguished from each other in their methods of leading beings to enlightenment. The Exoteric Teaching is none other than the scriptures preached by the Sambhogakāya and Nirmāṇakāya Buddhas. The Esoteric Treasury (*mitsuzō*) consists of the Dharmakāya Tathāgata. The Exoteric (*ken*) revolves around the six pāramitās of cause and effect. It endorses the practice of

> bodisattvahood, which is none other than the teaching gate of expedient means and accords with the languages of its audience. By contrast, the Esoteric (*mitsu*) is a teaching consisting of the eternally unceasing three mysteries (*honnu sanmitsu*), which is the language of suchness (*nyogigo*) that immediately describes the [Dharmakāya's] inmost enlightenment (*naishō*).[53]

The idea that the esoteric tantric teachings differ from the exoteric Mahāyāna is a common one, with the tantric traditions featuring secret teachings relating to practice that can rapidly lead to awakening. But Kūkai goes beyond this, claiming a higher and more authoritative source for the esoteric. He notes that the exoteric teachings are the teachings of the "manifestation body" *nirmāṇakāya* buddha, that is, a buddha who has assumed a physical form to teach corporeal beings, in this case Śākyamuni Buddha, or of a "beatific body" *saṃbhogakāya* buddha, that is, one of the buddhas, such as Amitābha, who exist perpetually in their buddha lands that they created out of compassion, which were a focus of a number of Mahāyāna traditions. His claim is that the esoteric teachings are a direct expression of the "reality body" *dharmakāya* buddha, which is none other than the very mind of awakening realized by all buddhas and possessed by all beings. It is thus the ultimate teaching of awakening that in fact pervades all other teachings and is implicitly present in the exoteric teachings.

But this ultimate teaching was not expressed in a clear and direct manner, as were the exoteric teachings directed toward those of the human realm and expressed to facilitate human understanding. Kūkai, again evidently following Huiguo, considered mantras and *dhāraṇī* "spells" to be the direct expression of the reality body level of buddha embodiment, and since *dhāraṇī* are also found in many exoteric sutras, the esoteric was, in his view, embedded within exoteric teachings, but not recognized as such by the exoteric schools that study them. But this hidden meaning can be revealed if one possesses the proper exegetical approach. In his *Interpretation of the Lotus Sūtra*, Kūkai wrote the following:

> The exoteric is to consume many words to denote one meaning. The esoteric is to unleash countless meanings within each letter of a word. This is the secret function of dhāraṇī. Because of this, dhāraṇī is translated as *sōji,* the container of all. However, this meaning has been kept secret by the Dharma transmitters of the past. This is what I have now introduced as the mantra treasury (*shingonzō*).[54]

For Kūkai and Huiguo, the esoteric, as the highest teaching, also provides the interpretive framework for properly understanding the exoteric teachings as well. While Kūkai thus created a hierarchy of Buddhist teachings, with the esoteric at the top, he did not further subdivide the esoteric teachings, probably because the number of esoteric texts received by him was relatively small. The Shingon tradition eventually did develop a relatively simple twofold system for categorizing esoteric teachings. The Tokugawa era scholar Ekō (1666–1734) proposed distinguishing "pure esoteric teachings" (*seijunmikkyō* 正純密教 or *junmitsu* 純密), the texts transmitted to Japan during the Heian era focusing on the Adamantine Pinnacle collection and the *Awakening of Mahāvairocana Tantra*. Ekō contrasted with this "miscellaneous esoteric teachings" (*zōbu mikkyō* 雜部密教 or *zōmitsu* 雜密), by which he meant various esoteric texts employing *dhāraṇī* in rituals for mundane ends.[55] While this was a relatively late formulation, it became very influential in Shingon study circles, and the *zōmitsu* category was used as a catchall to include all esoteric Buddhist works not transmitted to Japan during the Heian period, which includes the vast majority of extant tantric literature.[56]

4.3 Canonical Collections

Perhaps the earliest attempt to bring together tantric texts into a collection is the "Wizard Collection," *vidyādharapiṭaka,* which apparently began as a Dhammagutta collection of magical literature and was also the name of a seventh-century text that compiled magical lore. The use of this term implies a growing awareness that tantric Buddhism was distinct from earlier forms of Buddhism, which would ultimately lead to labels for the tradition such as the "mantric method" (*mantranaya*), "mantric path" (*mantrayāna*), or "adamantine path" (*vajrayāna*). Despite these early attempts to set aside a collection of tantric texts, due to the decentralized nature of Buddhist traditions, there does not appear to have been an organized, centralized attempt to collect and catalogue tantric Buddhist texts that were consistently maintained over time. Probably the most influential early effort in this regard was the attempt to develop collections of tantras, notably the eighth-century collections of eighteen tantras. As the number of tantras increased, however, this attempt was abandoned by the late eighth century.

Instead, each monastery where tantric Buddhism was practiced would collect its own library of texts for the traditions practiced there. These texts could be copied by those visiting the monastery, thus slowly facilitating the spread of new texts and traditions. This system, of each monastery preserving its own textual collection, was maintained in the Kathmandu Valley of Nepal, the only non-ethnic Tibetan region in South Asia where tantric Buddhism survived. The collections preserved by the Newar Buddhists were substantial and remarkable; most extant Sanskrit Buddhist texts were preserved there. Not only did the Newari Buddhists preserve ancient Buddhist manuscripts by copying and recopying them frequently, but also each generation of Vajrācāryas would compose new works, such as commentaries, ritual manuals, and contemplative manuals termed *samādhi*s, which over the generations led to the substantial growth of textual collections held by these monasteries.[57] The Kathmandu Valley was also an important regional center of tantric Buddhism that facilitated the spread of Buddhism to Tibet, and the Newar Buddhists' preservation of Sanskrit manuscripts have dramatically advanced our understanding of tantric traditions in South Asia.

When Chinese, Southeast Asian, and Tibetan monk pilgrims traveled to South Asia, they would have the opportunity to study at the monasteries with masters living there and to make copies of texts once they had received the authorization by receiving the requisite initiations and teachings. This would typically require making offerings to the master, which a number of Tibetans reported required a significant amount of cash in the form of gold.[58] If one is inclined to accuse the Indian and Nepali masters of greed, it is important to keep in mind that due to the esoteric nature of these traditions, it would not be possible to receive permission to study the tantras without first being initiated, and initiation requires that a substantial fee be paid to the master. Having received teachings as well as copies of the texts, they would return to their homelands bearing them, which they would often endeavor to translate.

These new translations were added to the growing canons of Buddhist literature in Tibet and China, which were maintained via official catalogues kept by the imperial states to oversee their translation efforts, and later, in Tibet, by scholars who assumed the oversight role formerly maintained by the state. As the number of tantric texts in translation grew, they were incorporated into the canons and subjected to various levels of organization. In China, for example, the Northern Song Dynasty catalogue produced in 1013 CE by the imperially sponsored translation institute divides the canon into three categories, namely a "Hīnayāna Scriptural Collection" (小乘經藏), a "Mahāyāna Scriptural Collection" (大乘經藏) and "The Esoteric Portion of the Mahāyāna Scriptural Collection" (大乘經藏秘密部). The latter is somewhat nebulous and includes all translations of the tantras and tantric literature, including all *dhāraṇī* collections, evidently following the position of Huiguo and Kūkai that *dhāraṇī* (spells) are intrinsically esoteric.[59]

The best known East Asian edition of the Buddhist canon is the Taishō canon ("New Edition of the Buddhist Canon Compiled During the Taishō Era" 大正新脩大藏經), compiled in Japan from 1924 to 1934, and consisting of one hundred volumes overall, with eighty-five volumes of actual canonical texts. It includes a four-volume "section on esoteric teachings" (*mikkyōbu*, 密教部), volumes 18–21. This section contains 573 works, including multiple translations for some of them, for a total of 618 texts. This section is further subdivided into fourteen subsections. The first volume contains translations of tantras, divided into three sections, on the *Awakening of Mahāvairocana Tantra* and related texts, the Adamantine Pinnacle collection and related texts, and the *Susiddhikara Sūtra* and related texts. The second is a catchall category, as it also includes many of the Northern Song dynasty translations, including of unexcelled yoga tantras such as the *Guhyasamāja, Hevajra,* and *Māyājāla Tantras*. The remaining eleven sections, spanning four volumes, deal with various ritual manuals, such as *homa* fire sacrifice and initiatory (*abhiṣeka*) manuals, as well as *dhāraṇī* ritual texts.[60] However, some of these sections also contain translations of tantras, so the distinction between revealed scripture (*tantra, kalpa,* and so forth) and ritual texts is blurred in this collection.[61] There were also various esoteric texts preserved in East Asia that were not included in the canonical collections. They include texts preserved in Japan that purport to be Tang era translations, as well as Chinese translations preserved in the Mogao Caves in Dunhuang as well as in the Beitangdian (北湯天) temple in Dali in Southwest China, a region in which the practice of esoteric Buddhism was preserved up until the early modern period.[62]

In Tibet during the imperial period, translation activity was sponsored by the state and monitored, with catalogues kept of translated works. Following the collapse of the imperial state, centralized monitoring of the canon ceased. Nonetheless, the early translations were preserved, and "they were copied and circulated piecemeal, within the limited circles of affiliated lineages or with the sponsorship of local rulers, but without the patronage or machinery of a unified state."[63] At this point, it appears that in Tibet, as in India and Nepal, each monastery kept copies of the texts available to them, and texts spread gradually as copies were made and distributed to other institutions.

In the Nyingma tradition, the translations made during the early dissemination period of the eighth through tenth centuries came to be known as the "canonical scripture collection" (*bka' ma*), which was distinguished from the collection of treasure texts (*gter ma*) revealed subsequent to the early dissemination period, and which eventually grew to a much larger size. The canon of treasure texts is a living, growing canon, with texts continuing to be discovered and compiled by modern tradents, as Cathy Cantwell has shown in her study of the treasure texts revealed by Dudjom Rinpoche, or Dudjom Jikdral Yeshe Dorje (*bdud 'joms 'jig bral ye shes rdo rje*, 1904–1987).[64] The *bka' ma* and *gter ma* collections reflect a distinction in the Nyingma tradition between two types of scripture; their canonical collections are organized in terms of the ninefold Buddhist path (*theg pa dgu*).

The first Tibetan attempt to organize what had become a very large canon was undertaken at Narthang (*snar thang*) monastery in the early fourteenth century, where the canon was organized into two large collections, the "translated scriptures," or kanjur/kangyur (*bka' 'gyur*), containing translated works believed to be awakened speech (*buddhavacana*), and the "translated treatises," or tenjur/tengyur (*bstan 'gyur*). It appears to have been inspired by a scholar named Jampé Yang ('jam pa'i dbyangs), who studied at Narthang and later became the court chaplain of Buyantu Khan, the Yuan emperor of China (r. 1311–1320). As Robert Mayer has noted, there is "little doubt that 'Jam pa'i dbyangs' interest in the development of Kanjur had a lot to do with a wish to emulate the Chinese model of a canon, regulated according to stringent bibliographical analysis and sponsored by the state."[65] The inclusion of the word "translate," *'gyur*, in the titles of these canonical collections was intended to emphasize their origin in India and to exclude works deemed apocryphal that originated in Tibet.

Efforts to assemble canons of Buddhist scripture were further advanced by Butön Rinchendrup, a Sakya scholar who assembled a very large collection of scriptures at Zhwa Lu Monastery,[66] and he composed an extremely influential catalogue for the collection. His catalogue established the organization for subsequent editions of the Kanjur and Tenjur. Controversially, he omitted from the collection many older tantras preserved by the Nyingma school that he considered apocryphal, although some of these texts were restored in later editions of the Kanjur.

The best known edition of the Tibetan canon, the Degé (*sde-dge*) edition, has 472 texts preserved in the tantra section of the Kanjur, along with nineteen texts preserved in the "Ancient Tantra" *rNying rgyud* section, which is a group of texts that Butön controversially rejected as apocryphal but were later restored. Following Butön's proposed organization, the tantra section is organized in accordance with the Sarma fourfold classification of tantras, in descending order. Since Butön was a member of the Sakya school, which holds the *Hevajra Tantra* to be the preeminent tantra, the tantra collection begins with the *Hevajra* cycle, then moves on to other unexcelled yoga tantras before moving to the yogatantras, and so forth. There are also an additional 2,623 texts preserved in the tantra section of the Tenjur, which consists of translations of Indian commentaries and ritual texts.[67] The Tenjur tantric texts follow the same pattern, organizing them according to class in descending order.

The Nyingma tradition preserved their tantras considered translations of Indic originals in a canon called "The Nyingma Collected Tantras" (*rnying ma rgyud 'bum*), of which multiple editions survive. The compilation of this canonical collection was also undertaken in the early fourteenth century, by the Nyingma scholar Zur Zanpo Pal (zur bzang po dpal), who, like Jampé Yang, taught at the court of Buyantu Khan, where a print of the canon was made in 1317 CE.[68] This canon preserves the most important "inner tantras." In the Degé (*sde dge*) edition of this collection, the

Mahāyoga section is the largest, with 229 texts contained in sixteen volumes. The Anuyoga section is much smaller, with twenty-eight texts in two volumes, while the Atiyoga section is somewhat larger, with 160 texts in six volumes.[69]

The Tibetan canons preserve the largest known collections of tantras and tantric literature, and they have played a major role in the preservation of this literature, and well as the preservation and dissemination of tantric traditions. They have been disseminated along with Tibetan Buddhism to the various regions where Tibetan Buddhism has spread, most notably Mongolia and China, as well as Mongol ethic regions in Russia, and, with the Tibetan diaspora of the twentieth century, around the world. Many print editions of the Kanjur and Tenjur have been published, and digital scans have also been published online.[70] The 84000 Foundation, an institution founded by the contemporary lama Dzongsar Kyentse Rinpoche, launched in 2009 in an effort to translate the Tibetan Kanjur into English and to make the translations freely available online.[71] Dzongsar Kyentse Rinpoche also launched the Kumarajiva Project, with the aim of translating texts from the Tibetan canon into Chinese; this translation effort would primarily focus on tantric texts, since most of the Tibetan translations absent from the Chinese Buddhist canon are tantric.

5
Transgression, Censorship, and Interpretation

5.1 Transgression, Translation, and Censorship

One of the most striking features of the Buddhist tantras is the transgressive passages that describe sexual or violent practices. This content, while not in every single tantra, is quite pervasive, being found in early seventh-century works such as the *Subāhuparipṛcchā Tantra*, which was translated into Chinese by Śubhakarasiṃha in 726 CE and contains charnel ground imagery and description of a ritual for summoning a female dryad spirit (*yakṣī*) for sexual enjoyment,[1] while the eighth-century "Compendium of the Realities of All Tathāgatas" *Sarvatathāgatatattvasaṃgraha-nāma-mahāyāna-sūtra* contains descriptions of sexual initiatory rituals, as discussed in section 2.3.2.1. The unexcelled yoga tantras, composed from the eighth century onward, even more prominently feature transgressive content, often in the opening background verse, as discussed in section 2.2.1.

The tradents of the tantras were often quite radical in their desire to challenge their readers. Violent and erotic content both presented a serious challenge to Buddhist identity as nonviolent and to the long-established practice of celibacy as a marker of elite spiritual status in Buddhist communities. This section will explore the impact this transgressive content had on the transmission of the Buddhist tantras, as well as the creative strategies taken by translators and commentators to overcome the resistance

The Buddhist Tantras. David B. Gray, Oxford University Press. © Oxford University Press 2023.
DOI: 10.1093/oso/9780197623831.003.0006

it engendered. It will thus attempt to shed light on this fascinating feature of tantric literature, which has attracted attention and triggered condemnation wherever these texts have been transmitted.

5.1.1 The Politics of Translation

Tantric Buddhism has often portrayed itself as a particularly efficacious form of Buddhism, one that, by virtue of its rich array of ritual and contemplative techniques, is potent in both spiritual and secular spheres. Tantric Buddhist texts and teachers have often claimed the ability to protect the state via their rituals and have accordingly been able to secure royal patronage. A notable example of this phenomenon is Amoghavajra's long years of service to several Tang emperors, discussed in section 3.1. But this same claim for power could also serve as an obstacle to securing support, particularly in East Asian cultural contexts. This is because insofar as these claims are accepted, esoteric Buddhist institutions could be seen as a competing locus of power—even a potential threat to imperial power. This is particularly the case with regard to the esoteric Buddhist texts that advocate or describe the rites of black magic, *abhicāra,* which the adept can use to kill or overpower his enemies, including the king or emperor. The transgressive rhetoric contained in many esoteric Buddhist scriptures could be seen as a threat to the political order as well as to traditional systems of morality and thus the social order.

These factors affected the reception and translation of esoteric Buddhist scriptures in both Tibet and China. There are many similarities in the reception of esoteric Buddhist works in both contexts during the eighth century. Most importantly, the translation of Buddhist scriptures was supported by both the Chinese and Tibetan imperial states. In both cases, there is evidence suggesting that this reception was selective, with more transgressive texts repressed, most likely by the translators themselves, insofar as their activities were supported and closely monitored by imperial authorities. However, during the Northern Song Dynasty, that is, the tenth and eleventh centuries when the officially sponsored translation of Buddhist texts resumed in both Tibet and China after a hiatus of over a century, we see a significant divergence in these two contexts. In China, where translation activity continued under imperial patronage, self-censorship on the part of the translators continued. Tibet, however, was by this time fragmented into numerous smaller, regional polities, so the translation of the tantras there occurred in a largely decentralized political environment, with less oversight from political authorities. While several rulers of western Tibet sought to control the dissemination of tantric texts, they failed, and their failure was a contributing factor to the largely unrestricted dissemination of tantric works and practices in Tibet.

The association between translation and the imperial state was very strong in China. As Wolfgang Behr has noted, the very term in Chinese that is considered to be the equivalent of the English term "translate," namely *fanyi* (翻譯), originated in one of the terms (*fan*, 譯) used for government officials responsible for oral interpretation and translation during the Han Dynasty.[2] The modern term *fanyi* (翻譯) was first used to describe Buddhist translation activity, and this activity gave rise to the earliest Chinese theorization about translation.[3] Translation was thus seen in China as preeminently a government activity.

The translation of Buddhist works was viewed as a component of Chinese foreign policy. Ancient records show that government bureaucrats responsible for translation were present as early as 1100 BCE,[4] which led in later dynasties to the formation of translation academies.[5] As Elsie Chan has argued, Buddhist translators accepted institutional support in exchange for their obedience to the throne.[6] As such, it is definitely not the case that the Chinese Buddhist canonical collections are a passive repository, containing translations of any and all Indian Buddhist scriptures that happened to reach China. Nor were the translations preserved within them the products of a free and unrestrained translation activity. Since Buddhist translation work in China was imperially sponsored, the translators were subject to surveillance by the Imperial Censorate.[7] Such monitoring undoubtedly influenced the resulting translations. When one compares the Chinese translations of the tantras with Sanskrit source texts and Tibetan translations, transgressive passages are often obscurely translated or omitted entirely. This was likely the result of either direct oversight or indirect pressure to produce translations that would accord, or at least not grossly offend, Han Chinese cultural sensibilities.

From the first century onward China received a steady stream of Buddhist missionaries and texts that they either brought with them or composed themselves. As Robert Buswell has noted, "The success or failure of such texts—and ultimately of the foreign missionaries who would have created them—would have been heavily dependent on their reception by Chinese officialdom."[8] Translation sometimes became a politicized act, as was the case with Bodhiruci's translation activity under Empress Wu (武則天, r. 690–704), as Antonino Forte has shown.[9] The formation of imperial bibliographies and canons was also often contentious.[10] The work of the translation and transmission of Buddhist scriptures was never free of political implications, and when it occurred within highly centralized political environments, such as China during the Tang and Song Dynasties, translators could not ignore the power of the imperial state to which they were beholden.

It is not surprising that tantric Buddhist texts, which reached both China and Tibet during the eighth century, would present a real challenge to the imperially sponsored translation teams. The Buddhist tantras are particularly notable for their focus on the achievement of "worldly powers" (*laukikasiddhi*) in addition to the "ultimate achievement" (*lokottarasiddhi*) of buddhahood. These "worldly powers" were achieved by magical ritual procedures such as mantra repetition and *homa* fire sacrifices as discussed in section 2.3.2.2. Many advocates of esoteric Buddhism, such as

Amoghavajra in Tang China, emphasized the positive and protective aspects of tantric ritual, and they claimed that it offered powerful means for defending and enriching the imperial state that patronized it.

Despite Amoghavajra's success, it seems that during the eighth century, when the tantras were first translated into their language, the Chinese may not have been particularly receptive to texts containing descriptions of dangerous ritual procedures. As discussed in section 1.5.1, there are both Tibetan and Chinese reports of a collection of eighteen tantras, the "Great Yoga" Mahāyoga and Adamantine Pinnacle collections, respectively. The latter collection, described by Amoghavajra, contains the "Compendium of the Realities of All Tathāgatas" *Sarvatathāgatatattvasaṃgraha-nāma-mahāyāna-sūtra*, "Esoteric Community" *Guhyasamāja*, the "Ḍākinīs' Network That Unites All Buddhas" *Sar vabuddhasamāyogaḍākinījālasaṃvara*, and the "Glorious Supreme Prime" *Śrīparamādya* tantras.[11] These texts all contain transgressive content, including sexual practices and violent rituals, as the selections translated in this volume indicate.

In an account recorded by his disciple Amoghavajra, Vajrabuddhi claimed to have acquired a complete set of the Adamantine Pinnacle collection of eighteen tantras, which he described as a massive text of 100,000 stanzas. He attempted to bring it with him on his return trip to China, which concluded when he reached Southern China in 719 CE. This voyage was disastrous and resulted in Vajrabuddhi losing the 100,000-stanza version of the tantra collection that he was carrying with him in a typhoon. Amoghavajra recorded the following account of the story:

> I set out from the Western Lands by way of the southern seas with a fleet of more than thirty great ships, each of which had five or six hundred passengers. At one point, when we had reached the middle of the sea while crossing the ocean, we hit a typhoon. The other ships, together with their passengers, were scattered and

> sank. The ship on which I was traveling was also about to sink. I had been keeping the two scriptures[12] close to me to worship them. When the captain saw that the ship was about to sink, he had everything on board cast into the sea. At that time, I was terrified and forgot to put away the scriptures. As a result, the hundred thousand stanza [text] was cast into the ocean, and only the abbreviated text remained. I then began to mentally recite and perform the rite for mitigating disaster, to end the typhoon. The wind and water became calm for more than 500 meters around the ship.[13]

Vajrabuddhi may very well have lost his collection of tantras, and while this would have been unfortunate, the history of tantric Buddhism was not likely highly impacted by this disaster. For even if he had successfully reached China in 719 with these texts, it is highly unlikely that the more transgressive texts would have been translated adequately, if at all. For, as Ronald Davidson notes, Vajrabuddhi's colleague Śubhakarasiṃha produced a translation in 726 of the *Subāhaparipṛcchā Tantra* that fails to clearly translate the transgressive content of this text, which includes descriptions of "cemetery-based ghoul (*vetāla*) practices, the employment of corpses in the center of the maṇḍala, the selling of human flesh, and its use in ferocious homa rituals."[14] It is certainly possible that Śubhakarasiṃha's obscure translation in precisely the most transgressive section of the text was intentional, in order to prevent the censorship of the entire text. This certainly would have been warranted. As Orzech noted:

> When he arrived in Ch'ang-an, Śubhakarasiṃha was met with considerable suspicion by the T'ang emperor Hsüan-tsung. The emperor was as interested in Taoism and the occult as he was suspicious of persons of reputedly vast power and insight. He impounded forthwith Śubhakarasiṃha's Sanskrit texts (and we can presume) placed him under careful surveillance. Apparently

> convinced that Śubhakarasiṃha's knowledge would be of more use than harm, the emperor returned the texts, and the *ācārya* was ensconced in an imperial monastery and put to work translating the texts he brought with him.[15]

While we do not know if the Sanskrit text(s) upon which he based his translation were identical to those used later by Tibetan translators, the bowdlerization of transgressive passages in Chinese translations is so common that it is highly unlikely to be the result of differences in the Indic manuscripts.

Such obscure translation may have been necessary in Tang China. Destructive magical practices were proscribed in China,[16] as was also the case in the Greco-Roman world.[17] This was apparently due to the fact that the efficacy of magic was widely accepted, although in both cultural contexts skepticism existed concerning this.[18] As Howard Goodman and Howard Wechsler have shown with regard to the late Han and Tang dynastic periods, imperial ritual was deployed as a powerful force for political legitimation.[19] In other words, the Chinese imperial state sought to control ritual power, to deploy it as a form of imperial power, and to restrict or prohibit illicit rituals that could be used to destabilize the imperium. While the eighth century Tang court patronized the translation of tantric texts and the performance of tantric rituals, these activities were highly scrutinized, and the more transgressive texts may not have been tolerated.

In Tibet, translation was also a political activity. The imperial state played a central role in the development and promotion of writing and literature in Tibet during the imperial period, circa the seventh through ninth centuries.[20] As in China, this translation activity had a political dimension. The Tibetan imperial court deployed tantric ritual and symbolism, particularly that associated with the Buddha Mahāvairocana, as part of its legitimation strategy.[21]

The oversight that accompanied the imperial sponsorship of translation activity in eighth- and ninth-century Tibet resulted in the censorship of some tantric scriptures. Samten Karmay concluded that "towards the end of the 8th century A.D. there was the question of whether the tantras, especially the [unexcelled yoga tantras],[22] were to be practiced literally. Finally, it was decided that such tantras should be translated into Tibetan only when royal permission was given."[23] According to the Tibetan scholar Butön Rinchendrup, during the late eighth and early ninth centuries,

> Tibet's king and high-ranking ministers observed that dishonest sentient beings of the future would not understand the profound intentional import [of the texts] and would consider the literal sense authoritative. Without even the slightest unification of art and wisdom, they would be educated in the mantras without being bound to even a single commitment concerning [what behaviors are] to be avoided or cultivated. These practitioners of the immodest, deviant, semblant tantras of the heretics would denigrate the Teachings of the Buddha and engage in a method of destroying both self and other. Hence it was decided through royal proclamation that there was to be no translation of the Mahāyoga Tantras except when permission is granted.[24]

As Butön was almost certainly aware, Emperor Tridé Songtsen (khri de srong btsan, r. 804–815) is reputed to have declared the following in his introduction to the *Two Fascicle Lexicon* (*Sgra sbyor bam po gnyis pa*), an early ninth-century work:

> The tantras of secret mantra, according to the texts, are to be kept secret. It is also not appropriate to explain and teach them to the unqualified. Still, in the meantime, though it has been permitted to translate and practice them, there have been those who have not deciphered what is expounded allusively, and seizing upon literal understanding have practiced perversely. It is stipulated that, among the tantras of mantra, there have also been some haphazardly translated into the Tibetan language. This being so, hereafter it is not permitted to translate haphazardly the tantras

> of mantra and the mantra terms except for those *dhāraṇīmantras* and tantras whose translations are enjoined on order from above.[25]

As Matthew Kapstein notes, this work reflects "the close relationship between the political and religious dimensions of Tibetan imperial authority, and their connection to questions of language."[26]

The Tibetan kings evidently viewed the translation of Buddhist works as an important aspect of government policy and acted accordingly. Under Tridé Songtsen, a religious council and editorial board were established to implement the policies outlined in the *Two Fascicle Lexicon*.[27] Later in the ninth century, under the emperor Tritsuk Detsen (khri gtsug lde btsan, r. 815–838), also known as Ralpachen, the translation of some of the more transgressive tantras, specifically the "Mother Tantras," or *yoginītantras*, were banned outright.[28] There is also evidence that some were selectively translated, with transgressive passages excluded.[29]

In Tibet during the late tenth century, King Lha-lama Yéshé-ö's doubts concerning the tantras, which were triggered by their transgressive content, were allayed by Rinchen Zangpo and Atiśa. Despite this, reticence lingered. One of Lha-lama Yéshé-ö's successors, King Zhiwa-ö (zhi ba 'od), would ordain the following in 1092, with obvious resignation: "Although the 'Mother tantras' are excellent, they nevertheless cause many monks to break their monastic vows as a result of not knowing the implications of certain terms. There will not be any contradiction if they are not practiced at all."[30]

The wish of Zhiwa-ö was not fulfilled; the "Mother Tantras" became extremely popular in Tibet and the kings of Guge Pu-hrangs in western Tibet lacked the power to restrict their translation and dissemination in Tibet. Here, the Tibetan and Chinese contexts diverged considerably. For while the Northern Song translation effort did result in the translation of a number of unexcelled yoga tantras that were notable for their transgressive character—such as the *Guhyasamāja*, *Hevajra*, and *Vajrabhairava Tantras*—the

Northern Song translations are notable for their relatively restrained character, and they failed, ultimately, to serve as the basis of viable traditions of practice in East Asia.[31] There also was an edict in China restricting translation of the more transgressive tantras. A Buddhist chronicle published in 1269 claims that there was an imperial edict issued in 1017 which stated the following:

> [B]lood sacrifices are inimical to the True Vehicle and foul curses are contrary to the exquisite principle. This newly translated *Vināyaka sūtra* in four *juan* is not permitted to be entered in the canon. From now on this [sort of] scripture will not be translated.[32]

While this reflects Chinese concerns regarding the black magical rites found in many of the tantras, it does not appear that the translation of any texts was blocked during this period. Instead, they were translated in a manner intended to ameliorate such concerns.

Tibet proved to be a far more receptive environment for these traditions. In Tibet, translation activity during the tenth through fourteenth centuries took place with little or no government oversight. Rather, it occurred in a decentralized fashion, typically at the initiative of scholar-monks who would travel to India or Nepal and secure the assistance of Buddhist scholars using funds that they had raised in their communities. There was often significant competition among the translators, which led to the more popular scriptures being translated several times, and then revised by subsequent generations of scholars, who would compare them with existing manuscripts, making changes according to the developing standards of Tibetan translation conventions.

5.1.2 Translation Strategies

Having outlined the contexts in which tantric scriptures were translated and disseminated in Tibet and China, it appears that these contexts shaped how tantric texts were translated. First, it is important to note the limits of our knowledge. Although Sanskrit manuscripts of many esoteric Buddhist works survive, it is also clear that there was significant variation in the manuscripts that were circulating circa the tenth through twelfth centuries.[33] So we cannot assume that a "mistranslation" of a given passage represents an intentional effort to obscure the meaning of a transgressive passage. That said, in the Chinese translations of the tantras, the pattern of obscure translation of transgressive passages is so clear that it is almost certainly the case that this phenomenon is not solely the result of misunderstanding and variant Sanskrit readings.

Second, translation is inherently an interpretative enterprise. There are various approaches to the art of translation, ranging from the conservative, which, as the name implies, seeks as much as possible to *conserve* the diction of the original, accurately transmitting it within the target language, to the liberal, which seeks to transmit the spirit of the original, if not the exact wording. However, the conservative approach, despite its pretense to accurate transmission, is still interpretive, as it inevitably privileges one interpretation of the text over others. This is not problematic in unambiguous textual passages, but in ambiguous contexts it becomes a serious issue—and the tantras were notorious for their deliberately ambiguous passages. Indian Buddhists developed sophisticated hermeneutical strategies for the interpretation, but these were tendentious insofar as they tended to downplay the literal meanings and privilege "inner" or "secret" meanings that are by no means obvious from the text itself.[34]

The Tibetans were generally conservative in their approach, in that they tended to emphasize the conversion of meaning via literal translation. Although Tibetan, a member of the Tibeto-Burman language family, is quite distinct from Sanskrit, the Tibetans devised a translation language that called for the use of standardized translation equivalents, as detailed in works such as the *Mahāvyutpatti / Bye brag tu rtogs par byed pa chen po.* Despite the persistent myth of the precision of Tibetan translations from Sanskrit, Tibetan translations do vary in the degree to which they aim for literal translations, using equivalents such as those proposed by lexicons, such as the *Mahāvyutpatti*, or more fluent and flexible translations. Given the significant differences between Tibetan and Sanskrit, it is of course impossible that the former could precisely correspond to the latter.[35] The Tibetan attempts to mirror the Sanskrit, while not free of ambiguity, typically yielded a stilted form of the language that is almost incomprehensible to ordinary Tibetan readers and, in fact, requires some knowledge of Sanskrit to be properly understood. Despite these problems, the Tibetan translation of the Sanskrit Buddhist canon, in the form that took shape in North Indian monasteries from the tenth through thirteenth centuries, stands as a remarkable cultural achievement.[36]

Perhaps due to the radical difference between the Sanskrit and Chinese languages, there is no myth of direct correspondence between Chinese translations and the Sanskrit texts on which they were based. Yet the Chinese translators, like their Tibetan counterparts and translators everywhere, faced the same dilemma. Should the translator strive for fidelity to the original, at the expense of clarity in the target language, or clarity at the expense of literal fidelity? Different translators, naturally, took different strategies, and popular texts such as the *Vimalakīrtinirdeśa Sūtra* often received multiple translations. For example, Kumarajīva's fluent and clear Chinese translation was followed by Xuanzang's technically more precise translation. Not surprisingly, it is the former, rather than the latter, that remains the most beloved translation, despite its problems.[37]

Both Tibetan and Chinese translations vary with respect to their fidelity to the Sanskrit originals. Moreover, the Sanskrit "originals" on which these translations are based are ultimately unknowable since we cannot assume that extant Sanskrit manuscripts are identical to the manuscripts used by the translators during the Tang and Northern Song dynastic periods. However, the examination of the translations of transgressive passages reveals patterns of translation and mistranslation that are almost certainly not the result of variations in the Sanskrit. These patterns involve what appear to be translation strategies designed to lessen the impact of these passages. They include failure to translate, euphemistic translation, and the interpolation of text that attempts to contextualize the offending passage, often by establishing an interpretive framework that renders the passage less offensive.

These strategies are all more common in the Chinese translations. The Tibetan translations show less tendency to bowdlerize transgressive passages. This is almost certainly due to the absence of a centralized political authority capable of exercising control over the translations made during the latter dissemination period and the competition among translators. On the one hand, of particular significance was the Tibetan access to Indian Buddhist masters, such as Atiśa, who validated the authenticity of these scriptures and transmitted with them oral explanations that included sophisticated exegetical systems. In Northern Song China, on the other hand, the translators were subject to imperial control and appear to have lacked the full transmission of the oral instructions connected with the tantras.

One of the strategies employed by translators, faced with shockingly transgressive passages, was simply to not translate the passages fully. Tibetan and Chinese translators, like many translators in other cultural contexts—including some modern Western translators—occasionally did not translate offending passages.[38] One of the most common strategies is to transliterate, rather than translate, sensitive terms. We find this, for example, in most Tibetan translations of the infamous erotic background verse that first appeared in the *Guhyasamāja Tantra,* which articulates the setting of the tantra "in the vulvae of the adamantine ladies." In most Tibetan translations of this passage, the Sanskrit term *bhageṣu,* "in the vulvae," is simply transliterated as "in the *bhagas*" (*bha ga rnams la*), transliterating the Sanskrit term and adding Tibetan grammatical particles.[39] This, of course, serves to obscure the meaning of the text for Tibetan readers who do not know Sanskrit.[40]

The same strategy is found in some Chinese works as well. Amogavajra, in his *Index of the Adamantine Pinnacle Scripture Yoga in Eighteen Sections,* diplomatically transliterated rather than translated the Sanskrit *yoṣidbhageṣu*, "in the vulvae of the adamantine ladies," reading as *yu shi po jia* 喻師婆伽, which is a simple transliteration.[41] Interestingly, he glosses this "place" as "the Perfection of Wisdom palace," which points to the sophisticated exegetical systems developing at that time.[42] However, his decision to transliterate rather than translate here obscures the literal meaning, which was likely his intention.

Dharmapāla, in his Song dynastic translation of the *Hevajratantra,* produced a hybrid translation-transliteration-interpolation of the Sanskrit *vajrayoṣidbhageṣu*, which might be rendered "in the secret, the adamantine *yoṣidbhageṣu*" (金剛喻施婆伲數祕密中).[43] The only Sanskrit translated here is the relatively innocuous *vajra,* here meaning "adamantine," along with the locative case, which is rendered redundantly by both translation and transliteration. Perhaps to make up for the bewilderingly unclear transliteration, Dharmapāla interpolated here the term "secret" (祕密); his translation here does indeed have the effect of making the Buddha's abode a secret.

Another strategy, common in Chinese translations of the tantras, but less common in the Tibetan, is interpretive translations that, in the context of transgressive passages, are euphemistic. We can see an example of such a euphemistic translation in Dānapāla's Song dynastic translation of the opening line of the *Guhyasamāja*. Unlike Dharmapāla, he did not transliterate *yoṣidbhageṣu*. Instead, he simply did not translate this compound at all, instead he emended the text to place the Buddha's teaching in a "pure state" (清淨境界).[44] Such renderings are not uncommon in the Chinese translations of the tantras.

Contra the common claim that Tibetan translations are exact and literal translations of the Sanskrit, it is not particularly difficult to find nonliteral, interpretive Tibetan translations.[45] However, outright euphemistic translations of transgressive passages are uncommon. One possible case occurs in chapter 11 of the *Cakrasaṃvara Tantra.* The chapter describes a special individual, a person "born seven times as a man," whose body contains a concretion that can confer magical powers. The chapter appears to describe the sacrifice of this person and the consumption of his empowering bodily constituent. While the extant Sanskrit manuscript clearly calls for "eating him" (*taṃ bhakṣayitvā*) and describes the powers attained "just by having eaten it" (*prāśitamātreṇa*), the canonical Tibetan translation replaces the verbs of eating with the verb *bsten,* "to serve," "rely upon," suggesting a nonviolent and non-transgressive way to attain the same end. This appears to be a euphemistic translation, based on one of the commentaries. Moreover, the Sanskrit commentaries give multiple readings of the chapter, suggesting that Indian Buddhists had already attempted to revise this chapter to reduce its transgressive impact. This passage thus appears to constitute a limit of tantric discourse, which challenged even the relatively unrestrained Indian and Tibetan Buddhist communities, apparently due to the direct challenge that it posed to Buddhist identity.[46]

Interpolations are common in both Tibetan and Chinese translations. This was also a strategy employed by translators to mitigate the impact of transgressive passages, since a well-placed word or phrase could easily transform how such passages were understood. For example, Bhavabhaṭṭa, in his commentary on the first chapter of the "Supreme Bliss of the Wheels" *Cakrasaṃvara Tantra,* at one point quotes the following passage: "Thus it is said: 'One of firm intelligence should eat the secret semen with eyes wide open. This is the worship of body, speech and mind with all mantras.' "[47] Interestingly, the Tibetan translators of this commentary added the term "mentally" to this passage, to read as follows: "One of firm intelligence should mentally eat the secret semen with eyes wide open."[48] This minor interpolation significantly shifts the texts' import, implying that the consumption of "impure" sexual fluid is to be visualized rather than actually performed.

Interpolation is much more commonly deployed in the Chinese translations. While many of the Chinese translations of the tantras are quite bowdlerized, to the extent that the transgressive passages are completely obscured, this is not the case with all Chinese translations of the tantras. Generally speaking, it appears that erotic elements are more frequently subject to this sort of treatment, as opposed to violent elements. An example of a clearer translation is Dharmabhadra's Chinese translation of the *Śrī-Vajrabhairava Tantra*,[49] which was translated between 989 through 999.[50] This text, in both the Chinese and Tibetan translations,[51] contains a chapter on a fierce *homa* fire sacrifice for the purpose of destroying enemies that appears to be less bowdlerized than other Chinese translations of the tantras.[52] However, it does not contain significant erotic content. Perhaps for this reason, the text is translated in a significantly clearer fashion. Violent rites, however, are problematic insofar as they are seen as a threat to the imperial monopoly of ritual power. To ensure the reader that the ritual power promised by the text is not to be used in a destabilizing manner, the translator(s) appended to the beginning of the first chapter the following prologue, which is not found in the Tibetan version:

> Then Vajrabhairava addressed the Buddha saying, "As I now desire to benefit sentient beings, I will teach the method of all magical powers. I beg that you, Buddha, compassionately bestow fearlessness upon me."
>
> The Buddha replied, "Excellent, Bhairava! Teach widely in order to benefit the licentious." Then Bhairava, receiving the command of the Buddha, manifested to the host of humans and gods a very fierce demeanor, and taught all of the method of the magical powers.
>
> [He proclaimed,] "If there are wizards who wish to practice this teaching of mine, they should first give rise to an attitude of

> [wishing] great benefit for all sentient beings. Then, seeking to receive consecration from the adamantine master they will attain consecration. [Then they can] make use of the various methods in the text to fix the magical powers.
>
> "Moreover, a wizard may see sentient beings of evil karma who rebel against the king's mandate, throw off all restraint in rebellion and are not filial to their parents, harbor hateful intentions toward the master, destroy the Three Jewels and defame the Mahāyāna and Secret Teachings, or who disrespectfully transgress their commitments, and passionately and perversely give rise to peril and harm. With regard to this sort of person, one should make use of this teaching to subdue him, and even give instruction to those who repent. Yet should a wizard harbor in his or her own mind childish envy toward ordinary, passionate beings or virtuous people, and perversely use this teaching to distress them, when he arrives at the karmic consequence of this he will enter the Howling Hell."[53]

This apology, with its recourse to the Confucian virtues of loyalty and filial piety, is an obvious attempt to characterize the potentially subversive rituals described in the text in positive fashion, by presenting them as tools to be compassionately deployed in the service of empire, against its foes. It thus sends a stern warning to those un-filial and disloyal practitioners who might be tempted to use them against the state. This particular attempt to reposition the text and the practices it described, while superfluously successful in that outright censorship was avoided, apparently failed, in that the practice tradition associated with the text was evidently not successfully transmitted to China, perhaps in part due to anxiety concerning the dissemination of these destructive ritual technologies, which could be employed by the state but also against it.

There are also passages that show evidence of all the translation strategies discussed above, namely omission, interpolation, and euphemistic mistranslation. A particularly notable example occurs in Dānapāla's translation of the *Guhyasamāja Tantra*, in the notorious fifth chapter, in which Vajradhara Buddha presented a discourse that astonished his audience, an assembly of bodhisattvas, causing them to question him and then faint out of fear. The initial section of this astonishing discourse occurs as follows, in my translation from the Sanskrit, with reference to the canonical Tibetan translation:

> [1] The clans of anger, lust, and delusion,[54]
> Arisen from the nonconceptual aim,
> Bring about the ultimate achievement
> On the path that's highest and unexcelled.
>
> [2] The Caṇḍālas, flute makers and so forth,
> Who're predisposed to the aim of killing,
> Will succeed on this highest of the paths,
> Which is the unexcelled Mahāyāna.
>
> [3] And those who have committed the great sins,
> Including even the sins that are boundless,[55]
> Will succeed on this path of the buddhas
> In the ocean of the Mahāyāna.
>
> [4] Only those ones who slander the master
> Will not succeed in this discipline (*sādhana*).
> However, those beings who destroy life,
> And who take pleasure in deceptive speech,
>
> [5] Those who are satisfied by others' wealth,
> Who always delight in passionate sex,
> And those who consume feces and urine,
> Are truly suited to this discipline.

> [6] Should that very practitioner have sex
> With his mother, sister, or his daughter,
> He will attain magnificent success
> In the supreme Mahāyāna teachings.[56]
>
> [7] He is not defiled even having sex
> With the mother of the chief of buddhas.
> One who is non-conceptually wise
> Will then attain one's own awakened state.[57]

The canonical Tibetan translation of this passage is quite close to the extant Sanskrit, exhibiting only minor differences. The only translation that might be interpreted as euphemistic is the honorific translation of *kāmayan*, "desiring, loving, or having sex with," as *mnyes par byas* when used with "the mother of the Lord Buddha" as its object, in place of the *'dod byas* used to translate *kāmayet* when the objects are "mundane" female relatives. This was likely inspired by a desire to show respect to such a lofty figure, although it is somewhat misplaced in the context of this verse. It is a euphemistic translation since the basic meaning of *mnyes par byas* is to "please" or "honor." It thus has the effect of rendering the verse nonsensical; how could one be defiled by "honoring" the Buddha's mother?

However, the Tibetan translation is a model of fidelity to the Sanskrit when compared to Dānapāla's translation of the same passage. It reads as follows in my translation, with interpolations in italics, and euphemistic renderings underlined:

> Reality arises in the manner of desire, hatred, and stupidity. *The equality of existents is the equality of the three secrets.* Understanding the reality of this is unexcelled awakening. Understanding thus, one succeeds in everything. Should there be in the world [people of] the Caṇḍāla or [other] despised castes, who always give rise to minds [desiring to] kill sentient beings, *if they are able to expound and cultivate the secret by means of pure*

> *faith* (淨信), the people of these classes will all succeed, and will be able to establish themselves in the secret of the Mahāyāna. Moreover, if sentient beings who have committed the boundless sins and who have widely performed great evil and grave sins are *able to give rise to pure faith and cultivate the secret*, they too will attain all of the ultimate powers. If there are sentient beings who destroy life, who do not give but take, who experience depraved contaminants, who produce false speech, and who engage in evil actions in this manner, *yet are able to arouse pure faith to expound and practice the secret teaching*, even these types of people will thus attain power. *Why is that? Great heroes who understand the secret teaching are all equal, whether they are polluted or pure, angry, or loving. If they understand, they will be able to establish themselves in the secret essence of reality of the ultimate Mahāyāna, and will then attain the Buddha nature. Therefore, one should be free of doubt regarding all things.* Only those who slander the master should be avoided. That sort of person, even though he or she earnestly seeks the secret teaching, will never attain it.[58]

The attentive reader will note that there are also numerous omissions; the shocking and arguably blasphemous passages referring to incestuous sex and to sex with the Buddha's mother are omitted entirely, and replaced with a lengthy interpolation, and repeated references to "pure faith" (淨信) as the mode of practice to be cultivated, reflecting either discomfort on the part of the translator or concern that the passage would not be well received by the translation's intended audience. Unlike the fierce *homa* fire sacrificial rite contained in the Chinese *Śrī-Vajrabhairava Tantra*, this tour de force of sexual transgression was evidently not acceptable to the Northern Song milieu in which Dānapāla was translating. Fierce fire sacrificial rites had, after all, been known to Chinese Buddhists for centuries. Dānapāla certainly succeeded in "purifying" this passage, but his highly bowdlerized translation makes the entire chapter inconsistent and confusing. The reader wonders why the bodhisattvas in the audience object to this passage and faint out of fear.

What would motivate a learned Buddhist scholar, who was presumably dedicated to the successful transmission of Buddhist scriptures and traditions to China, to translate the text in this fashion? It almost certainly was not the result of careless error. Rather, the translators working with imperial support during the Northern Song Dynasty were almost certainly driven by conflicting desires: to render the texts into Chinese accurately but to avoid triggering rebuke, censorship, and/or the revocation of state support. Charles Willemen concluded as much in his study of the Chinese translation of the *Hevajra Tantra*. He argued that the text's euphemistic translations were not the product of misunderstanding but of diplomatic compromise. Concerning, for example, the erotic process of initiation described in the text, Willemen wrote:

> The Chinese *Hevajratantra* is very mysterious and appears to avoid clarity. Knowledge of the initiations is assumed by the Chinese text. Without such prior knowledge, it is unclear what the Chinese text actually means. On the other hand, the Indian text is much more explicit. I am convinced that Dharmapāla rendered the Indian original in a very tactful, deliberately abstruse way, but remaining true to the actual proceedings of the Indian original. The coherence of the Chinese "mistranslations" only proves Dharmapāla's sound philological abilities and his remarkable talent for tactfulness. It would be a mistake to discard the Chinese *Hevajratantra* as a faulty translation. Dharmapāla delivered a translation which was morally acceptable and in line with the existing Chinese esoteric texts, yet ambiguous enough to leave room for the right interpretation.[59]

Since it is unlikely that the text's lack of fidelity to the presumed Sanskrit original is due to simple, inadvertent mistranslation, it appears that political considerations or pressures, as well as possibly the outright fear or threat of censorship, are responsible for the texts' studious avoidance of explicit or controversial language. Willemen certainly did not regard these problems as accidental; we might note that Willemen's defense of Dharmapāla's translation presumes that the translation was accompanied by the transmission of the oral instructions that would provide the initiate with the authoritative exegetical system for interpreting the text. While this may have been Dharmapāla's intention, it appears that the associated practice traditions were not successfully established in China, leaving these works jettisoned, relics of Chinese Buddhist history preserved in the canon.

The central question that has animated this section—why were the transgressive mahāyoga and yoginītantras successfully transmitted to Tibet but not to China?—is naturally complex enough that it cannot be definitively answered here. The Northern Song Chinese centralized state likely served as, at least, a minor obstacle, leading, almost certainly, to some of the unusual features of the tantras translated into Chinese at the time. The decentralized Tibetan political situation in the tenth century apparently was much less of an obstacle. Another factor may have been China's strong, indigenous systems of moral, social, and political thought, namely Confucian thought and the neo-Confucian thought that was emerging during the Song Dynasty. This likely made the Chinese at least somewhat less receptive to new and controversial systems of Buddhist thought and practice emerging in India. While many Chinese Buddhists did idealize India as the homeland of Buddhism, Chinese cultural chauvinism likely mitigated the impact of this idealization.[60] The Tibetan idealization of India, and its lack of an established competing system of sophisticated indigenous thought,[61] likely made Tibetans far more receptive to the cutting-edge traditions advocated by contemporary Indian Buddhist masters such as Atiśa.

The most important factor of all may have been purely accidental. The proximity of southern Tibetan population centers to major centers of learning in South Asia, such as Kashmir, Magadha, and the Kathmandu Valley, made it far easier for interested Tibetans to gain access not only to the tantras themselves but also to the living practice traditions associated with them, without the need for state support. The failure of the unexcelled yoga tantra practice traditions to take root in China may have been largely due to the much greater distance from China to these centers of learning. The resulting successful transmission to Tibet, as well as unsuccessful transmission to China, is likely the result of multiple factors and certainly cannot be solely attributed to the more restrictive Chinese translation programs.

5.2 Exegetical Strategies

As the previous section should have made clear, translation is an interpretive art, so the first step in making texts understood in a new context is translating them. The way they are translated can serve to seemingly clarify the meaning, by making a straightforward literal reading the default for the reader, or to obscure the meaning, by problematizing the reader's instinctual attempt at making sense of the text. There is not necessarily a "right" or "wrong" approach here. Since the tantras are often obscure in the Sanskrit text in which they were compiled, a literal translation may in fact be very difficult to understand.

Given the inherent challenge of reading the tantras, recourse to the commentaries can be very helpful for one seeking to understand them. These commentaries often take different strategies in explaining the tantras. When the texts are unclear, they will often attempt to clarify them for the reader. Sometimes, however, the texts are all too clear, and the commentaries function to ameliorate concerns raised by transgressive passages by elucidating the "real" meaning of the passage, which fortunately is not as shocking as the literal meaning seems to indicate.

To shed light on how tantric commentaries functioned to shape the understanding of the tantras as well as facilitate their acceptance by concerned Buddhists, the focus on this section will be on the "Esoteric Community" *Guhyāsamāja Tantra,* a relatively early eighth-century tantra replete with transgressive rhetoric, that gave rise to very influential commentarial traditions that shaped how tantras were understood in India and beyond.

As noted above, the *Guhyasamāja* appears to be the earliest tantra with an erotic opening context verse. This is the first and most obvious instance of transgressive rhetoric in the text. Perhaps not surprisingly, one of the earliest dateable commentaries on the scripture focuses on precisely this verse. This text is Vilāsavajra's "Exposition of the Guru's Oral Instructions on the Background Verse of the Glorious Esoteric Community Tantra." Since Vilāsavajra was active in the mid- to late-eighth century,[62] it almost certainly predates the copious works produced by the Ārya school of Guhyasamāja exegesis, which likely date to the early ninth century and later.[63] He comments on the place in which the Lord is depicted as dwelling as follows:

> With respect to the line, "residing in the vulvae[64] of the adamantine ladies, the essence of the body, speech and mind of all tathāgatas," [the text] "body, speech, and mind" refers to the nature of all [of these]. Since it is the nature of body, etc., of all tathāgatas, this refers to the vajra of body, speech, and mind. The "essence" is its seed. With respect to residing in the vulvae of the ladies of Mahāvairocana, the "lady" is the symbolic consort.[65] The "vulva" is her lotus; it is therein that he resides. In what manner does he reside? He resides as the nature of the gnosis of Mahāvairocana, in the manner of something that is like water, yet white and pure like the moon. With respect to this, this should also be shown in another formulation from "Thus" (*evaṃ*) up to "residing in the ladies' vulvae." That is, *e* is the vulva (*dharmodaya*),[66] *vaṃ* is the vajra, and *ma* is Mahāvairocana's

> gnostic seed. *Yā*[67] is characterized by the action of excitation and refers to the emergence of semen (*śukra*). Regarding the "Lord" (*bhagavān*), since he resides at that time in the place of the *bhaga*, the place of pleasure of Vajradhātvīśvarī, he is called *bhagavān*.[68] The "essence of the body, speech, and mind of all tathāgatas" refers to the vajra, and applies to its moon-like seed. "Resides in the ladies' vulvae" indicates that it resides in the place of the lotus of Vajradhātvīśvarī, the "adamantine lady of the body, speech, and mind of all tathāgatas."[69]

This passage is fascinating for several reasons. First, it unabashedly explains the erotic significance of the text, and it does so via "atomic analysis" commentarial style, in which words are broken down into their constituent syllables. He equates the buddha with semen, pointing to the sacramental use of sexual fluids in Mahāyoga tantras such as this one.[70] Vilāsavajra continues by noting the "great wonder" of the Buddha's dwelling place, as follows:

> The meaning of *yoṣit* is consort, and it is a great wonder that the Lord dwells in her place, the place of the vulva (*dharmodaya*). At this point some people might object that while it is acceptable that this be taken to be awakened speech (*buddhavacana*), there is no necessity for "Thus have I heard," since some tantras [begin] with "and then" *atha,* and if one takes it to be a conjunction, it connects [the text to a larger source text with a context verse], which is excellent. Why is this so? If [a text] is stated after the Lord [Śākyamuni]'s cessation, then it is of the class [of texts] that state "Thus have I heard." Why are texts that [state] "Thus have I heard" not of the contemporary time when the Lord exists manifestly? The answer is they are of that type. "Thus have I heard" occurs in all tantras, and "the Teacher has passed into cessation" is not stated in any tantras either. Someone might object that others have said that concise tantras lack it. Why is that? They say it is because these tantras exist in a nondual fashion. The reply

> to that is that others might wonder how these tantras could exist is they lacked an interlocutor. It is to clarify these [doubts] that "Thus have I heard" is stated.[71]

While Vilāsavajra notes the "great wonder" of the *Guhyasamāja Tantra's* opening verse, he cleverly deflects the reader's attention to the question of whether a background verse is necessary. Rather than answering the obvious objection, that the erotic language here could not have been spoken by the Buddha, he attempts to draw attention to scriptures that lack an opening verse.[72] He implies that having an erotic opening verse is less problematic than lacking one and dodges the objection to its erotic quality.

Vilāsavajra likely did not feel compelled to address this issue, for it is addressed within the tantra itself. The tradents of the *Guhyasamāja Tantra* certainly understood that this scripture was radical and was likely to evoke a strong reaction in their readers. This expected reader response was addressed in chapter 5 of the scripture. The preceding section featured a translation of the first seven verses of this chapter, comparing the Sanskrit with the Tibetan and Chinese translations. Given the importance of this text, herein is the remaining section of this chapter; it opens with an objection voiced by a bodhisattva with the very interesting name, "He who bars [the door] to all disturbances," Sarvanivaraṇaviskambhin. It occurs as follows:

> At this point the great bodhisattvas, beginning with Sarvanivaraṇaviskambhin, were overcome with astonishment and amazement. They asked, "Why does the Lord, the Master of All Tathāgatas, speak such poorly spoken speech amidst the assembly of all Tathāgatas?"
>
> Then all of the Tathāgatas heard the astonished speech of the great bodhisattvas, beginning with Sarvanivaraṇaviskambhin, and they said to those bodhisattvas, "Do not say this, sons of the clan!

[8] "This is the purified reality
Of the buddhas' quintessential gnosis;
It's the state of awakening practice,
Born of the essential teaching's import."

At this point the bodhisattvas—as many as the atoms of Mount Sumeru of inexpressible Buddha lands—were frightened, and fainted, terrified. Then the Lord Tathāgatas saw the insensate bodhisattvas, and said the following to the Lord, the Sovereign of the Body, Speech, and Mind of all Tathāgatas: "Lord, rouse these bodhisattvas!"

Then the Lord, the Tathāgata Vajra of the Body, Speech, and Mind of all Tathāgatas, settled into the concentration called "the space-like nondual vajra," and soon as he settled into it, the bodhisattvas stood in their own places just through contact with the radiance of the Adamantine Sovereign of the Body, Speech, and Mind of all Tathāgatas. Then all the tathāgatas, overcome with astonishment and wonder and overflowing with joy, stated the following dharma song:

[9] "Aha, the Teaching! Aha, the Teaching!
Aha, the birth of the Teaching's import!
Homage to selflessness, Teaching's pure aim,
Which is known as the Adamantine King.

[10] "Homage to the Body, to Speech and Mind,
Fully purified, the space-like abode,
Which is immutable, not appearing,
And is called the adamantine body.

[11] "Homage to the supreme mind, the Thus Gone,
Abiding on the path of the three times,
To the great space that exists as a realm,
And which is known as the import of space.[73]

[12] "Homage to the supreme of the teachings,
Which is known as the station of practice,
The mind of space, born from space's body,
And which does abide in the speech of space.[74]"[75]

This entire chapter was composed in anticipation of the response many readers would have to this text. Following Mahāyāna scriptural precedent, the "great bodhisattvas" represent the presumed Mahāyāna Buddhist audience, just as they would in a Mahāyāna sutra. However, the "disciples" (*śrāvaka*), or Buddhist monks, are not even present in the audience here, as there was surely no need to dramatize their presumed reaction—total rejection. Presumably, members of the conservative Buddhist traditions were not expected to read as far as the fifth chapter. Most would likely not have read further than the opening verse. The bodhisattvas exemplified by Sarvanivaraṇaviskambhin react to the Buddha's transgressive speech with surprise and disapproval, mirroring the expected reaction of the reader, but they are firmly corrected. The Buddha's message to them is clearly directed toward the numerous readers who were expected to experience similar feelings of shock, wonder, or disgust. This passage thus can be taken as an apologetic defense of the use of such rhetoric.[76]

The reason for the great bodhisattvas' anxiety is clear. The Buddha's message here is indeed that immoral behavior—transgressive sexuality, violence, lying, theft, consumption of impure substances—is not only permissible but also is "truly suited to this discipline,"[77] and it can be characterized as the "state of awakening practice, born of the essential teaching's import." Not only is one not defiled by undertaking such practices, but one can attain the highest goal, awakening, by means of them as well.

The tradents of this text were correct in their assumption that passages such as these would attract attention. Indeed, Amoghavajra, in his summary of this text in his *Index of the Adamantine Pinnacle Scripture Yoga in Eighteen Sections*, focused precisely on the background verse and the fifth chapter. His summary reads as follows:

> The Fifteenth Assembly is called *Yoga of the Esoteric Community*, and it was expounded in a secret place, that is to say, it was expounded in the *yoṣidbhaga* place, which is called the Prajñāpāramitā palace. Herein the teachings, mandala,[78] mudrās and mantras, and abiding by prohibitory precepts are explained by imitating the like of mundane speech consonant with lust and defilement. Among the assembly, the Bodhisattva [Sarva] nivaraṇaviskambhin and others rose from their seats, paid homage to the Buddha, and said, "O World-Honored One, a great person should not utter coarse language or words consonant with contamination." The Buddha said, "You [bodhisattvas], what are the characteristics of speech that is consonant with purity? This speech of mine empowers the written word and draws [people] into the path of the Buddha by expedient means in accordance with the circumstances of those to be converted; it is, moreover, without characteristics and creates great benefits. You should not engender any doubts." Thereupon he explained extensively the concentration (*samādhi*) of the true aspect [of reality], and the bodhisattvas each explained the four kinds of mandalas and the four mudrās.[79]

This brief summary corresponds quite closely to several important sections of the tantra itself, namely the erotic opening verse and chapter 5. Amoghavajra here also invokes what would become the primary strategy for legitimating the transgressive rhetoric found in the tantras, which is the notion of skillful means. It is also quite clear that the text of the *Guhyasamāja Tantra* was quite transgressive in the form in which it existed in the eighth century, which explains perhaps why Vajrabuddhi needed to lose it en route to China.

The radical message of the text is reinforced in the ninth chapter of this scripture, which introduces the mandalas of the five buddhas and equates each one to the performance of one of the sins. The Buddha Akṣobhya, for example, is equated with murder, in a form that is both sacrilegious and astonishingly extensive. The passage reads as follows:

> [3] Visualize a Buddha mandala
> Positioned amidst the space element.
> Visualize that Akṣobhya Vajra
> Manifests with a vajra in his hand.
>
> [4] He is surrounded by a mass of sparks,
> And he is filled with the five light rays.
> Visualize the buddhas of the three times,[80]
> And pulverize them all with the vajra.
>
> [5] Imagine that the eight vajras pulverize
> Body, speech, and mind's unification.[81]
> It's the supreme visualization
> That produces the power of the mind (*cittasiddhi*).
>
> [6] Should one murder all sentient beings
> With this vajra which is a secret,
> They will be [born as][82] sons of the Jina
> Of the Buddhaland that's adamantine.
> This is known as the hatred clan's union,
> Which is sublime among all of the clans.[83]

This is followed by similar descriptions of the mandalas of the other four buddhas. Vairocana is associated with the passion delusion and the crime of "theft of all wealth."[84] Amitābha is associated with passion, and the meditator is instructed to visualize him in union with goddesses, and to "enjoy them all through the union of the two organs; this is the meditation on the three indivisible bodies of all buddhas."[85] Lastly, Amoghasiddhi is associated with the sin of "lying,"[86] and Ratnaketu with the injunction to undertake "abusive speech."[87]

As in the case of chapter 5, this teaching astonished and amazed the assembled bodhisattvas, who again asked the Buddha why he would state this. The Buddha responded by reassuring them, warning them not to call this base or disgusting. He asserts instead that "the practice of passion (*rāgacaryā*) is the practice of bodhisattvas (*bodhisattvacaryā*), the highest practice."[88]

This, naturally, is extremely provocative; the practice or conduct of awakening beings, *bodhisattvacaryā*, here is a far cry from the selfless, compassionate conduct advocated in Mahāyāna sutras or influential works such as Śāntideva's *Bodhicaryāvatāra*.[89] Rather, the aspiring adept is advised to practice a modified version of the five misdeeds, which were exactly what mainstream Buddhists are taught to avoid by practicing the five precepts, the fundamental elements of Buddhist moral practice. These are the avoidance of (1) violence, (2) theft, (3) sexual misconduct, (4) lying and wrong speech, and (5) intoxication. The last of these, avoiding intoxication, is absent here, perhaps because this was traditionally considered to be the lightest transgression, since it does not directly harm others, but can indirectly lead to harm by clouding one's judgment.[90] In place of the fifth precept, the fourth precept is divided into its two major components, lying and wrong speech,[91] both of which are commended here. This was a radical move, as moral conduct, in accordance with the five precepts, traditionally constituted one of the bulwarks of Buddhist identity.

Now, one might wonder how transgressive passages such as these are explained by the commentators. There was some variation here. One of the earliest commentators, Vilāsavajra, did not attempt to explain away the transgressive content of the opening verse, but explained it clearly in terms of sexual practices, as we saw above. However, over time, there was a general move toward more internalized and abstract explanations of these transgressive passages, which had the effect of neutralizing the transgressive passages by claiming that they did not mean what they seem to mean.[92] One might recall Vilāsavajra's "atomic analysis" of the opening verse text; he analyzed the first four syllables *e, vaṃ, ma,* and *yā* in terms of the female sex organ, male sex organ, "gnostic seed," and the act of excitation. Compare that to the atomic analysis to which the entire opening verse is subjected in the "Glorious Adamantine Rosary Discourse Great Yoga Tantra" *Śrīvajramālābh idhānamahāyogatantra*, an explanatory tantra associated with the *Guhyasamāja Tantra*. It is a ninth-century text compiled by tradents associated with the "Noble" Ārya school of Guhyasamāja exegesis, which was more philosophically oriented and advocated a more complex and rarified exegetical approach to the study of the tantras than did the earlier Jñānapāda school, with which Vilāsavajra was associated.[93] The fifty-ninth chapter of this work analyzes the entire opening verse, dedicating a verse to the exegesis of each syllable. The meaning revealed is much more abstract and internalized compared to Vilāsavajra's interpretation. The following are the seven verses analyzing the "setting" of the text, *vajrayoṣidbhageṣu*:

VA
By uniting the vajra and lotus,
One knows the aspects of the three gnoses.[94]
One always blissfully resides in that,
One's mind being tainted or untainted.

JRA
With the illusory concentration
One manifests as the nature of all.
One resides within the established state,
Performing awakened activities.

YO
One should manifest oneself in union,
In utmost union and in great union,

As the *vajrī*[95] and the *ḍākinī* are
Both themselves in that very union.

ṢĪD
Having undertaken the cessations
And renouncing action and inaction,
Know that one's nature will not be tainted,
As the lotus is untainted by mud.

BHA
Being endowed with the eight qualities,
All sentient beings will have a clan.
One should wander with a gnostic body
In all worlds and realms without exception.

GE
Wherever the sovereign might wander,
The space that is around one is one's home.
One always takes pleasure in that as well
Through the concentration of the great bliss.

ṢU
Here, through distinctions of luminance,
Twilight, along with the day and the night,
Are taken to be worldly conventions
So as to indicate the three gnoses.[96]

Analyzed in this manner, the literal meaning is not prioritized, since these words are "worldly conventions" pointing ultimately toward gnosis. The reader is also assured that she or he will not be tainted, just as the lotus flower is not tainted by the mud from which it arises. Exactly what one would be doing is not at all clear, since it will evidently entail neither "action" nor "inaction"; the text's references to union, utmost union, and great union imply that internalized yogic practices will be central to the practice system advocated by the tradents of this work. Its reference to the three gnoses connects the text being commented on here to perfection stage yogic practices. Overall, it is a far more abstract commentary pointing toward secret contemplative practices in comparison to Vilāsavajra's much more straightforward interpretation in terms of the act of sexual union that is the text's literal meaning.

Candrakīrti, the author of the "Illuminating Lamp" *Pradīpoddyotana* commentary on the "Esoteric Community" *Guhyasamāja Tantra*, begins his work with a discussion of how to interpret tantras, and he proposes a complicated and sophisticated system of analysis, involving six "ornaments" or modes of analysis,[97] leading up to the seventh, which is perfection stage practice, the details of which are the ultimate hidden meaning that can be decoded using his exegetical strategy.[98] When Candrakīrti discusses the erotic opening verse, needless to say he does not opt for the literal meaning. He comments as follows:

> Beginning from the words "he resided" the meaning of the *Esoteric Community Tantra* is sealed with the six parameters and four interpretations according to this very process. Not understanding this and relying only on the literal meaning, sentient beings who are [still] attached to objects engage in transgressions and weird activities, due to which they come under the power of [negative] evolutionary action.[99]

He then quotes a series of passages from the explanatory tantras, including the *Vajra Rosary Tantra*'s atomic analysis of the syllables, as well as a passage from the "Revelation of the Intention" *Sandhivyākaraṇa* explanatory tantra that warns darkly about evil yogis who mistakenly act out the literal meaning of the tantras and "taking it in its literal sense, fall into a bad way."[100]

For a further example, we might look at how Candrakīrti explains the notorious sixth verse in the fifth chapter, which is in my translation:

Should that very practitioner have sex
With his mother, sister, or his daughter,
He will attain magnificent success
In the supreme Mahāyāna teachings.[101]

Candrakīrti first relates the "interpretable meaning," which entails union with an "actual consort" (*karmamudrā*), who is not really a blood relative but who merely has a "wish to benefit one like a mother, sister or daughter,"[102] so no incest is called for, fortunately. For the definitive meaning of this passage, he again quotes the "Revelation of the Intention" *Sandhivyākaraṇa* explanatory tantra, as follows:

With Transcendent Wisdom as the wisdom,
The reality body's unique matrix,
One should make love in "unreality,"
Through union with her nondual suchness.

Born the same as the beatific [body],
Just as she is claimed as "the sister,"
One should make love with her mantra body,
Having union with one's own ideal deity.

The performer should realize her,
The emanation body being his daughter.

The yogi/ni who makes love with just that sort
Of mother, sister, and daughter,
Should progress to the magnificent attainment,
In the supreme realities of the universal vehicle.

Such is the definitive meaning explanation.[103]

Candrakīrti explains the three female relatives in terms of the three levels of embodiment, a Mahāyāna philosophical theory often connected to tantric contemplative practice. Here again the reader is led in a very different direction from the apparent transgressive eroticism of the root tantra. With the definitive explanation stated so clearly by Candrakīrti, we might expect that the matter may be settled, and that no one would want to be like those evil yogis who act out the literal sense of the tantras. This, however, was not the case.

While en route to Tibet, the great pundit Atiśa Dīpaṅkaraśrījñāna, no doubt informed of skepticism concerning the orthodoxy of the tantras held by some members of the royal family in western Tibet, composed his very well-known verse text, the "Lamp for the Path to Awakening," *Bodhipathapradīpa*, a concise introduction to the tantric Buddhist path of practice. In this work, he briefly addressed the sexual initiatory rites, the second "secret consecration," and the third "consort gnosis consecration," which entail sexual practices if interpreted literally, as discussed in section 2.3.2.1. He argues that neither monks nor nuns should receive them, since they would entail the violation of the celibacy vow.[104] In his auto-commentary he explains this suggested prohibition as follows:

> Regarding consecrations there are two types: those applicable to householders, and those applicable to the celibate. Those applicable to householders include everything taught in the tantras, while the celibate from amongst those should avoid the secret and gnosis of the consort consecrations. Why should they avoid those two? Celibacy is understood to be one of the virtues that occurs as a point of doctrine, in reliance upon the Buddha's teaching. Those two consecrations are regarded as not in accordance with the practice of celibacy. Hence it is said that the two consecrations would bring about the end of celibacy, and the end of celibacy would be the end of the Buddha's teaching. And by its ceasing the continuum of merit making would be broken. Since from that basis there would arise innumerable non-virtuous people, the celibate should thus avoid those two.[105]

Atiśa clearly understands these consecrations as entailing actual sexual practices, as literally described. His solution is simply that these consecrations should only be taken by the laity since they would entail breaking the celibacy vow for the monastic community. He makes it clear that the stakes are high here, as he equates the celibacy with the preservation of the Buddha's teachings.

His recommendation may have been based on current practice in India at the time, or it may have been a more conservative solution for a more conservative audience, his western Tibetan hosts. However, Atiśa's solution to this problem had an unfortunate consequence; it excluded the monks from full participation in what was considered, in Indian Buddhist tantric circles at least, the highest and most efficacious system of tantric practice. This was not a sustainable state of affairs; it would not be easy for a Buddhist community to sustain the monastic community if the monks were excluded from practice of the "highest" teaching, nor would this solution be acceptable for the monks, who traditionally served as spiritual leaders for Buddhist communities. Not surprisingly, some Buddhist leaders sought alternative solutions for this problem.

We see this in the work of Abhayākaragupta, who lived shortly after Atiśa, from approximately 1064 to 1125. Like Atiśa, he also served as a teacher at Vikramaśīla in northeastern India.[106] Of relevance here is his work the *Vajrāvalī*, "The Diamond Array," a manual relating to mandalas from a wide range of tantras. In this work, when describing the secret consecration, Abhayākaragupta uses verbs such as "visualize" (*bsam par bya*),[107] implying that the liturgy is, at least in part, visualized. Abhayākaragupta also addresses the question of whether the sexual aspects of the rite are to be performed with an actual partner or consort, typically referred to as an "actual consort" (*karmamudrā*) in this literature, or with a "gnostic consort" (*jñānamudrā*), that is, a consort who is visualized. It turns out that the way initiation should be bestowed depends upon multiple factors. Abhayākaragupta comments as follows:

> "There is no infraction even if a monk experiences the limits of the bliss of the two organs with an outer consort who is seen in a dream, if seen with discernment of the habitual tendency of the bliss of union that is so experienced." One should understand this as a teaching on monastic discipline. However, in the case of an alternate instance, when within the experiential scope of an evil person, the secret and consort gnosis consecrations should be bestowed with a gnostic consort on such occasions. If there are no evil persons, then an actual consort only [is acceptable]. A monk who, while faithful, is not steadfastly intent upon reality should be prohibited from receiving consecration with an outer wisdom-consort.[108]

Abhayākaragupta begins with a quote from an unknown source, which notes that erotic dreams are not considered to be a violation of the monastic vow of celibacy. This connects with the traditional Buddhist literature on monastic discipline, which emphasizes intention rather than the physical action when considering whether the action is a violation by the disciple. As Bernard Faure noted, "In all cases of sexual misconduct, at issue is not just control of the genital organs, but, more importantly, control over a higher organ, the mind. The source of the passions that Buddhists combat is not the penis per se but rather the mind."[109]

Abhayākaragupta then proposes a twofold set of conditions to determine whether the rite of sexual union should be performed actually, with a human partner, or mentally, with a visualized partner. His first condition concerns the presence or absence "evil people" (*skye bo ngan pa*), presumably outsiders who would not understand such subtleties. In other words, the actual sexual rite should only be performed in private, with an insider audience. The second condition implies a hierarchy of disciples, the idea being that only the most advanced disciples, who fully understand the nature of reality, and hence presumably are in control of their minds, are qualified for the actual practice. For such disciples, due to their advanced level of understanding, there would be no transgression or sin. Lesser disciples who lack this high degree of realization should not practice the actual ritual and should practice only its internally visualized version. In accordance with such a hierarchy, Jean Filliozat suggested that the violations of morality in the Buddhist tantras

> do not merely consist in allowing free-play to impulses. These violations are based on certain procedures into which the adept is initiated by the master and they generally take place only after a probation of asceticism which is intended to bestow a kind of immunity against the consequences of such violations. . . . It is to be remembered, above all, that self-mastery is the essential element of the psycho-physiological techniques of *yoga* to which the Buddhist techniques are related. The influence of these techniques intervenes, then, to discipline the activity and to give it another significance than the one found in the ordinary libertine.[110]

What might these practices entail for advanced practitioners? This is not clear due to the intense secrecy surrounding sexual yogic practices. Insofar as sexual yogas are practiced by tantric Buddhists, it appears that they are not intended to simply provide hedonistic release. The eighth-century scholar Buddhajñāna, the founder of the Jñānapāda school of Guhyasamāja exegesis and disciple of Vilāsavajra, described, in his "Oral Instructions Called the Two-Staged Meditation on Reality" *Dvikramatattvabhāvana-nāma-mukhāgama,* a sexual yogic practice involving stimulation of subtle channels present in the vicinity of the vulva, as follows:

> Rub the mandala of the lotus with your left hand, and stimulate it with your tongue. Gazing at it from above and from below, desire it with your mind. Then that joyful lady says the following, displaying her lotus: "Lord of Self-Arisen Great Bliss! Enter this

> lotus. Seek out your channel wheels through realization of the winds and channels." Then you should open the great channel wheel that abides within the lotus, and which is ornamented with eight petals, a corolla, filaments, and the five essences. Seek out the three channels [called] the Vowel and Consonant Mantra (*ālikālimantra*), the Turtle (*kūrmaka*) and the Rabbit (*śaśaka*). The channel which is the Lord of the Adamantine Realm within the vulva, free of subjectivity and objectivity, must be known with the finger through the power of the Guru's oral instructions.[111]

This practice was evidently carried out for the mutual discovery and manipulation of elements of the subtle body by a trained *yogin* and *yoginī*, and it appears to differ significantly from mundane sexual behavior; the very specificity of this passage suggests that we are no longer in the realm of pure rhetoric, but practice. Or rather, we are dealing with a textual representation of praxis; it is probably not possible to ascertain the extent to which descriptions such as this were deployed in practice. Yet the fact that this passage comes from a text in the "oral instructions" genre that accompanied a specific tradition's lineage of practice suggests that it was deployed to some extent, even if we cannot know by whom or under what circumstances, or even exactly *what* took place.

Abhayākaragupta's solution provided Buddhist institutions, and the monastics members of these communities, with a way to teach and engage in tantric practice in a non-transgressive fashion, the manner that is appropriate for most "ordinary" practitioners, involving visualization of transgressive elements only. This is in fact how these rituals are performed in contemporary Tibetan Buddhist communities. If advanced practitioners perform them bodily, with an actual consort, they do so in private. This would explain the cases of surreptitious consort sexual practices conducted by lamas who outwardly adhere to celibacy. Unfortunately, it also creates occasions for sexual abuse,[112] given the secrecy that shroud these practices.

The tantras are enigmatic, and one of the questions that they raise is why Indian Buddhists felt compelled to compose texts that so directly challenged Buddhist identity. In so doing, tantric Buddhists inverted the typical way in which identity is constructed, with the "self" or the group with which one identifies constructed as good and virtuous, with the "other" or the outsider group labeled as bad, immoral, demonic, and so forth. This may very well have been a brilliant but risky strategy for deconstructing Buddhist identity to facilitate the transformation of identity in the context of creation stage deity yoga practice. In other words, it represents a form of psychological jiujitsu, a rapid but dangerous attempt at spiritual transformation at all costs. This is because one of the central goals of tantric practice is dissolving one's sense of, and attachment to, self as an ordinary, conventional being, to generate a new sense of self as an awakened deity. For this to be successful, one would need to destabilize the foundations of one's ordinary sense of self, namely dualistic constructions such as self/other, good/evil, deluded/awakened, and so forth. The shock to the Buddhist sense of identity presented by texts such as the *Guhyasamāja Tantra* may have served to facilitate this by challenging dualistic constructions of identity. While this may have been the case, such passages have also clearly raised obstacles to the dissemination of the tantras, which may have spread more widely had they not been deemed objectionable, at least when read in terms of the literal meaning of these challenging and mysterious texts.

Notes

Introduction

1. Here "red thread" refers to Bernard Faure's (1998) work, an important study of gender and sexuality in Buddhist literature.

Chapter 1

1. See Urban 2003 for a detailed exploration of the history of Western fascination with and appropriation of the tantric traditions of South Asia.
2. Davidson 2002a, 26–30.
3. Regarding the Euro-American reception of Buddhism see Almond 1988 and Inden 1990.
4. Orzech 1998, 8.
5. Slouber 2017, 7.
6. Padoux 2002, 18.
7. Gray and Overbey 2016, 2.
8. These folia were provisionally identified by Alexis Sanderson (2009, 50) as deriving from the *Devītantrasadbhāvasāra.*
9. Translated in White 2003, 207. See as well Sircar 1965, 399–405.
10. One of the earliest Śaiva tantric texts is the *Niśvāsatattvasaṃhitā,* the oldest section of which dates to c. 450–550. See Sanderson 2013, 234 and Goodall 2015, 71–73.
11. Kimura 1999.
12. My translation of the Sanskrit text edited in Gnoli 1960, 163. See also Gray 2005a, 51.
13. Sanderson 2001, 11–13, n. 10.
14. Hodge 2003, 14–15.
15. Davidson 2002a, 118; Lin 1935.
16. Hodge 2003, 10.
17. See Skilling 1992 for a discussion of the *rakṣā* protective spells preserved by Buddhist traditions, and Van Schaik 2020 for an excellent overview of the practice of magic in Buddhist traditions.

18. Davidson 2009, 113.
19. Dalton 2016a, 202.
20. Shinohara 2014, 194–195.
21. Sen 2003, 203–211.
22. Giebel 1995.
23. Davidson 2002a, 77–80.
24. Ibid., 84–87.
25. See Li 1996 for an English translation of this work.
26. That is, Orissa in East India.
27. The term "empty flower," 空花, is likely a pejorative reference to Mahāyāna arguments for the unreality of objective phenomena.
28. Translated in Li 1995, 130.
29. White 1996, 306.
30. Hodge in fact went further, arguing that the text was likely composed in a forest retreat associated with Nālandā. See Hodge 1994, 72–74.
31. Mayer 2020, 37–38.
32. Regarding this formula see Lopez 1995.
33. Mayer 2020, 41.
34. Gray 2012, 6–12.
35. Sanderson dates Padmavajra to the late eighth century based on the fact that Āryadeva quotes the *Guhyasiddhi* in his *Caryāmelāpakapradīpa,* following Tomabechi's (2008, 175) dating of that text to the early ninth century (2009, 114, n. 332). Wedemeyer, however, follows Ronald Davidson's early ninth-century dating of Padmavajra (2007, 13).
36. Padmavajra, *Guhyasiddhi* 8.8c-16b, translated in Sanderson 2009, 144–145.
37. My translation of *Guhyasamāja Tantra* 16.93-94 from Matsunaga's edition (1978, 95) and D fol. 137b.
38. Jing-zhou (荆州) was a large province in Central China consisting of what is now the province of Hunan, as well as most of Hubei and Guizhou Provinces. Jiang-ling (江陵) was its capital.
39. Literally, before he received his cap, at age twenty.
40. 裸國, which according to Takakusu refers to the Nicobar Islands (1896, xxxviii–xxxix).
41. 羅茶國, which is not identified but restored by Takakusu as *Lāṭa,* which he suggests may be equivalent to *rāṣṭra* (1896, 9). However, it is almost certainly a region in Gujarat; see Sircar 1983, 46.
42. This list would not be out of place in any of the later tantras, which typically include lists of the powers (*siddhi*) attainable through their practice.

43. My translation from Yijing, *Records of Eminent Monks of the Great Tang Who Sought the Dharma in the Western Regions,* T. 2066.51.6c-7a. Takakusu (1896) translated not this work but Yijing's account of his own travels; this work is, however, a useful resource for the translation of his biographies. This work has not been fully translated to my knowledge, although an excerpt from it is translated in Hodge 2003, 10. The exact dates of Daolin are not known, aside from the fact that he was a predecessor of Yijing, whose journey lasted more than two decades, from 671 to 695 (Takakusu 1896, xv). According to Ch'en (1964, 239), the fifty-six biographies recorded in Yijing's text narrate lives of monks who journeyed to India during the seventh century, generally from the reign of Emperor Tai-zong up to that of Empress Wu (c. 627–705).
44. Regarding this myth see Walser 2005, 73–75.
45. Collins 1990, 92–93.
46. Matsunaga 1977, 169.
47. Abé 1999, 108–111.
48. The Chinese translation Kūkai encountered employed the Chinese term usually used to designate Buddhist scripture, *jing* (經), which is usually translated as "sutra." However, it is important to note, as Iain Sinclair pointed out, that this term "translates a range of Sanskrit terms such as *āgama, sūtra, kalpa,* and *tantra*" (2016, 29, n. 2).
49. My translation, Kūkai (空海), *Dainichikyō kaidai* (大日经开题), in T.2211.58.1a24-b1, and in the Kōbō daishi zenshū, ed. Hase Hōshū, 4:2.
50. There are remarkable parallels between tantric Buddhist and Vedic Hindu mythic discourse. These parallels include both the claim that Vedas are eternal and supramundane and that the Vedic literature preserved by the Brahmanical community is an incomplete and imperfect manifestation of this corpus. Regarding this see Pollock 2005.
51. Abé 1999, 213–235.
52. The Indian monk Vajrabuddhi is better known in English literature as Vajrabodhi. However, as Iain Sinclair pointed out (2016, 390–391), the Sanskrit reconstruction of his Chinese name, 金剛智 as *Vajrabodhi is almost certainly incorrect, as the Chinese character 智 can translate *buddhi* but never *bodhi.* There are other reasons to support the Vajrabuddhi reconstruction as Sinclair points out.
53. Chou 2006, 47–48.
54. Regarding this collection see Giebel 1995.
55. Translated in Orzech 1995, 317.
56. Ibid., 317–318.

57. Regarding this see Almogi 2014.
58. My translation of Jñānamitra's *Prajñāpāramitānaya-śatapañcāśatikā-ṭīkā*, 272b-273a; cf. Davidson 2002a, 242–243. As Davidson notes, this text is extremely early, being listed in the imperial catalogue of Denkar Library, which dates to about 810 CE.
59. Davidson 2002a, 244.
60. For a discussion of this myth see Dalton 2016b, 10–19.
61. Templeman 1989, 9–10.
62. See Chimpa and Chattopadhyaya 1990, 243. Many thanks to Professor José Cabezón for bringing this narrative to my attention.
63. My translation, Indranāla, *Sarvabuddhasamayogaḍākinījālasaṃvaratantr ārthodaraṭīkā,* To. 1659, D rgyud 'grel vol. ra, fol. 245a.
64. I would tentatively date Indranāla to the eleventh century, largely on the basis of similarity between his work and the works of the early Kālacakra commentators, such as the claim that the text derives from the Ādibuddhatantra and the provision of quotations from it. This feature, along with his invocation of classifications of explanatory tantras—which also appears to be relatively late—suggests that Indranāla was active no earlier than the eleventh century. If the paṇḍit Vidyākara who assisted in its translation is the same eleventh-century Vidyākara who compiled the famous poetry collection, this would confirm this estimate. See D rgyud 'grel vol. ra, fol. 389a.
65. My translation, Indranāla, *Sarvabuddhasamayogaḍākinījālasaṃvaratantr ārthodaraṭīkā,* fol. 246b.
66. Gray 2012, 6–8.
67. My translation of *Ḍākārṇava Tantra* 50.4.53, fol. 242b-243a.
68. My translation, Vīravajra, *Padārthaprakāśikā-nāma-śrīsaṃvaramūlatantraṭīkā,* fol. 355b.
69. Templeman 1995, 3.
70. Regarding Western reappropriations of the term "witch" see Berger and Ezzy 2009. Regarding tantric Buddhist valorization of the ḍākinīs see Simmer-Brown 2001.
71. My translation of *Laṅkāvatāra Sūtra*, 8.14-15; Vaidya 1963, 105; cf. Suzuki 1932, 221.
72. Hodge 2003, 163.
73. Chou 2006, 44.
74. The substance 牛黃, "bovine concretion," is a calculus or bezoar found in the digestive tracts of cattle. It was used in both traditional Chinese and Indian Ayurvedic medicine, and it was renowned as an antidote for poisoning. See Chen and Chen 2004, 184–185 and Wujastyk 2003, 138, n. 94.

75. The text reads here 降伏三世法門, SET F I interpret as a translation of *trailokyavijayadharmaparyāya*. This is reference to the deity Trailokyavijaya, a Buddhist deity particularly associated with the subjugation of Śaiva deities. Regarding this deity see Iyanaga 1985. Dr. Iyanaga has informed me that this is a probably a reference to the second *Trailokyavijaya* chapter of the *Sarvatathāgatatattvasaṃgraha Sūtra*, which contains a brief account of the subjugation of the ḍākinī at T.18.882.374c16-375a19; for a discussion of this passage see Kuo 2003.
76. My translation Śubhakarasiṃha and Yixing, 大毘盧遮那成佛經疏T.1796.39.687.b17-c11; cf. Iyanaga 1994, 857–860 and 1999, 51–53.
77. The Tibetan version of this text occurs at fol. 49a-53b; the Sanskrit is edited in Yamada 1981, 157–169.
78. This line, *'jig rten gyi khams rab 'byams sprin rgya mtsho thams cad na* (fol. 50a), indicates that Mahādeva summoned all sorts of beings, including the terrestrial, celestial, and aquatic.
79. My translation, Indrabhūti, *Śrīcakrasaṃvaratantrarāja-saṃvarasamuccaya-nāma-vṛtti*, fol. 49b-51a. This is immediately followed by Indrabhūti's account of the conversion of Bhairava by Heruka, a fierce buddha manifesting in Śaiva guise, which is the origin myth of the Cakrasaṃvara tradition. See Gray 2005a, 46–51.
80. For a discussion of Vajrapāṇi's rise in Mahāyāna and Vajrayāna traditions see Snellgrove 1987, 134ff.
81. This describes the development of the mandala as the traditional Buddhist "wedding cake" cosmos, which is composed of the elemental disks, topped by Mt. Sumeru, on which are positioned the five Tathāgatas.
82. My translation, *Jñānatilaka-yoginītantrarāja-paramamahādbhuta*, 134b-135a.
83. It is thus datable due to references in the text to the Kuṣāṇa King Kaniṣka, who reigned in North India c. 135–158 CE. See Strong 1992, 24.
84. For an account of this myth see Strong 1992, 26ff.
85. Concerning Faxian see Ch'en 1964, 89–93.
86. See Legge 1886, 29.
87. Regarding Śiva's portrayal in Hindu mythology see O'Flaherty 1973.
88. Concerning this hierarchy and the dialectical opposition between the buddhas and the "demonic" see Kapferer 1983, 172–178.
89. My translation, *Āryavidyottama-mahātantra*, 200b. This text almost certainly dates to the eighth century given its association with the Indian great adept Padmasambhava. Regarding this see Beckwith 1987, 2, 170–171.
90. Ibid. 1996, 73, insert mine.
91. My translation, *Śrīguhyagarbhatattvaviniścaya*, fol. 26a-b.

92. Regarding this see Dalton 2011 and Kapstein 1992.
93. Sanderson 2009, 223.
94. Newman 1998.

Chapter 2

1. Chattopadhyaya noted that "inscriptions from the seventh century alone, from differing regions of India, begin to produce elaborate genealogies, either aligning the alleged local roots of ruling lineages with a mythical tradition or by tracing their descent from mythical heroic lineages. The emergence of genealogy has been taken as a shift from 'yajña to vaṃśa,' indicating a change in the nature of kingship, but in the totality of its geographical distribution, the genealogical evidence has a more significant implication: the proliferation of actual ruling lineages defining the domain of political power" (1994, 204–205). This observation has also been made by D. C. Sircar, who describes in great detail a number of the lineage claims made during this period. See Sircar 1983, 73–94.
2. Wu 2018, 132.
3. White 1996, 79.
4. Gold 1987, 197.
5. Ibid., 1987, 48.
6. Reinders 1997, 257.
7. The name of this text, Hevajra, is also the name of its central deity. It is not readily translatable. *Vajra* can mean diamond, thunderbolt, or a ritual scepter. The Sanskrit term *he* is a vocative particle, which could be translated as "hey!," "ho!" or "oh!" "Hey Diamond" might be the best translation, but since it is a proper name, it is probably best left untranslated.
8. Davidson argues, correctly I believe, that the *Hevajra* dates no earlier than the late ninth century. See Davidson 2002c, 65, 77–78, n. 69.
9. *Hevajra Tantra* 2.7.2-4, trans. in Snellgrove 1959a, 1.115, with emendations by me.
10. Wolff 1950, 355, emphasis in original.
11. McMahan 1998, 252.
12. See Hurvitz 1976, 49–83.
13. Hurvitz 1962, 247–248.
14. A well-known example is the opening scene of the *Avataṃsaka Sūtra,* wherein the Buddha, by virtue of the "Coming Forth of the Lion Samādhi," transforms the Jeta grove into an inconceivably magnificent pure land.

This vision, however, is not perceived by *śrāvaka*s such as Śāriputra because they lacked the corresponding "roots of goodness." See Cleary 1993, 14–23.

15. McMahan 1998, 272.
16. Harrison 1978, 51.
17. See Nagao 1991, 76. The *Mahāyānasūtrālaṃkāra* 9.3 defines a sutra as follows: "A *sutra* is [so called] because it communicates by means of context, characteristics, reality and import." (My translation of the text edited in Bagchi 1970, 55).
18. However, we should note that the Mahāyāna tradition attributes this text to the bodhisattva Maitreya, who transmitted it to Asaṅga via a revelatory process.
19. My translation of *Mahāyānasūtrālaṃkāra*, 9.3 auto-commentary (Bagchi 1970, 56).
20. Sthiramati's comments occur in his *Sūtrālaṃkāravṛttibhāṣya,* in the context of his elucidation of the *Mahāyānasūtrālaṃkāra* 9.3. He wrote: "Moreover, in the *sūtra*s it is stated: 'Thus have I heard: at one time the Blessed Lord resided in Rājagṛha together with many monks and bodhisattvas.' 'Rājagṛha,' etc. shows the context in the sense of the place wherein it was taught. 'Blessed Lord' shows the context in the sense that it is He by whom it was taught. The persons [mentioned] show the context in the sense of the persons for whom the discourse was taught." (My translation, vol. mi fol. 157b.)
21. Luhrmann (1988 and 2012) has argued that immersion in visualization practice can cause a proclivity toward visionary experiences in some individuals. Since visualization is a central tantric Buddhist practice, it is not unreasonable to expect that visionary experiences would be relatively common among its practitioners, a hypothesis that is confirmed by biographies and autobiographies of dedicated practitioners.
22. Obeyesekere 2012.
23. See Cleary 1993, 55ff.
24. Dharmacakra Translation Committee, *The Noble Sovereign Ritual of Amoghapāśa,* Introduction i.3.
25. Ibid., i.2.
26. See Hikosaka 1998.
27. My translation from the *Sarvatathāgatatattvasaṃgraha-nāma-mahāyāna-sūtra,* fol. 1b-2a and Yamada 1981, 3–4.
28. My translation, *Sarvatathāgatakāyavākcittarahasya-guhyasamāja-nāma-mahākalparāja*, fol. 90a and Matsunaga 1978, 4.

29. Variants of it include the *nidāna* of the "Array of Esoteric Ornaments" tantra, *Sarvatathāgatakāyavākcitta-guhyālaṃkāravyūha*, which is similar to the Guhyasamāja background verse but somewhat less erotic, as it places the "Lord" *bhagavān* in the company of male deities such as Vajrajñānayogamaheśvara of the "body, speech and mind of all tathāgatas" (fol. 83b). This is followed by a feminine version of the background verse, which again placed the Lord not in the vulva, but in the company of the "adamantine lady" known as Prajñāpāramitā (fol. 84a). Another variant occurs in the "Fierce Great Anger" *Caṇḍamahāroṣaṇa Tantra* as follows: "Thus have I heard: at one time the Blessed Lord Vajrasattva was residing in the vulva of the Adamantine Realm Lady (Vajradhātvīśvarī), the essence of the body, speech and mind of all Tathāgatas, with many hosts of adamantine yogins and yoginīs" (George 1974, 18). This verse is also interesting in that it corrects the unusual locative plural "in the vulvas" *bhageṣu* to the locative singular "in the vulva" *bhage*.
30. My translation from the *Śrī-tattvapradīpa-nāma-mahāyoginītantrarāja*, fol. 137a.
31. The syllable *hūm*, the seed syllable of the Adamantine Clan (*vajrakula*), was often broken down into its component parts, with even the *bindu*, or "dot," signifying the nasal receiving esoteric significance. See, e.g., Kūkai's essay "The Meaning of the Syllable *Hūṃ*," translated in Hakeda 1972, 246–262.
32. This occurs in ch. 59 of the tantra. See Kittay and Lozang Jamspal 2020, 353–359.
33. According to Vajragarbha's "Commentary on the Concise Meaning of *Hevajra*" *Hevajrapiṇḍārthaṭīkā*, the background verse of the *Hevajra Tantra* has thirty-seven syllables, which is achieved by subtracting the three-syllable word *hṛdaya* from the *nidāna* of the GS. See fol. 7a-b. Snellgrove's edition includes the word *hṛdaya*, "essence," but he notes that two of the three Sanskrit manuscripts he used omit the word, which suggests that his edition may have to be emended (1959a, 2.2); at the very least, the thirty-seven-syllable version was an important and well-attested variant.
34. Concerning the *Saṃpuṭa Tantra* see the fourth chapter of the first *kalpa*, which is translated and edited by Elder 1978 and edited by Skorupski 1996. The import of this background verse is also discussed in chapter 2 of Kāṇha's "Light on the Secret Reality" *Guhyatattvaprakāśa*.
35. Vajragarbha's comments occur in his *Hevajrapiṇḍārthaṭīkā*, fol. 7aff.
36. The Tibetan version of the "Adamantine Pinnacle" *Vajraśekhara Tantra* also begins with *atha* (*de nas*), (fol. 142b), as does the "Great Sovereign

Tantra Called the Glorious Moon's Secret Drop" *Śrīcandraguhyatilaka-nāma-mahātantrarāja* (fol. 247b).

37. Translated in Gray 2007, 155.
38. Regarding his dates see Gray 2012, 6–8, n. 14.
39. My translation from Jayabhadra's "Commentary on the *Supreme Bliss of the Wheels*" *Cakrasaṃvarapañjikā,* 41b and Sugiki 2001, 105. When translating tantric commentaries, I place the text being commented on in bold font.
40. Jayabhadra, fol. 41b and 2001, 106.
41. My translation, *Sarvabuddhasamāyoga-dākinījālasaṃvara Tantra,* fol. 151a.
42. My translation of *Cakrasaṃvara Tantra* 1.2c-3b (Gray 2012, 49, 249); cf. Gray 2007, 155–156.
43. The alternate background is subjected to atomic analysis in chapter 42 of the "Adamantine Warlock" *Vajraḍāka Tantra.* See Sugiki 2002, 94–95. It is correlated with the standard background verse in the first chapter of the "Ocean of Warlocks" *Ḍākārṇava Tantra*; see fol. 138a-139a.
44. Wallace 2004, 4.
45. Kittay and Lozang Jamspal 2020, 112–115.
46. See, e.g., *Śrīḍākārṇava-mahāyoginī-tantrarāja,* fol. 140a.
47. Bubenik 2003, 207–208.
48. Salomon 2018, 1.
49. Collins 1990, 101.
50. Edgerton 1936, 1953.
51. Some tantric works were composed in other regions of Asia, most notably the *gter ma* treasure texts of the Tibetan Nyingma (*rnying ma*) tradition, which will be discussed in chapters 3 and 4.
52. Davidson 2002a, 265.
53. Dalton 2016b, 4–5.
54. Giacomella Orofino has written an article on this rite (1994a) and discusses the passages on this rite in the "Pointing Out Consecration," *Śekoddeśa,* a Kālacakra text that is believed to be a fragment of the "Supreme First Buddha" *Paramādibuddha Tantra,* the source text for the *Kālacakra Tantra.* See Orofino 1994b, 63–64. The rite is also briefly described in ch. 43 of the *Cakrasaṃvara Tantra.* See Gray 2007, 345.
55. My translation of Jayabhadra, *Śrīcakrasamvara-mūlatantra-pañjikā* from the text edited in Sugiki 2001, 120. I am indebted to Dr. George Cardona for his assistance in translating this passage.
56. Wallis 2008, 253.
57. Translated in Newman 1988, 125–127.

58. See Newman 1998, 342–343.
59. See Davidson 2002a, 270–271.
60. Bubenik 2003, 209.
61. *Ḍākārṇava Tantra* 23.20-24, fol. 194b-195a and Chaudhuri 1935, 141. Translated by Gray et al., forthcoming.
62. *Hevajra Tantra* 2.4.6-8. Translated in Snellgrove 1959a, 1.101.
63. Davidson 2002a, 262–269.
64. Sanderson 2001, 41–47.
65. Translated in Gray 2007, 241.
66. Bagchi 1939, 50–51.
67. *Hevajra Tantra* I.7.8-9; translated in Snellgrove 1959a, 1.68.
68. Davidson 1999, 35.
69. Gray 2012, 9–10.
70. Gray 2007, 21–24.
71. Regarding the Tibetan debates on this issue see Vose 2009 and Stearns 2010.
72. The main exception here is the "Noble" Ārya school of *Guhyasamāja* exegesis, which advanced a Prāsaṅgika Madhyamaka approach in both the commentaries as well as several of the explanatory tantras associated with this school, which is fitting, given that the tradition claims Nāgārjuna, his disciple Āryadeva, and Candrakīrti as central authority figures; see chapters 4 and 5 for more information on this school. The *Kālacakra Tantra* directly expresses affiliation with the Madhyamaka philosophical view, although it is not clear to me at least if at adheres to either of the approaches identified by Tibetans. See Wallace 2001, 170.
73. For an extended discussion of this idea in Chan Buddhism see Faure 1991.
74. Emptiness was explained to me thusly by a former graduate student of mine at Rice University, who came to serve as one of my Buddhist teachers, the Chungtai Chan Buddhist monk, Ven. Jianying.
75. My translation, *Guhyasamāja Tantra* 2.4, fol. 94a-b and Matsunaga 1978, 10. Concerning the importance of this verse in Tantric exegetical literature see Namai 1997.
76. Wallace 2011, 100.
77. See Cantwell and Mayer 2012, 103–108; regarding the text's background see 1–2.
78. My translation of Rong-zom Chos-kyi-bzang-po's *gsang sngags rdo rje theg pa'i tshul las snang ba lhar sgrub pa,* 127–128.
79. Sferra 1999, 84.

80. My translation of Rong-zom Chos-kyi-bzang-po's *gsang sngags rdo rje theg pa'i tshul las snang ba lhar sgrub pa*, 130.
81. My translation, *Śrīsamvarakhasama-tantrarāja*, fol. 262a.
82. *Kālacakra Tantra* 4.6, translated in Wallace 2010, 23. The insert is mine, based upon Wallace's summary of Bu-ston's commentary at 23, n. 82.
83. My translation from the *Sarvabuddhasamāyogaḍākinījālasaṃvara Tantra*, fol. 151a-b.
84. My translation of Tripiṭakamāla, *Nayatrayapradīpa*, 7a.
85. The "deity yoga" (*devatāyoga*) and "buddha yoga" (*buddhayoga*) are synonyms since the mandala deities with whom one identifies are understood to be awakened. In the Buddhist tantric context that the "deity" is not an absolutely existent entity whom the practitioner approaches as a supplicant as in theistic religions; rather, it is an embodiment of the ideal of awakening that the practitioner seeks to activate via meditative identification.
86. My translation of *Abhidhānottaratantra* 3.12, fol. 251b.
87. See Gomez and Harrison 2022 and Cleary 1993.
88. See Cook 1977, as well as Cleary's (1983) translations of relevant works from this school.
89. See the translation of this text in Hakeda 1972, 157–224.
90. My translation, Kūkai, *Sokushin jōbutsugi*, 100; cf. Hakeda 1972, 232.
91. My translation from the Chinese version of the *Sarvarahasya-nāma-tantrarāja*/一切祕密最上名義大教王儀軌. T 888, 18.537. The Tibetan version differs somewhat; see To. 481, *D rgyud 'bum* vol. ta, 2b. This passage is also cited by Tsongkhapa in his "Great Mantric Process," *sngags rim chen mo*; cf. Hopkins 1977, 131.
92. Translated in Hopkins 1977, 48–49, with insert by me. This explanation began with the traditional etymology of mantra as "that which protects the mind," which is why the notion of protection occurs throughout it.
93. If one engages in deity yoga practices without having realized emptiness, there's the danger that one will merely strengthen one's coarse attachment to self and egotism, one's "ordinary pride." The proper practice of deity yoga undermines rather than strengthens attachment to self. This is because the deity yoga practice of visualizing oneself as arising as a deity out of emptiness and then dissolving the vision back into emptiness again is believed to be a powerful tool for strengthening one's realization of emptiness. See Cozort 1986, 28, 58.
94. Chinese: 五身; Tibetan: *'byung lnga*.

95. 實智 , literally "true knowledge" or "knowledge of reality." A translation of *jñāna* in its supramundane or *lokottara* aspect.
96. Chinese version of the *Sarvarahasya-nāma-tantrarāja*/一切祕密最上名義大教王儀軌, vv. 1-4, T 888.536, and D fol. 1b.
97. My translation, *Sandhivyākaraṇa-nāma-tantra*, 178a.
98. My translation of the *Āryaḍākinīvajrapañjara-mahātantrarājakalpa*, fol. 31a,b; cf. Hopkins 1977, 117. For lists of the thirty-two signs and eighty marks of a great being see Thurman 1976, 156–157.
99. See Hopkins 1977, 118–122.
100. "mandarin, n.1," OED Online. March 2022. Oxford University Press. https://www-oed-com.libproxy.scu.edu/view/Entry/113292?rskey=ANTv5n&result=1&isAdvanced=false.
101. Dharmacakra Translation Committee, *The Bhūtaḍāmara Tantra*, 7.1-7.2.
102. The typical list of the "seven precious things" *saptaratna* include gold, silver, blue beryl, crystal, pearl, red precious stone (*lohitikā*), and coral (*musāragalva*). See Liu 1994, 93–94.
103. My translation from Asaṅga, *Mahāyānasaṃgraha*, fol. 41a.
104. The *Mañjuśrīmūlakalpa* is a composite text that was compiled over time by multiple tradents. Glenn Wallis argues that it mainly dates to the eighth century (2002, 10–11, 171–173).
105. Translated in Snellgrove 1959b, 206–207.
106. My translation, Nāgabuddhi, *Samājasādhanavyavasthāna*, 121b.
107. Ibid., my translation. This description is very close to Vasubandu's in the *Adbhidharmakośa*, which very well may have been the source for this account; cf. La Vallée Poussin 1988, 2: 451–456.
108. Two of the Dalai Lama's performances of the Kālacakra rite of initiation in 2002 were the focus of Werner Herzog's 2003 documentary *Wheel of Time*. Mandala-related rituals also feature prominently in Richard Kohn's 2001 study on the Mani Rimdu festival in Nepal. See as well Cozort 1996 for a description of this ritual practice.
109. *Cakrasaṃvara Tantra* 2.1-3, translated in Gray 2007, 164.
110. My translation of *Cakrasaṃvara Tantra* 2.6c-13a; cf. Gray 2007, 165–167.
111. These are the five types of gnosis (*jñāna*) that are antidotes to the five poisons of anger, pride, greed, jealousy, and ignorance.
112. My translation of *Abhidhānottaratantra* 4.12-21 along with associated prose passages but with most of the mantras omitted, from my forthcoming edition of the Sanskrit text and the Tibetan at fol. 253b-254b.
113. My translation of *Abhidhānottaratantra* 4.45-46 along with an associated prose passage, from my forthcoming edition of the Sanskrit text and the Tibetan at fol. 256a.

114. Cozort 1986, 68–88.
115. For more information on these practices, see Cozort 1986 and Mullin 1996.
116. Kohn 2001, 147.
117. Ibid., 148.
118. See Davidson 2002a, 122–127.
119. Translated in Abé 1999, 135–136.
120. For a detailed discussion of these rituals see Snellgrove 1987, 213–243.
121. The *Śrīparamādya* is one the tantras contained in both the Tibetan Mahāyoga and Chinese Adamantine Pinnacle collections of eighteen tantras. Two texts with this title are preserved in the Tibetan canon (To. 487 and 488); while they were translated later, circa the tenth and eleventh centuries, they seem to genuinely preserve older material. The *Cakrasaṃvara Tantra,* which was most likely composed during the ninth century, mentions this work by name, so it definitely postdates it.
122. The term *mudrā* here could designate a "consort," which would accord with the initiation ritual as it came to develop, as we will see later in the chapter. It could also indicate the disclosure of a secret hand gesture.
123. My translation, *Śrīparamādya-mantrakalpakhaṇḍa*, fol. 185a-b.
124. Sanderson 2009, 133, n. 311.
125. Sanderson 2001, 12–13.
126. My translation, *Sarvabuddhasamāyoga-ḍākinījālasaṃvara Tantra,* fol. 178b.
127. For more information on the ubiquity of rituals involving possession in South Asia see Smith 2006.
128. See Saunders 1960, 10–13. On the relationship between Indian dance and drama with tantric traditions see Shekhar 1960, 27–30.
129. See Renou and Filliozat 1947, 570; quoted in Saunders 1960, 12–13.
130. For more information on the range of meanings of the term *mudrā* in this literature see Gray 2013.
131. That is, a wheel with eight spokes, a well-known Buddhist symbol.
132. My translation, *Sarvatathāgatatattvasaṃgraha-nāma-mahāyāna-sūtra,* Yamada 1981, 483, and D fol. 118a-b. Many thanks to Prof. Christian Wedemeyer for his assistance with the translation of this passage.
133. My translation, *Sarvatathāgatatattvasaṃgraha-nāma-mahāyāna-sūtra,* Yamada 1981, 288–289 and D fol. 77a.
134. My translation from the *Śrīparamādya-nāma-mahāyānakalparāja,* fol. 171a.
135. That is, *dngos grub thams cad kyi dam tshig zhes bya ba'i phyag rgya'i dkyil 'khor, *sarvasiddhisamaya-nāma-mudrāmaṇḍala.*

136. That is, such people should not be admitted to the mandala and initiation. Presumably they are people who have already received initiation into rival, "heretical" tantric traditions.
137. This text here, *drag po'i dam tshig* might be read as "commitment of Rudra," one of the names of the Hindu deity Śiva.
138. That is, one will not be killed and, presumably, eaten at any tantric feast gathering (*tshogs*). This is important to note given the cannibalism that seems to be recommended here.
139. My translation from the *Śrīparamādya-nāma-mahāyānakalparāja,* 171a-b. For a more detailed study of this text see Gray 2013, 449–451.
140. These include Mahākāla, the "mothers" (*ma mo, mātṛkā*), and possibly Rudra. During the early period of tantric Buddhist development, namely the seventh through ninth centuries, many Śaiva deities were adopted by Buddhist groups and transformed into tantric Buddhist deities, as illustrated by the conversion myths discussed in chapter 1.
141. My translation, *Sarvatathāgatatattvasaṃgraha-nāma-mahāyāna-sūtra,* Yamada 1981, 492, and D fol. 120b.
142. Ibid., my translation.
143. My translation of *Cakrasaṃvara Tantra* 3.7-8, from my edition of the Sanskrit and Tibetan (Gray 2012, 63, 257); cf. Gray 2007, 174.
144. That is, sexual fluids.
145. My translation from Jayabhadra's *Śrīcakrasamvara-mūlatantra-pañjikā,* 13b-14a and Sugiki 2001, 114. The text in bold are quotations from the root tantra text.
146. These are the three subtle states of consciousness that emerge from (or, in reverse order, lead to) the clear light consciousness, namely "luminance" (*āloka*), "radiance" (*ābhāsa*), and "immanence" (*upalabdhaka*). Regarding them see Wedemeyer 2007, 95–96.
147. My translation, Atiśa, *Abhisamayavibhaṅga,* 197a.7-b.4.
148. Orzech 1996, 219–220.
149. Translated in McBride 2018, 58, from the 佛說隨求即 得大自在陀羅尼神呪經, T. 1154, 20.637 b27-c4.
150. Giovanni Verardi has argued for the early Buddhist appropriation of the *homa* rite in his (1994) monograph. For more information concerning the Buddhist *homa* rite, see Payne 1991 and Payne and Witzel 2016.
151. For an overview of Indian sorcery practices see Türstig 1985 and Goudriaan 1978. For an excellent introduction to Buddhist sorcery see Van Schaik 2020, a work that contains a complete translation of a Tibetan book of spells.

152. *Cakrasaṃvara Tantra* 12.2.7, translated in Gray 2007, 212.
153. Translated in Gray 2017, 273.
154. Kubera is a worldly deity associated with wealth.
155. Dharmacakra Translation Committee, *The Practice Manual of Noble Tārā Kurukullā,* 3.27.

Chapter 3

1. Sen 2014, 50.
2. Sundberg and Giebel 2011, 134.
3. Sen 2015, 454.
4. Sundberg 2003 and 2004.
5. Nihom 1998, 251.
6. Chou 2006, 40; Sundberg and Giebel 2011, 152.
7. Orzech 1998, 137.
8. Yang 2018, 23–26.
9. Orzech 1998, 160–161.
10. Yang 2018, 61–65.
11. Sinclair 2016, 33–38.
12. The text here indicates that he gave the dogs *dam tshig*, or *samaya,* which here likely designates the sacraments, i.e., consecrated food and drink, offered to deities in the tantric feast. It implies that he celebrated the tantric feast (*gaṇacakra*) rite with his canine companions.
13. These are (1) knowledge of miraculous procedures, *ṛddhividhijñāna*; (2) clairvoyance, *divyaṃcakṣus*; (3) clairaudience, *divyaṃśrota*; 4) mind-reading, *paracittajñāna*; (5) and recollection of past lives, *pūrvanirvāsānusmṛtijñāna* (Rigzin 1986, 95–96).
14. The "Glorious Supreme Prime" *Śrīparamādya* does in fact contain embedded within it a short esoteric sutra, the "Hundred and Fifty [Stanzas] on the Method of the Perfection of Wisdom" *Prajñāpāramitā-naya-śatapañcāśatikā*. Regarding this text see Astley-Kristensen 1992.
15. My translation of Jñānamitra's "*Commentary on the Method of the Perfection of Wisdom in 150 Stanzas*" **Prajñāpāramitānaya-śatapañcāśatikā-ṭīkā*, 273ab.
16. The title of the text in Chinese is 最上大乘金剛大教寶王經, which we might translate as "Sutra of the Adamantine King of Wealth, the Highest Great Teaching of the Mahāyāna." However, I follow Nanjiu's (1883, #869) Sanskrit reconstruction, *Vajragarbharatnarāja-tantra*. It was most likely translated during the late tenth century or very early eleventh

century, as its translator was Dharmadeva (法天), who passed away in 1001 (Orzech 2006, 140).

17. The text here lists the four main social classes in India, the warrior aristocracy (*kṣatriya*), the priests (*brāhmaṇa*), commoners (*vaiśya*) and servants (*śūdra*). This text follows the Buddhist precedent of listing first the warrior class, into which Śākyamuni Buddha was born.
18. My translation from the *Vajragarbharatnarāja-tantra*, T. 1128 p. 543.3; cf. Bagchi 1944, 39.
19. In the Newāri context, in which the Buddhists have been constituted as a "caste" within the context of the larger Hindu society, the Vajrācārya as a profession has evidently been assimilated with the brahmin, serving, in Greenwold's (1974) terms, as "Buddhist brahmins." This assimilation was facilitated by the transmission of *vajrācārya* status through birth lineage, following the brahmanical model.
20. Davidson 2002a, 51–61.
21. Gellner 1991, 161.
22. This "conundrum" has been explored in depth by Heesterman, who has argued that renunciatory ideology became the key for the brahmin to maintain his purity while engaged in guarded involvement with the world. See Heesterman 1985, 43.
23. See Robinson 1979, 150–152.
24. This term, "adamantine seat" (*vajrapīṭha*) refers to sacred pilgrimage sites that are also correlated to mandala deities. They play a prominent role in yoginītantras such as the *Cakrasaṃvara* (Gray 2007, 54–76) and *Hevajra* (Snellgrove 1959a, 1.69–70). Regarding a pilgrimage tradition connected to one of these sites, see Huber 1999.
25. The text refers to the *Śrī-Jñānatilaka-yoginītantrarāja-paramamahādbhuta*, a Tantra that focuses on Vajrapāṇi.
26. My translation, *Śrī-tattvapradīpa-nāma-mahāyoginītantrarāja*, 142b. The text refers to the stages that bodhisattvas must pass through on the path to awakening, which are variously enumerated from ten to fifteen (see Dayal 1970), as well as the theory that buddhas possess multiple levels of embodiment, including their physical or "emanation bodies," as well as other levels that can manifest in different realms and survive physical death. Regarding this idea see Makransky 1997.
27. My translation of *Cakrasaṃvara Tantra* 3.10-14, from my edition of the Sanskrit and Tibetan (Gray 2012, 63–64, 257–258); cf. Gray 2007, 175.
28. The Wuzong emperor, a devout Daoist, proscribed Buddhism and all other "foreign" religions for apparently both economic and religious

reasons. He ordered the confiscation of Buddhist property, destruction of temples, and the laicization of monks and nuns. The mainstream Buddhist orders were decimated by this persecution, which lasted from 841 to 846. This event was a turning point in Chinese religious history, and it led to the rise of two traditions, Chan and Pure Land, that were less dependent at that time on royal patronage. Regarding the Wu Zong persecution see Weinstein 1987, 117–134.

29. Tinsley 2011, 692.
30. Abé 1995, 104–105.
31. Tendai is the Japanese pronunciation of the Chinese name Tiantai (天台); he was establishing a Japanese branch of this school.
32. Abé 1995, 108; insert mine. See as well Groner 1984, 66–68.
33. Abé 1995, 123–124.
34. Dolce 2011, 752.
35. Ibid., 753.
36. Abé 1999, 118–127.
37. Tinsley 2011, 699.
38. Ibid., 706–707.
39. See Abé 1999, 359ff.
40. Ibid., 384–385.
41. Snellgrove 1987, 414–415.
42. For a traditional Tibetan account of this see Ahmad 1995, 17–21 and Roerich 1976, 39.
43. Walter 2009, 219.
44. In fact, there is little evidence for Buddhism in Tibet prior to King Tri Songdetsen's reign. See Snellgrove 1987, 414.
45. Śāntarakṣita 2011, 85.
46. His name literally means "Lotus Born," marking his origin in a lotus blossom that appeared in a lake in Oḍiyāna. See Yeshe Tsogyal 1978, 85ff.
47. See Dudjom Rinpoche 1991, 516 and Dowman 1984, 21ff.
48. Padmasambhava's visit to Tibet is recorded in an old dynastic historical account, the *Testament of Ba* (*sba bzhed*, an account written by a member of Tri Songdetsen's court (Van Shaik 2013, 34–35). Interestingly, the earliest sources emphasize that he attempted to introduce new irrigation technology to Tibet, and that his subjugation of spirits was connected with this, given the widespread association in South Asia of water sources with serpent deities (*nāga, klu*); see Dalton 2004a, 769. While this seems to confirm that he did in fact visit Tibet and helped with the construction of Samye Monastery, this account provides little additional information

about his activities in Tibet. The Tibetan hagiographies were composed centuries later. For a traditional hagiography see Yeshe Tsogyal 1978.

49. Herrmann-Pfandt 2002, 132.
50. According to Tibetan historical sources, three catalogs of translated texts were made during the Tibetan imperial period. These include the *Lhan/lDan kar ma*, which has been dated to 812 (Herrmann-Pfandt 2002, 129), and the *'Phang-thang-ma*, which has been dated to 842 (Dotson 2007, 4). The third catalog, the *mchims phu ma*, is apparently lost.
51. Dalton and Van Schaik 2006, xxi.
52. See Beckwith 1987, 168–169 and Davidson 2005, 65–66.
53. Cantwell and Mayer 2012, 7–8.
54. Kapstein 2006, 81.
55. Orzech 2011a, 320.
56. See Keyworth 2011 and Wu 2018.
57. See Capitano 2011.
58. Orzech 2006, 140 and 156, n. 6.
59. Sen 2002.
60. Sørensen 2011b, 587.
61. Sørensen 2006a, 67–70.
62. Cantwell and Mayer 2012, 6–9.
63. Davidson 2005, 69.
64. Karmay 1980a, 154.
65. Ibid., 151.
66. This is due to its large amount of transgressive content and relatively small amount of Buddhist content, as discussed in section 2.3.1.
67. Decleer 1995.
68. Van Schaik 2013, 59–60.
69. On the final days of Buddhism in India see Verardi 2011. As Verardi argues, the decline and disappearance of Buddhism in most of India was complex, and it wasn't only due to the destruction of Buddhist monasteries by Turks, but also hostility from Hindu groups, as well as hostility from Theravāda monks from Sri Lanka toward the tantric Mahāyāna centers such as Nālandā (Verardi 2011, 360–372). Here we might also note that the Abhayagiri Monastery in Sri Lanka, famed as a center of tantric studies, with a well-documented collection of tantric works, was destroyed in the twelfth century by King Parakkamabāhu I (1153–1186), at the urging of the dominant Theravāda tradition. See Gombrich 1988, 159 and Chandra 1984.
70. For an introduction to the Nyingma school and its tantric teachings, see Khetsun Sangpo 1996 and Dudjom Rinpoche 1991.

71. Samuel 1993, 460.
72. Cassinelli and Ekvall 1969, 6–7.
73. According to Rerikh, before summoning Sakya Paṇḍita to the Mongol court in Lan-zhou, Godan dispatched reconnaissance troops under the command of Dorda-darkhan into Tibet to access the state of the country. He concluded that Sakya Monastery was of greatest influence. His report led to Godan's invitation to Sakya Paṇḍita. See Rerikh 1973, 43–45.
74. Petech stresses regarding Sakya Paṇḍita that "the Tibetans had not elected or conferred a mandate on him. The Mongols simply wanted an influential monk to employ for their own purposes in Tibet" (1983, 180–181).
75. See Ruegg 1991, 443. This letter is translated in Tucci 1949, 10.
76. Concerning the translation of these terms see Ruegg 1991, 446–447.
77. Rerikh 1973, 46.
78. Petech 1990.
79. Franke 1981, 308, Bade 2016, 143–144.
80. Sperling 1994.
81. I refer to the conversation Polo reports with Khubilai Khan, regarding "Why the Great Khan did not convert to Christianity" (Waugh 1984, 68–70). While there are numerous reasons to doubt elements of Polo's narrative, there is no doubt his observation that the Mongols were impressed by Buddhist's magic is accurate.
82. For a translation of the relevant passage see Van Gulik 1961, 260. See also Van der Kuijp 1991, 305–306, n. 35.
83. Kapstein 2006, 129–134.
84. Taupier 2015, 23–28.
85. Kapstein 2006, 137–138.
86. Sørensen 2006a, 72.
87. See McBride 2018.
88. Sørensen 2006b.
89. Sanford 2006, 164–174.
90. Bodiford 2011.
91. Payne 2021.
92. Payne 2016.
93. Iyanaga 2011, 811.
94. This was argued in Sanford 1991.
95. Iyanaga 2011, 812.
96. Pranke 1995, 343.
97. Ibid., 344.
98. Van Schaik 2020, 98–99.
99. Pranke 1995, 344.

100. Foxeus 2016, 429.
101. See Sharrock 2012.
102. See Sharrock 2013.
103. Sharrock and Bunker 2016, 252.
104. Bade 2016, 148–149.
105. Kapstein 2009, 9.
106. Tuttle 2005, 79–81.
107. See Tuttle 2005, 87–102 and Meinert 2009.
108. There apparently were earlier attempts to translate Tibetan works into Chinese during the Yuan Dynasty. Regarding an extra-canonical collection of works in Chinese attributed to the Tibetan lama Pakpa Lodrö Gyeltsen (*'phags pa blo gros rgyal mtshan,* 1235–1280), see Beckwith 1984.
109. Bianchi 2009, 304–305.
110. Tuttle 2005, 204.
111. Tuttle 2009.
112. These translations were published in a two-volume set, published in Hong Kong and Taipei in 1997. Their titles and publication information occur as follows: 吉祥集密大續王，勝樂略續。寶 法 稱 and 仁欽曲扎, 譯者。香港：佛教慈慧服務中心，台北：盤逸有限公司。
113. For an overview of the Chinese occupation of Tibet see Van Schaik 2013, 207–269. For information on the almost total destruction of Buddhism in Mongolia see Wallace and Murphy 2017, 162–163.
114. LeVine and Gellner 2005, 251–253.
115. Zablocki 2009a, 387–394.
116. Kapstein 2009, xv.
117. Germano 1998, 68.
118. Wallace and Murphy 2017, 165.
119. See Lu 1995, iii. This work is a good English-language introduction to the teachings and practices of the True Buddha School.
120. For an excellent translation based on the recently discovered Sanskrit manuscript see Gómez and Harrison 2022; cf. Thurman 1976.
121. See Yee 2008. This is a fascinating work that is largely dedicated to "proving" the author's claim that he is an incarnation of Vajradhara Buddha. Evidence offered includes reports of miracles allegedly performed by him, as well as letters from various Tibetan lamas, which are used to support his claims. It also includes reproductions of his own artworks. While I do not know how many copies of this work were

distributed, I presume that its distribution was wide, since a copy was sent, without my having requested it, to my academic address in 2009.

122. Robouam 2011, 1037–1038.
123. For a short, critical biography of Chögyam Trungpa Rinpoche see Gardner 2021.
124. Regarding Geshe Wangyal's impact see Urubshurow 2013.
125. See Zablocki 2009b.
126. See Eastman 2009 for a discussion of a failed Shingon temple in Oregon.
127. Regarding this practice and the controversy it has engendered, see Gayley 2018.

Chapter 4

1. Gyatso 1992, 100.
2. To. 1401–1411.
3. To. 1180–1189.
4. To. 1347–1354, if you count commentaries on the "Consecration Instructions" *Sekoddeśa,* which, understood as a fragment of the larger *Paramādibuddha Tantra,* is also understood as a primary revelation for the Wheel of Time tradition.
5. To. 1622–1625.
6. To. 1784–1787.
7. I can only speculate on its date of composition. It clearly was composed by the late tenth century, as it was one of the texts translated by Rin chen Zang po along with the Kashmiri pundit Śraddhākaravarma. It was likely composed sometime in the ninth or early tenth centuries. Detailed study of the *Guhyasamāja* commentarial literature and explanatory tantras would likely enable us to narrow down the date range significantly.
8. See Matsunaga 1964 for a discussion of how these texts are interrelated.
9. Wedemeyer 2007, 47–48.
10. Gray 2017, 34–36.
11. My translation from Bu ston Rin chen grub, "Illumination of the General Meaning of the Supreme Bliss Light Tantra" *bde mchog nyung ngu rgyud kyi spyi rnam don gsal,* 47–48.
12. See Wedemeyer 2007, 47, n. 100.
13. For more information on their contributions to the Guhyasamāja tradition see Wedemeyer 2007, 49–58.

14. See Wallace 2001, 3. This is one of three "bodhisattva commentaries," as Tibetans deem them. The other two are commentaries on the *Hevajra* and *Cakrasaṃvara* that will be mentioned later in the chapter. All three comment from the perspective of the Kālacakra tradition and thus appear to be an ambitious attempt by advocates of the Kālacakra to expand their exegetical reach into what appear to be the two most popular Buddhist tantric traditions in eleventh-century India, when the Kālacakra tradition was revealed. The commentaries on the *Hevajra* and *Cakrasaṃvara* are attributed to the bodhisattvas believed to be the tantra's interlocutor, Vajragarbha and Vajrapāṇi respectively. These attributions were clearly made to bolster the authority of these ambitious, and somewhat controversial, works. Regarding this see Gray 2009, 193–195.
15. This is his "Commentary on the Consecration Instructions Called the Compilation of Ultimate Import," *Paramārthasaṃgraha-nāmasekoddeśaṭīka,* To. 1351.
16. These are Vajragarba's "Commentary That Summarizes the Hevajra" *Hev ajrapiṇḍārthaṭīkā* (To. 1180), one of the Kālacakra-inspired bodhisattva commentaries, the "Hevajra Commentary Called a Garland of Yogic Jewels," attributed to Kṛṣṇācārya (To. 1183), and the "Commentary on the Magical Two Precepts of the Hevajra Great Sovereign Tantra Called the Origin of Mindfulness" *rgyud kyi rgyal po chen po dgyes pa' rdo rje zhes bya ba sgyu ma brtag pa gnyis pa'i dka' 'grel dran pa'i 'byung gnas zhe bya ba* attributed to Kāṇha (To. 1187); Kāṇha and Kṛṣṇācārya are alternative names for the same great adept.
17. To Ḍombipa is attributed two meditation manuals (To. 1232 & 1305), a ritual manual for tantric feasts (To. 1231), and two oral instruction texts (To. 1230 & 1266).
18. The "Path and Result" system of teachings is based on multiple transmissions from Indian masters. The Sakya organized these into two "pith instruction" lineages attributed to Vīrupa and Nāropa and six "great chariot" transmissions, one of which is attributed to Ḍombīheruka and one to Śāntipa. See Sobisch 2008, 2.
19. Davidson 1992, 109. Insert is mine.
20. Lūipa is reputed to be the author of the "Realization of Cakrasaṃvara" *Cakrasaṃvarābhisamaya* meditation manual.
21. Kṛṣṇācarya/Kāṇha is believed to have authored important works that address the path of creation and completion stage practice in the Cakrasaṃvara tradition. These include his "Spring Drop" (*vasantatilakā,* To. 1448), his "The Four Stages" (*olicatuṣṭaya*) and its

auto-commentary (To.1451 & 1452), and his "Light on the Secret Reality" (*guhyatattvaprakāśa,* To. 1450). Attributed to him are also a meditation manual (*Śrīcakrasaṃvarasādhana,* To. 1445), a fire sacrifice ritual manual (*Śrīcakrasaṃvarahomavidhi,* To. 1447), and a mandala ritual manual (*Bha gavacchrīcakrasaṃvaramaṇḍalavidhi.* To. 1446).

22. Ghaṇṭāpāda/Vajraghaṇṭa is the reputed author of an important text on practice in this tradition called "The Five Stages of the Śrī Cakrasaṃvara" (*Śrīcakrasaṃvarapañcakrama.* To. 1433). Two meditation manuals are also attributed to him (To. 1432 & 1436), as well as ritual texts on mandala construction (To. 1430) and the bestowal of consecrations therein (To. 1431).
23. This is the "Commentary on the Light Tantra," *Laghutantraṭīkā* (To. 1402, Sanskrit edited in Cicuzza 2001).
24. These texts are Kambala's "Sādhana Treasury Commentary on the Discourse of Śrī Heruka" *Śrīherukābhidhāna-sādhananidhi-pañjikā* (To. 1401) and Indrabhūti's "Commentary on the Glorious Binding of the Wheels King of Tantras Called the Assembly of Supreme Bliss" *Śrīcakrasaṃvaratantrarāja-saṃvarasamuccaya-nāma-vṛtti* (To. 1413). The Tibetan commentator Tsongkhapa (1357–1419) relies particularly on the former work and incorporates large amounts of Kambala's commentary into his own work. See Gray 2019, 7.
25. Verardi 2011, 362.
26. For a discussion of how this fourfold system developed in Tibet see Dalton 2005, 158–161.
27. The Nyingma scheme is part of their analysis of the Buddhist path as ninefold (*theg pa dgu*). The first three stages of the path are exoteric, consisting of the "Disciple Path" (*nyan thos kyi theg pa*), the path of the early Buddhist traditions; the "Solitary Buddha Path" (*rang rgyal ba'i theg pa*), the path of the "solitary buddhas" who reach awakening but do not teach, and the "bodhisattva path" (*byang chub sems dpa'i theg pa*) of the classical Mahāyāna. Regarding these nine paths see Cabezón 2013.
28. Buddhaguhya's exact dates are unknown, but he is known to be a contemporary of King Khri-srong-lde-brtsan, who ruled Tibet from 754 to 797, and who invited him to Tibet. Buddhaguhya's letter reply of reply, in which he declined the king's invitation, is preserved in the gTam-yig section of the Tibetan canon. For a survey of the data concerning Buddhaguhya's life and dates see Lo Bue 1987.
29. This refers to the classical Mahāyāna, which focuses on the cultivation of the perfections (*pāramitā*) of a bodhisattva.

30. These are the *trivimokṣamukha,* namely emptiness (*śūnyatā*), signlessness (*animittatā*), and wishlessness (*apraṇihitatā*).
31. My translation, Buddhaguhya, *rnam par snang mdzad mngon par byang chub pa'i rgyud chen po'i 'grel bshad* 261a-b.
32. Variants of the terms *ubhayatantra* include *upayoga,* which might be translated as "conduct" or "subsidiary yoga" and *upāyayoga* "expedience yoga." These terms are found in a relatively small number of texts, namely early Indic texts, such as Buddhaguhya's from the eighth century, as well as texts of the Nyingma school, which developed from a transmission of texts and practices to Tibet during the eighth century. Snellgrove holds that *upayoga* is most likely the original term and *ubhayayoga* and *upāyayoga* are later variants. This may be true, but clearly by the eighth century the term *ubhayayoga* referred to a category of texts considered intermediary between the *kriyā* and *yoga* tantras, sharing the qualities of "both" (*ubhaya*) types. The term is more meaningful than the alternatives, in my opinion. See Snellgrove 1988, 1363.
33. Dalton 2005, 124–126.
34. Verardi 1994 discusses the ample evidence indicating widespread Buddhist performance of *homa* rituals in Gandhāra during the Kushan era, namely first century BCE through fourth century CE.
35. The issue of the development of Buddhist iconography has been the subject of extensive research and debate. It is generally agreed that it took place during the Kushan period, i.e., the first two centuries of the common era; see Abe 1995.
36. Stanley Abe (1990) has argued that some Buddhist images in the Mogao Caves in northwestern China appear to have been produced to facilitate visualization practices that are known to have been popular when the images were produced in the fifth century CE.
37. The distinction between outer ritual actions and inner contemplative practices is ancient and goes back to the Upaṇiṣads of ancient Hinduism. Concerning the tendency in Vedic Hindu thought toward "interiorization" see Heesterman 1985, 212n72. Buddhists here were simply following a venerable trend.
38. Dalton 2004b, 2.
39. My translation, Śraddhākaravarma, *rnal 'byor bla na med pa'i rgyud kyi don la 'jug pa bsdus pa zhes bya ba,* 105b; cf. Dalton 2005, 155.
40. The text gives two names for this class, *brtag pa'i rgyud* "analytical tantra" (fol. 106b.3) and *btags pa'i rgyud* "conceptual tantra" (fol. 106b.4). I follow

the latter as the distinction between natural and conceptual seems more meaningful.

41. My translation, Śraddhākaravarma, *rnal 'byor bla na med pa'i rgyud kyi don la 'jug pa bsdus pa zhes bya ba,* 106b. He quotes the *Uttaratantra,* vv. 34–35 of in Matsunaga's Sanskrit edition (1978, 115). Cf. the partial translation in Dalton 2005, 155–156.
42. My translation, Śraddhākaravarma, *rnal 'byor bla na med pa'i rgyud kyi don la 'jug pa bsdus pa zhes bya ba,* 107a.
43. Here it is worth mentioning that the association of women with wisdom is not necessarily empowering, as Śraddhākaravarma's text makes clear, since here the gender dichotomy is linked to the insider/outsider dichotomy, with women placed in the subordinate role. Bernard Faure argued that "far from extolling wisdom and women as a superficial reading would suggest, this imagery presupposes and reinforces the inferiority of women. Max Weber has already noted that the symbolic abrogation of gender difference usually goes along with a dichotomic system of gender segregation" (2003, 124).
44. Dalton 2005, 152.
45. My translation, *Sarvatathāgatakāyavākcitta-kṛṣṇayamāri Tantra,* 150a.
46. My translation, ibid., 153a-b.
47. My translation of Kukurāja's *dpal rdo rje sems pa'i gsang ba'i don rnam par dgod pa shes bya ba,* 124b.
48. The five "awakenings" *abhisambodhi*s are creation stage mediation techniques leading to awakening, involving (1) discernment of the sixteen voids; (2) creating the spirit of awakening; (3) contemplating the mind as adamant; (4) contemplating the voidness of the vajra-mind; and (5) contemplation of the equality of all Tathāgatas. See Rigzin 1986, 96.
49. Translating *gnas bzhi,* with the assumption that *gnas* is an atypical translation of *bhūta.*
50. My translation of Indranāla's *Sarvabuddhasamāyogaḍākinījālasaṃvarata ntrārthodaraṭīkā,* fol. 274a-b.
51. See the discussion of these practices in section 2.3.2.1.
52. Abé 1999, 190.
53. Ibid., 207.
54. Ibid., 264.
55. Ibid., 152–153.
56. Sharf 2002, 265–267.
57. For an overview of past and contemporary Newari *vajrācārya* masters' life and works see Lewis and Bajracharya 2016, 155–166.

58. The late twelfth- to early-thirteenth-century Sakya scholar Drakpa Gyaltsen (grags pa rgyal mtshan) reported in his *Chronicle of Tibet: The Lineage of Teachers* that the Tibetan translator Drokmi ('brog mi lo tsā ba, born c. 1000) offered 500 ounces of gold to receive teachings from the pundit Gayādhara. See Davidson 2005, 165–167.
59. Orzech, Payne, and Sørensen 2011, 11.
60. Giebel 2011, 27–31.
61. For example, the tenth section, "Ritual Texts for Bodhisattvas," contains a translation of the *Bhūtaḍāmara Tantra,* the eleventh section, "Ritual Texts for Mañjuśrī," contains translation of the *Mañjuśrīnāmasaṃgīti* and the *Mañjuśrīmūlakalpa,* while the twelfth section, "Ritual Texts for Vidyārāja" contain tantras associated with fierce deities including Acala, Trailokyavijaya, Yamāntaka, Vajrabhairava, and Mahābala. See Giebel 2011, 33–34.
62. Sørensen 2011a.
63. Skilling 1997, 95.
64. See Cantwell 2020.
65. Mayer 1996, 17.
66. Ruegg 1966, 118.
67. Stanley 2005.
68. Kawa Sherab Sangpo 2013, 217.
69. See "Catalog of the Degé Edition of the Collected Tantras of the Ancients," Tibetan & Himalayan Library, n.d., https://www.thlib.org/encyclopedias/literary/canons/ngb/catalog.php#cat=dg.
70. See the Buddhist Digital Archives published by the Buddhist Digital Resource Center, https://library.bdrc.io.
71. Regarding this effort see https://84000.co.

Chapter 5

1. Regarding the dating of this text see Abé 1999, 151 and Davidson 2002a, 213. For a translation of the *yakṣī* summoning rite see Gray 2007, 87–88.
2. See Behr 2004.
3. Cheung 2005, 28–31.
4. Chan 2000, 187.
5. Behr 2004, 199.
6. Chan 2000, 194.
7. Regarding this institution see Hucker 1966. Translators in China were monitored and subjected to imperial control. The prominent translator

Śubhākarasiṃha, e.g., requested permission to return to India in 732, but the emperor denied his request. See Chou 2006, 46.

8. Buswell 1990, 18.
9. See Forte 1976 and 1990.
10. See the discussion of the politics that surrounded the development of imperial bibliographies and canons under Empress Wu and the Xuan-zong emperor in 695 and 730 CE in Lewis 1990, 230–231.
11. See Giebel 1995, 112–113.
12. That is, the full and abridged versions of the Adamantine Pinnacle Yoga scriptural collection.
13. My translation of Amoghavajra, "Instructions on the Gate to the Teachings on Secret Heart of the Great Yoga of the Adamantine Pinnacle Scripture" 金剛頂經大瑜伽祕密心地法門義訣, T.39.1798.808b17-23; cf. Orzech 1995, 317. The text uses the Chinese unit of measure word 里, which is approximately 500 meters or one third of a mile.
14. Davidson 2002a, 203 and 387, n. 110.
15. Orzech 1998, 139.
16. Regarding accusations of witchcraft and resulting persecution in Han China, see Raphals 1998, 78–86. She discusses the accusations of black magic (巫 蠱) made by members of the court of the Han Chengdi emperor (r. 32–6 BCE) recorded in the Han Shu (漢 書).
17. Regarding magic in the Greco-Roman world see Brown 1970, 17–45. For an example of accusations of witchcraft in second-century CE Roman North Africa see Apuleius's *Apologia,* translated in Hunink 2001.
18. Indeed, in both the Han Chinese and late Roman contexts those accused of magic are portrayed as expressing skepticism concerning its efficacy. See Empress Xu's (in Raphals 1998, 81) and Apuleius's (Hunink 2001, 49–88) refutations of accusations of witchcraft.
19. See Goodman 1998 and Wechsler 1985.
20. See Walter 2009, 3ff.
21. See Kapstein 2000, 60.
22. Karmay uses the hypothetical Sanskrit reconstruction "*anuttarayogatantras*," which is unattested; *niruttara-* rather than *anuttara-* is actually found in Sanskrit tantric Buddhist texts.
23. Karmay 1980a, 151.
24. My translation, Bu ston Rin chen grub, *Rgyud sde spyi'i rnam par gzhag pa rgyud sde rin po che'i mdzes rgyan zhes bya ba*, 127.
25. Translated in Kapstein 2000, 231, n. 60. While it is not known if this text was actually composed by the king, it was composed during his reign and under his patronage, and thus likely reflects the king's viewpoint.

26. Kapstein 2000, 76.
27. Karmay 1988, 5.
28. Ibid., 6.
29. Van der Kuijp 1992, 116.
30. Karmay 1980b, 17.
31. The reasons for this are complex but are most likely due to a failure to disseminate the oral practice tradition along with the scriptures. Regarding this see Orzech 2006, 145.
32. Orzech 2011b, 445.
33. Some commentators, such as Bhavabhaṭṭa in his *Cakrasamvaravivṛtti,* note variant readings in the multiple copies of the scriptures available to him. Many of the differences in the Tibetan translations appear to be due to variant readings in the Sanskrit texts that they were translating, as noted at many points in Gray 2007. See also Gray 2012, 6–22 and Wedemeyer 2006.
34. Much has been written on the subject of tantric exegetical strategies. See in particular Broido 1988 and Wedemeyer 2002. On tantric exegesis in general see Thurman 1988.
35. E.g., the Tibetan attempts to render the rich complexity of Sanskrit verb forms naturally led to ambiguity, with a single Tibetan verb form often used to translate several Sanskrit forms. For a discussion of this problem see Beyer 1992, 345–350.
36. For an excellent summary of Tibetan translation styles, as well as a critique of the myth of the absolute precision of Tibetan translations from Sanskrit, see Wedemeyer 2006, 149–152.
37. See Kumārajīva's translation, the 維摩詰所說經 (T.475.14.537a-557b), and Xuan-zang's, the 說無垢稱經 (T.476.14.557-587). Regarding the significance of this work in China see Mather 1968.
38. David Snellgrove, e.g., in his translation of the *Hevajra Tantra,* simply omitted several passages that he deemed offensive, such as *kalpa* 2, chapter 11, verse 15, which he includes in his Sanskrit edition, but does not translate into English. See Snellgrove 1959a, 2.98–99.
39. In the canonical Tibetan translation of the *Guhyasamāja Tantra,* we find a hybrid translation-transliteration, *bha ga rnams la,* affixing Tibetan grammatical particles indicating plurality and the locative case to the transliterated Sanskrit term. See fol. 90a2. A variant occurs in the canonical translation of the *Hevajra Tantra,* which drops the plural indicator, *rnams,* reading simply *bha ga la.* See Snellgrove 1959a, 2.3.
40. Or, we might add, any reader who does not know Sanskrit. This strategy was also employed by Alex Wayman, apparently following the precedent set by Tibetan translators; he translated *bhageṣu* as "in the bhagas" (1977, 108).

41. See T.869.18.287a.29.
42. Amoghavajra composed this text shortly after his return to China from South Asia in 746. Buddhaśrījñāna, the founder of the Jñānapāda school of Guhyasamāja exegesis, was active at this time. His reference to the "Perfection of Wisdom" (*prajñāpāramitā*) palace likewise points to the "integration of sūtra and tantra" that characterized mature esoteric exegetical systems. E.g., Kūkai argued for the complementary of the exoteric and esoteric scriptures, and the implicit presence of the latter's teachings in the former, in his works *The Ten Abiding Stages of Mind* and *Distinguishing the Two Teachings of the Exoteric and the Esoteric*. The latter is translated in Hakeda 1972, 151–157. See also Abé 1999, 237–271.
43. See T.892.18.587c.13. For a more elegant translation of the Chinese translation of the *Hevajra nidāna* verse, see Willemen 1983, 33–34.
44. See T.885.18.469c.26.
45. One example occurs in chapter 31 of the *Cakrasaṃvara Tantra* where the text cryptically describes the practice of "hand worship" (*hastapūjā*), in which the deities are visualized on one's hands. The text describes the parts of the hands symbolically, at one point reading "Vajrasattva abides by the tree." The Sanskrit here, *vajrasattvas tarave sthita*, is ungrammatical. Perhaps in response to this error, the canonical Tibetan translation does not translate literally here "at/on/by the tree," but instead interpretively translates "at/on/by the thumb," *mthe bor*, relying on the commentaries. While this translation is not incorrect, it is interpretive, and does not precisely correlate to what was almost certainly the Sanskrit text extant at the time, judging by the commentaries. Regarding this passage see Gray 2007, 298, n. 6.
46. See Gray 2005a and Gray 2007, 206–208.
47. My translation, Bhavabhaṭṭa. *Śrīcakrasamvarapañjikā*, edited in Pandey 2002, 1.23.
48. My translation, Bhavabhaṭṭa. *Śrīcakrasamvarapañjikā*, fol. 159a1.
49. That is, the 佛說妙吉祥瑜伽大教金剛陪囉縛輪觀想成就儀軌經 (T.1242). This title could be reconstructed as **Buddhabhāṣita-śrīvajrabhairava-mahāyogatantra-cakradhyāna-siddhikalpa*.
50. Orzech 2006, 150.
51. The corresponding Tibetan text is not, as the titles suggest, the *Śrīvajrabhairava-tantrarāja-siddhikalpa* (To. 470), but it is rather the *Śrīvajrabhairava-nāma-tantrarāja* (To. 468). Both texts are translated into English, on the basis of the Tibetan and Mongolian translations, in Siklós 1996.
52. Orzech 2006, 164, n. 53.

53. My translation from the Chinese *Śrīvajrabhairava Tantra*, 佛說妙吉祥瑜伽大教金剛陪囉縛輪觀想成就儀軌經, T.1242. 21.203b.9-25.
54. Here I follow the reading preserved in the Tibetan translation as well as some of the Sanskrit manuscripts noted by Matsunaga, *-mohakulām,* rather than *-mahākulāṃ*. See Matsunaga 1978, 15, n. 13.
55. These are the *pañcānantarya,* 五無間, which are (1) killing one's father, (2) killing one's mother, (3) killing an arhat, (4) intentionally shedding the blood of a buddha, and (5) causing a schism in the Buddhist community or Sangha.
56. Here I translate the reading contained in a minority of manuscripts, *mahāyānāgradharmeṣu* (Matsunaga 1978, 15, n. 27), rather than the reading Matsunaga adopted, *-dharmatām.* The former reading not only makes more sense but also more closely matches the Tibetan translation, *theg chen mchog gi chos su* (D fol. 97b).
57. My translation, *Guhyasamāja Tantra,* from the Sanskrit at Matsunaga 1978, 15, vv. 1–7; and Tibetan at D fol. 97a.5-b.
58. My translation, 佛說一切如來金剛三業最上祕密大教王經, T.885.18.474a.1-15.
59. Willemen 1983, 29.
60. See Behr 2004, 182–185, for a discussion of the cultural and linguistic chauvinism of China's elite.
61. While the Bon tradition of Tibet did develop sophisticated doctrinal systems, it seems to have done so with significant dependence upon Indian Buddhist systems, and this development was ongoing during the later dissemination period. While Tibetans did have complex ritual systems and oral textual traditions prior to the transmission of Buddhism, and, with it, writing, to Tibet, they do not reach at this time the level of sophistication of Confucian thought, which was, when Buddhism arrived in China during the Later Han Dynasty, a completely independent system of thought. For an excellent study of Bon thought that also highlights its interdependence with Buddhist traditions see Klein and Geshe Tenzin Wangyal Rinpoche 2006.
62. Vilāsavajra was one of the preceptors of Buddhajñānapāda, who served at the newly founded Vikramaśīla under King Dharmapāla. See Davidson 1981, 6 and 2002a, 311. He thus contributed to one of the major traditions of Guhyasamāja exegesis, the Jñānapāda school founded by Buddhajñānapāda.
63. Ronald Davidson has argued that the ninth century was the era when tantric commentarial systematization occurred (2002c, 56ff.), and based on

my own studies of tantric commentarial literature, I believe that this is a correct estimate. Mimaki and Tomabechi have argued that the Ārya texts were most likely composed during the ninth or tenth centuries (1994, ix). Wedemeyer has argued that Āryadeva's *Caryāmelāpakapradīpa* was composed c. 850–1000 (2007, 14). The ninth- to tenth-century estimate for the Ārya texts thus seems sound.

64. This text gives a somewhat uncommon translation of *bhageṣu,* namely *dkyil na,* which would probably be best translated as "within," given *dkyil*'s sematic range, i.e., "center, core, essence," etc. However, there is no doubt that this is a translation of *bhaga,* as the term is transliterated later in the chapter. See To. 1910, 91b.
65. During the eighth century when Vilāsavajra was writing, the term *samayamudrā* usually designated either symbolic hand gestures or attributes of buddhas and bodhisattvas (Saunders 1960, 36–37). I am not sure why he would gloss the term *yoṣit* in this manner, unless he considers her to be an attribute of Mahāvairocana here.
66. The term *dharmodaya,* "origin of things," is a well-known euphemism for *bhaga*. Regarding this see Gray 2007, 181, n. 1.
67. Here I read *ya* as *yā*.
68. Vilāsavajra is here is making a pun on the term *bhagavat,* which literally means "he who is possessed of *bhaga.*" The term *bhaga* has several meanings, one of which is vulva, the other being "booty" or "loot," a *bhagavat* being a successful war leader. This was a military term redeployed for religious use.
69. My translation, Vilāsavajra, *Śrīguhyasamājatantranidānagurūpadeśanavyākhyāna*, fol. 91b.
70. Regarding this see Dalton 2004b, 7–21.
71. My translation, Vilāsavajra, *Śrīguhyasamājatantranidānagurūpadeśanavyākhyāna*, fol. 92a.
72. Although Vilāsavajra does not explicitly state which text he is referring to here, there were several text circulating by the mid-eighth century that lacked a *nidāna* and begin with the word *atha* instead. These include two works with which he was definitely familiar, including the *Ma ñjuśrīnāmasaṃgīti,* on which he wrote a commentary (To. 2533), and the *Sarvabuddhasamāyoga-ḍākinījālasamvara Tantra,* which he repeatedly quotes in that work (see Gray 2007, 13, n. 41). One might note that the *Mahāvairocanābhisambodhi Tantra* also appears to have originally lacked the standard *nidāna*, and Buddhaguhya provides a fascinating justification of this absence (Hodge 2003, 47). Since Buddhaguhya was a

contemporary of Vilāsavajra (Hodge estimates that his commentary was composed c. 760; 2003, 17), it is possible that Vilāsavajra was responding to commentary such as his.

73. This translates the Sanskrit *ākāśārtha*. The Tibetan here reads "path of space" (*nam mkha'i lam*), which corresponds to the Sanskrit reading *ākāśapatha* found in a minority of manuscripts.
74. This translates the Sanskrit *ākāśavāk-*. The Tibetan here reads "path of space" (*nam mkha'i lam*), which corresponds to the Sanskrit reading *ākāśapatha-* found in a minority of manuscripts.
75. My translation from the Sanskrit edited in Matsunaga 1978, 15–16, and the Tibetan at fol. 97a-98a.
76. The placing of "doubts" in the mind of a straw man, which are then promptly dispelled by the Buddha or some other authoritative figure, is a rhetorical strategy commonly employed in Mahāyāna texts. A classic example is the *Vimālakīrtinirdeśa Sūtra,* in which Śāriputra repeatedly plays the role of the straw man (e.g., see Gómez and Harrison 2022, 15–16). This undoubtedly represents an attempt to preempt questions concerning the orthodoxy of the text. For a similar example in the context of Chinese tantric Buddhism see Orzech 1998, 83.
77. As indicated in verse 5, translated in section 5.1.2.
78. Here I translate the Chinese 壇 as maṇḍala, one of the possible meanings of the term, rather than "altar" like Giebel (1995, 193). While that is the most common meaning of the term, it does not seem appropriate in this context.
79. Translated in Giebel 1995, 193, with an emendation by me as noted above, from the text at T. 869, p. 287ab.
80. Here I follow the Tibetan, *dus gsum 'byung ba'i sangs rgyas rnams* (To. 422, 103a), a reading supported by the Sanskrit *taikālyasambhūtabuddhān* (Matsunaga 1978, p. 26 n. 18), which should be corrected to *traikālyasa mbhūtabuddhān.* Matsunaga adopts the reading "Buddha multitude," *buddhasya prabhūtāṃ* (1978, 26).
81. Here I translate the Sanskrit *kāyavākcittasaṃyogaṃ*; I understand this as referring to the group "all Tathāgatas" often associated in this text with "body, speech, and mind." Several manuscripts read *saṃbhogaṃ* instead of *saṃyogaṃ*, and this reading is supported by the Tibetan *sku gsung thugs kyi longs spyod* (fol. 103a).
82. This verb is omitted in the Sanskrit but occurs in the Tibetan (*skye bar 'gyur,* fol. 103a).

83. My translation of *Guhyasamāja Tantra* (GT) 9.3-6 from the Sanskrit edited in Matsunaga 1978, 26, and the Tibetan at fol. 103a.
84. I.e., *haraṇaṃ sarvadravyānāṃ,* GT 9.9a, Matsunaga 1978, 27.
85. My translation of GT 9.14 from the Sanskrit edited in Matsunaga 1978, 27, and the Tibetan at fol. 103b.
86. I.e., *mṛṣāvādaṃ,* GT 9.17a, Matsunaga 1978, 27.
87. I.e., *pāruṣyavacanādyais,* GT 9.20e, Matsunaga 1978, 28.
88. My translation of a GT prose passage from Matsunaga 1978, 28.
89. For a translation and study of this text see Śāntideva 2008.
90. Harvey 2000, 78–79.
91. This is usually defined as harsh or abusive speech, which more or less covers *pāruṣyavacana.* "Wrong speech" often is defined as including idle speech and gossip as well. See Harvey 2000, 76.
92. I have argued this with respect to the exegetical tradition associated with the *Cakrasaṃvara Tantra;* see Gray 2005b.
93. The *Śrīvajramālābhidhānamahāyogatantra* appears to be a product of the Ārya school of Guhyasamāja exegesis; it is quoted extensively by Candrakīrti is his "Illuminating Lamp" *Pradīpoddyotana* commentary, and it is also quoted by Āryādeva in his "Lamp That Integrates the Practices" *Caryāmelāpakapradīpa,* and it is intertextually connected to Nāgarjuna's "Five Stages" *pañcakrama* commentary. Given the dating of the Ārya tradition to circa 850–1000, it seems likely that this work was composed toward the beginning of the period, circa the mid-ninth century. See Kittay and Lozang Jamspal 2020, 5–6.
94. The "three gnoses" (*jñānatraya*) are, according to the Tibetan commentator Tsongkhapa, the "three luminances," luminance, radiance, and immanence (Kittay and Lozang Jamspal 2020, 520, n. 753), which are signs (*nimitta*) that appear with the dissolution and reappearance of the subtle body in perfection stage practice.
95. Literally, "he who has the vajra"; it refers here to the male partner in the visualized deity couple.
96. My translation, *Śrīvajramālābhidhānamahāyogatantra-sarvatantrahṛdayarahasyavibhaṅga,* fol. 265a-b; cf. Kittay and Lozang Jamspal 2020, 357–358.
97. E.g., the third ornament is the "six parameters," which entails analyzing scripture in terms of interpretable and definitive meaning, intentional and unintentional speech, and literal and symbolic speech, while the fourth ornament is the "four interpretations," which entails

distinguishing linguistic meaning, common meaning, hidden meaning, and ultimate meaning. See Campbell and Thurman 2020, 112–114.

98. For a translation of Candrakīrti's introduction see Campbell and Thurman 2020, 110–117. For an overview of Candrakīrti's exegetical system see Thurman 1988.
99. Translated in Campbell and Thurman 2020, 125.
100. See ibid., 125 ff.
101. See my translation in section 5.1.2.
102. Campbell and Thurman 2020, 217.
103. Ibid., 218.
104. For a translation of this text see Davidson 1995, 301.
105. My translation from Atiśa's *Bodhimārgadīpapañjikā*, fol. 290a-b.
106. See Bühnemann 1992, 122–123.
107. E.g., see Abhayākaragupta, *Vajrāvalī-nāma-maṇḍalasādhana*, fol. 61b.
108. My translation of ibid., fol. 67a.
109. Faure 1998, 86.
110. Filliozat 1991, 333.
111. My translation, Buddhajñāna, *Dvikramatattvabhāvana-nāma-mukhāgama*, fol. 6b.
112. See Campbell 1996 for an account of this behavior by a prominent Tibetan lama.

Bibliography

Primary Sources

Abhayākaragupta. *Vajrāvalī-nāma-maṇḍalasādhana*. dkyil 'khor gyi cho ga rdo rje phreng ba zhes bya ba [Meditation Manual for Mandalas Called the Diamond Array]. To. 3140, D rgyud 'grel vol. phu, 1b-94b.

Abhidhānottaratantra. mngon par brjod pa'i rgyud bla ma zhes bya ba [Discourse Appendix Tantra]. To. 369, D rgyud 'bum vol. ka, 247a-370a.

Amoghavajra [不空金刚]. 金刚頂经瑜伽十八会指归 [Index of the Adamantine Pinnacle Scripture Yoga in Eighteen Sections]. T.18.869.284c18-287.c14.

Amoghavajra [不空金刚]. 金刚頂经大瑜伽祕密心地法门义诀 [Instructions on the Gate to the Teachings on Secret Heart of the Great Yoga of the Adamantine Pinnacle Scripture]. T.39.1798.808a1-821a20.

Āryaḍākinīvajrapañjara-mahātantrarājakalpa. 'phags pa mkha' 'gro ma rdo rje gur zhes bya ba'i rgyud kyi rgyal po chen po'i brtag pa [Precept of the Great Sovereign Tantra Called the Noble Ḍākinīs' Adamantine Cage]. To. 419, D rgyud 'bum vol. nga, 30a-65b.

Āryavidyottama-mahātantra. 'phags pa'i rig pa mchog gi rgyud chen po [Noble Supreme Spell Great Tantra]. To. 746, D rgyud 'bum vol. dza 1b-237b.

Asaṅga. *Mahāyānasaṃgraha*. theg pa chen po bsdus pa [Summary of the Mahāyāna]. To. 4048, D sems tsam vol. ri, 1b-43a.

Atiśa Dīpaṅkaraśrījñāna. *Abhisamayavibhaṅga*. mngon par rtogs pa rnam par 'byed pa zhes bya ba [Analysis of *The Realization*]. To. 1490, D rgyud 'grel vol zha, 186a–202b.

Atiśa Dīpaṅkaraśrījñāna. *Bodhimārgadīpapañjikā-nāma*. byang chub lam gyi sgron ma'i dka' 'grel zhes bya ba [Lamp for the Path to Awakening Commentary]. To. 3948, D dbu ma vol. khi 241a-293a.

Bhavabhaṭṭa. *Śrīcakrasamvarapañjikā*. dpal 'khor lo sdom pa'i dka' 'grel shes bya ba [Commentary on the Glorious Supreme Bliss of the Wheels]. To. 1403, D rgyud 'grel vol. ba, 141a–246b. Sanskrit and Tibetan edited in Pandey 2002.

Buddhaguhya. *rnam par snang mdzad mngon par byang chub pa'i rgyud chen po'i 'grel bshad* [Detailed Commentary on the Awakening of Mahāvairocana Tantra]. To. 2663, D rgyud 'grel vol. nyu, 261a-351a.

Buddhajñāna. *Dvikramatattvabhāvana-nāma-mukhāgama.* rim pa gnyis pa'i de kho na nyid bsgom pa shes bya ba'i zhal gyi lung [Oral Instructions Called The Two-Staged Meditation on Reality]. To.1853, D rgyud 'bum vol. di 1b-17b.

Bu ston Rin chen grub. *rgyud sde spyi'i rnam par gzhag pa rgyud sde rin po che'i mdzes rgyan zhes bya ba* [General Arrangement of the Classes of Tantras Called the Precious Ornament of Tantric Classes]. In *The Collected Works of Bu-ston*, edited by Lokesh Chandra, vol. ba, 1–610. New Delhi: International Academy of Indian Culture, 1966.

Bu ston Rin chen grub. *bde mchog nyung ngu rgyud kyi spyi rnam don gsal* [Illumination of the General Meaning of the Supreme Bliss Light Tantra]. In *The Collected Works of Bu-ston*, edited by Lokesh Chandra, vol. cha, 1–118. New Delhi: International Academy of Indian Culture, 1966.

Cakrasaṃvara Tantra [Supreme Bliss of the Wheels Tantra]. *Tantrarāja-śrīlaghusaṃvara-nāma.* rgyud kyi rgyal po dpal bde mchog nyung ngu zhes bya ba [Sovereign Tantra Called Supreme Bliss Light]. To. 368, D rgyud 'bum vol. ka, 213b-246b. Sanskrit and Tibetan texts edited in Gray 2012.

Ḍākārṇava Tantra [Ocean of Warlocks Tantra]. *Śrīḍākārṇava-mahāyoginī-tantrarāja.* dpal mkha' 'gro rgya mtsho rnal 'byor ma'i rgyud kyi rgyal po chen po zhes bya ba [Great Yoginī King of Tantras Called the Ocean of Warlocks]. To. 372, D rgyud-'bum, vol. kha, 137a-264b.

Guhyasamāja Tantra. Sarvatathāgatakāyavākcittarahasya-guhyasamāja-nāma-mahākalparāja. Sanskrit edited in Matsunaga 1978.
Tibetan translation: de bzhin gshegs pa thams cad kyi sku gsung thugs kyi gsang chen gsang ba 'dus pa zhes bya ba brtag pa'i rgyal po chen po [Great Sovereign Precept Called the Esoteric Community, the Secret of the Body, Speech and Mind of all Tathāgatas]. To. 442, D rgyud 'bum vol. ca, 90a-148a.
Chinese translation: 佛說一切如來金剛三業最上祕密大教王經. T.885.18.469c-511b.

Hevajra Tantra. Sanskrit and Tibetan edited in Snellgrove 1959a.
Chinese translation: 佛說大悲空智金剛大教王儀軌經. T.892.18.587c-601c.

Indrabhūti. *Śrīcakrasaṃvaratantrarāja-saṃvarasamuccaya-nāma-vṛtti.* dpal 'khor lo sdom pa'i rgyud kyi rgyal po bde mchog bsdus pa zhes bya ba'i rnam par bshad pa [Commentary on the Glorious Binding of the Wheels King of Tantras Called the Assembly of Supreme Bliss]. To. 1413, D rgyud 'grel vol. tsa, 1a-119b.

*Indranāla [brgya byin sdang po]. *Sarvabuddhasamāyogaḍākinījālasaṃvarat antrārthodaraṭīkā.* dpal sangs rgyas thams cad dang mnyam par sbyor ba mkha' 'gro sgyu ma bde mchog gi rgyud kyi don rnam par bshad pa zhes bya ba [Detailed Exegesis of the Import of the Sarvabuddhasamāyogaḍākinījāla samvara Tantra]. To. 1659, D rgyud 'grel vol. ra, 245a-389a.

Jayabhadra. *Śrīcakrasamvara-mūlatantra-pañjikā* [Commentary on the Glorious Supreme Bliss of the Wheels Root Tantra].To. 1406, D rgyud 'grel vol. ma, 41a-69a. Sanskrit edited in Sugiki 2001.

Jñānamitra, *Prajñāpāramitānayaśatapañcāśatikāṭīkā*. 'phags pa shes rab kyi pha rol tu phyin pa tshul brgya lnga bcu pa'i 'grel pa [Commentary on the Method of the Perfection of Wisdom in 150 Stanzas]. To. 2647, D rgyud 'grel vol. ju, 272b-294a.

Jñānatilaka-yoginītantrarāja-paramamahādbhuta. dpal ye she thig le rnal 'byor ma'i rgyud kyi rgyal po chen po mchog tu rmad du byung ba [Supremely Wonderful Sovereign Yoginītantras Called the Gnostic Drop]. To. 422, D rgyud 'bum vol. nga, 96b-136b.

Kāṇha/Kṛṣṇācārya. *Guhyatattvaprakāśa*. gsang ba'i de kho nan yid ra btu gsal ba [Light on the Secret Reality]. To. 1450, D rgyud 'grel vol. wa, 349a-355b.

Kūkai (空海). *Dainichikyō-kaidai*. 大日經開題 [Introduction to the Mahāvairocana Sutra]. In T.2211.58.1.a1-12a17, and in *Kōbō daishi zenshū*, edited by Hase Hōshū, vol. 4, 1–10. Tokyo: Yoshikawa Kobunkan, 1911.

Kūkai (空海). *Sokushin jōbutsugi*. 即身成佛義 [Attaining Enlightenment in This Very Existence]. In Kōbō daishi zenshū, edited by Hase Hōshū, vol. 3, 90–104. Tokyo: Yoshikawa Kobunkan, 1910.

Kukurāja. dpal rdo rje sems pa'i gsang ba'i don rnam par dgod pa shes bya ba [Explanation of the Secret Meaning of Glorious Vajrasattva]. To. 1664, D rgyud 'grel vol. la, 116a-133b.

Laṅkāvatārasūtra [Descent to Laṅkā]. To. 107, D mdo sde vol. ca, 56a-191b. Sanskrit edited in Vaidya 1963.

Lūipa. *Cakrasaṃvarābhisamaya*. dpal bcom 'dan 'das mngon par rtogs pa zhes bya ba [Realization of the Cakrasaṃvara]. To. 1427, D rgyud 'grel vol. wa, 186b–193a. Sanskrit edited in Sakurai 1998.

Mañjuśrīnāmasaṃgīti. *MaMañjuMaśrMaīn*MaāmasaMa*ṃgñjuśrījñānasa ttvasya paramārthanāmasaṃgīti*. 'jam dpal ye shes sems dpa'i don dam pa'i mtshan yang dag par brjod pa [Litany of the Ultimate Names of the Gnostic Being Mañjuśrī]. To. 360, D rgyud 'bum vol. ka. Sanskrit edited in Davidson 1981.

Nāgabuddhi. *Samājasādhanavyavasthāli*. 'dus pa'i sgrub pa'i thabs rnam par gzhag pa'i rim pa zhes bya ba [Established Arrangement of the Community Meditation Manual]. To. 1809, D rgyud 'bum vol. ngi, 121a-130a.

Prajñāpāramitā-naya-śatapañcāśatikā. 'phags pa shes rab kyi pha rol tu phyin pa'i tshul brgya lnga bcu pa [Method of the Perfection of Wisdom in 150 Stanzas]. To. 489. D rgyud 'bum vol. ta, 266a-272a.

Rong-zom Chos-kyi-bzang-po. *gsang sngags rdo rje theg pa'i tshul las snang ba lhar sgrub pa* [The Attainment of Divine Vision in the Mantra-Vajrayāna]. In *Selected Writings (gsuṅ thor bu) of Roṅ-zom Chos-kyi-bzaṅ-po*, edited by 'Khor-gdoṅ Gter-sprul 'Chi-med-rig-'dzin, 125–151. Smanrtsis Shesrig Spendzod vol. 73. Leh: S. W. Tashigangpa, 1974.

Sampuṭa-nāma-mahātantra. yang dag par sbyor ba shes bya ba'i rgyud chen po [Great Tantra named "The Kiss"]. To. 381, D rgyud 'bum vol. ga, 73b-158b.

Sandhivyākaraṇa-nāma-tantra. dgongs pa lung bstan pa shes bya ba'i rgyud [Revelation of the Intention]. To. 444, D rgyud 'bum col. ca, 158a-208a.

Sarvabuddhasamāyogaḍākinījālasaṃvara [Ḍākinīs' Network That Unites All Buddhas]. *Śrī-sarvabuddhasamāyogaḍākinījālasaṃvara-nāma-uttaratantra.* dpal sangs rgyas thams cad dang mnyam par sbyor ba mkha' 'gro ma sgyu ma bde ba'i mchog ces bya ba'i rgyud phyi ma [Glorious Appendix Called the Ḍākinīs' Network that Unites All Buddhas]. To. 366, D vol. ka 151b-193a.

Sarvatathāgatakāyavākcittaguhyālaṃkāravyūha-tantrarāja. de bzhin gshegs pa thams cad kyi sku gsung thugs kyi gsang ba rgyan gyi bkod pa zhes bya ba'i rgyud kyi rgyal po [Sovereign Tantra Called the Array of Esoteric Ornaments of the Body, Speech and Mind of all Tathāgatas]. To. 492, D rgyud 'bum vol. tha, 83b-119a.

Sarvatathāgatakāyavākcittakṛṣṇayamāri-nāma-tantra. de bzhin gshegs pa thams cad kyi sku gsung thugs gshin rje gshed nag po zhes bya ba'i rgyud [Black Bane of Death, the Body Speech and Mind of All Tathāgatas Tantra]. To. 467, D rgyud 'bum vol. ja, 134b-151b.

Sarvatathāgatatattvasaṃgraha-nāma-mahāyāna-sūtra. de bzhin gshegs pa thams cad kyi de kho na nyid bsdus pa shes bya ba theg pa chen po'i mdo [Mahāyāna Sūtra Called the Compendium of the Realities of All Tathāgatas]. To. 479, D rgyud 'bum vol. nya, 1b-142a. Sanskrit text edited in Yamada 1981.

Sarvarahasya-nāma-tantrarāja [Universal Secret Sovereign Tantra].
Tibetan translation: thams cad gsang ba zhes bya ba rgyud kyi rgyal po. To. 481, D rgyud 'bum vol. ta, 1b-10a.
Chinese translation: 一切祕密最上名義大教王儀軌. T 888, 18.536-541.

Śrī-candraguhyatilaka-nāma-mahātantrarāja. dpal zla gsang thig le shes bya ba rgyud kyi rgyal po chen po [Great Sovereign Tantra Called the Glorious Moon's Secret Drop]. To. 477, D rgyud 'bum vol. ja, 247b-303.

Śrī-guhyagarbhatattvaviniścaya. dpal gsang ba'i snying po de kho na nyid rnam par nges pa [The Glorious Esoteric Essence that Ascertains Reality]. To. 832, D rnying rgyud vol. kha, 110b-132a.

Śrī-jñānatilaka-yoginītantrarāja-paramamahādbhuta-nāma. dpal ye shes thig le rnal 'byor ma'i rgyud kyi rgyal po chen po mchog tu rmad du byung ba zhes bya ba [The Supremely Wonderful Sovereign Yoginītantra Called the Gnostic Drop]. To. 422, D rgyud 'bum vol. nga, 96b-136b.

Śrīparamādya-mantrakalpakhaṇḍa. dpal mchog dang po snags kyi rtog pa'i dum bu zhes bya ba [Mantric Precept Division of the Glorious Supreme Prime]. To. 488, D rgyud 'bum vol. ta, 173a-265b.

Śrīparamādya-nāma-mahāyānakalparāja. dpal mchog dang po zhes bya ba theg pa chen po'i rtog pa'i rgyal po [Sovereign Mahāyāna Precept Called the Glorious Supreme Prime] To. 487, D rgyud 'bum vol. ta, 150b-173a; H rgyud vol. ja, 97a-135b; S rgyud vol. nya, 1b-35a.

Śrī-samvarakhasama-tantrarāja [Glorious Sky-like Great Bliss Sovereign Tantra]. To. 415, D rgyud 'bum vol. ga, 261b-263a.

Śrī-tattvapradīpa-nāma-mahāyoginītantrarāja. dpal de kho nan yid kyi sgron ma [Sovereign Yoginītantra Called the Glorious Light on Reality]. To. 423, D rgyud 'bum vol. nga 136b-142b.

Śrīvajrabhairava Tantra.

Tibetan translation: **Śrīvajrabhairava-nāma-tantrarāja*. dpal rdo rje 'jigs byed chen po'i rgyud ces bya ba [Great Tantra of Glorious Vajrabhairava]. To. 468, D rgyud-'bum vol. ja, 151b-164a.

Chinese translation: **Buddhabhāṣita-śrīvajrabhairava-mahāyogatantra-cakradhyāna-siddhikalpa*. 佛說妙吉祥瑜伽大教金剛陪囉縛輪觀想成就儀軌經 [Great Yogatantra of Glorious Vajrabhairava, Spoken by the Buddha, the Precept on Powers Through Visualization of the Wheel]. T.1242.21.203b–207b.

Śrīvajramālābhidhānamahāyogatantra-sarvatantrahṛdayarahasyavibhaṅga. rnal 'byor chen po'i rgyud rdo rje phreng ba mngon par brjod pa rgyud thams cad kyi snying po gsang ba rnam par phye ba zhe bya ba [Glorious Adamantine Rosary Discourse Great Yoga Tantra That Distinguishes the Secret That Is the Essence of all Tantras]. To. 445, D rgyud 'bum vol. ca, 208a-277b.

Sthiramati. *Sūtrālaṃkāravṛttibhāṣya*. mdo sde rgyan gyi 'grel bshad [Subcommentary on the Ornament of Sutras]. To. 4034, D sems tsam vol. mi, 1b-283a and vol. tsi, 1b-286a.

Śraddhākaravarma. *rnal 'byor bla na med pa'i rgyud kyi don la 'jug pa bsdus pa zhes bya ba* [Introductory Summary of the Import of the Unexcelled Yoga Tantras]. D rgyud-'bum vol. tsu, 104b-115a.

Śubhakarasiṃha (善无畏) and Yixing (一行). 大毘盧遮那成佛經疏 [Running Commentary on the Awakening of Mahāvairocana Sutra] T. 1796.39.579a-789c.

Tripiṭakamāla. *Nayatrayapradīpa*. tshul gsum gyi sgron ma [Light on the Three Methods]. To. 3707, D rgyud 'grel vol. tsu, 6b-26b.

Uttaratantra. rgyud phyi ma [Appendix Tantra]. To. 443, D rgyud 'bum vol. ca 148a-157b.

Vajraḍāka Tantra [Adamantine Warlock Tantra]. *Śrī-vajraḍāka-nāma-mahātantrarāja*. rgyud kyi rgyal po chen po dpal rdo rje mkha' 'gro shes bya ba [The Great Sovereign Tantra Called the Glorious Adamantine Warlock]. To. 370, D rgyud-'bum vol. kha, 1b-125a.

Vajragarbha. *Hevajrapiṇḍārthaṭīkā*. kye'i rdo rje bsdus pa'i don gyi rgya cher 'grel pa [Commentary on the Concise Meaning of Hevajra]. To. 1180. D rgyud 'grel vol. ka, 1b-126a.

**Vajragarbharatnarāja-tantra*. 最上大乘金剛大教寶王經 [Tantra on the Adamantine Womb King of Wealth]. T.1128.20.542-548.

Vajrapāṇi. *Laghutantraṭīkā*. mngon par brjod pa 'bum pa las phyung ba nyung ngu'i rgyud kyi bsdus pa'i don rnam par bshad pa shes bya ba To. 1402, D rgyud 'grel vol. ba, 78b-141a. Sanskrit edited in Cicuzza 2001.

Vajraśekhara-mahāguhyayogatantra. gsang ba rnal 'byor chen po'i rgyud rdo rje rtse mo [The Adamantine Pinnacle Secret Great Yoga Tantra]. To. 480, D rgyud 'bum vol. nya, 142b-274a.

Vilāsavajra. *Ārya-nāmasaṃgītiṭīkā-mantrārthāvalokinī-nāma*. mtshan yang dag par brjod pa'i rgya cher 'grel pa mtshan gsang sngags kyi don du rnam par lta ba [Commentary on the Noble Litany Called Beholding the Meaning of Mantra]. To. 2533, D rgyud 'grel vol. khu, 27b-115b.

Vilāsavajra. *Śrīguhyasamājatantranidānagurūpadeśana-vyākhyāna*. dpal gsang ba 'dus pa'i rgyud kyi gleng gshi bla ma'i man ngag gis bshad pa [Exposition of the Guru's Oral Instructions on the Background Verse of the Glorious Esoteric Community Tantra]. To.1910, D rgyud 'grel vol. phi 89b-97b.

Vīravajra. *Padārthaprakāśikā-nāma-śrīsaṃvaramūlatantraṭīkā. dpal bde mchog gi rtsa rgyud kyi rgya chen bshad pa tshig don rab tu gsal ba shes bya ba* [Commentary on the Glorious Bliss Root Tantra Called Light on the Word's Meaning]. To. 1412, D rgyud 'grel vol. ma, 353b-450a.

Yijing (義 淨). 大 唐 西 域 求 法 高 僧 傳 [Records of Eminent Monks of the Great Tang who Sought the Dharma in the Western Regions]. T.2066.51.1a1-12b12.

Modern Sources

Abé, Ryūichi. 1995. "Saichō and Kukai: A Conflict of Interpretations." *Japanese Journal of Religious Studies* 22.1–2: 103–137.

Abé, Ryūichi. 1999. *The Weaving of Mantra: Kukai and the Construction of Esoteric Buddhist Discourse*. New York: Columbia University Press.

Abe, Stanley K. 1990. "Art and Practice in a Fifth-Century Chinese Buddhist Cave Temple." *Ars Orientalis* 20: 1–31.

Abe, Stanley K. 1995. "Inside the Wonder House: Buddhist Art and the West." In *Curators of the Buddha: The Study of Buddhism Under Colonialism*, edited by Donald S. Lopez, Jr., 63–106. Chicago: University of Chicago Press.

Ahmad, Zahiruddin. 1995. *A History of Tibet by Ṅag-dBaṅ Blo-bZaṅ rGya-mTsho, The Fifth Dalai Lama*. Bloomington: Indiana University, Research Institute for Inner Asian Studies.

Almogi, Orna. 2014. "The Eighteen Mahāyoga Tantric Cycles: A Real Canon or the Mere Notion of One?" *Revue d'Etudes Tibétaines* 30 (October 2014): 47–110.

Almond, Philip C. 1988. *The British Discovery of Buddhism*. New York: Cambridge University Press.

Amoghavajra and Ian Astley-Kristensen. 1992. *The Rishukyō: The Sino-Japanese Tantric Prajñāpāramitā in 150 Verses, Amoghavajra's Version*. Tring, UK: Institute of Buddhist Studies.

Bade, David. 2016. "(Spi)ritual Warfare in 13th-Century Asia? International Reflections, the Balance of Powers, and the Tantric Buddhism of Kṛtangara and Khubilai Khan." In *Esoteric Buddhism in Medieval Maritime Asia: Networks of Masters, Texts, Icons*, edited by Andrea Acri, 141–159. Singapore: ISEAS-Yusaf Ishak Institute.

Bagchi, Prabodh Chandra. 1939. *Studies in the Tantra. Part I.* Calcutta: University of Calcutta.

Bagchi, Prabodh Chandra. 1944. "*Vajragarbhatantrarājasūtra:* A New Work of King Indrabodhi." *Sino-Indian Studies* 1.1: 23–59.

Bagchi, S., ed. 1970. *Mahāyāna-sūtrālaṅkāra of Asaṅga.* Buddhist Sanskrit Texts no. 13. Darbhanga: Mithila Institute of Post-Graduate Studies and Research in Sanskrit.

Beckwith, Christopher I. 1984. "A Hitherto Unnoticed Yüan-Period Collection Attributed to 'Phagspa." In *Tibetan and Buddhist Studies Commemorating the 200th Anniversary of the Birth of Alexander Csoma de Korös*, edited by Louis Ligeti, vol. 1, 9–16. New Delhi: Munshiram Manoharlal Publishers.

Beckwith, Christopher I. 1987. *The Tibetan Empire in Central Asia.* Princeton: Princeton University Press.

Behr, Wolfgang. 2004. "'To Translate' Is 'To Exchange' 譯者言易也—Linguistic Diversity and the Terms for Translation in Ancient China." In *Mapping Meanings: The Field of New Learning in Late Qing China*, edited by Michael Lackner and Natascha Vittinghoff, 173–209. Leiden and Boston: Brill.

Berger, Helen A., and Douglas Ezzy. 2009. "Mass Media and Religious Identity: A Case Study of Young Witches." *Journal for the Scientific Study of Religion* 48.3: 501–514.

Beyer, Stephan V. 1992. *The Classical Tibetan Language.* Albany: State University of New York Press.

Bianchi, Ester. 2009. "The 'Chinese Lama' Nenghai (1886–1967): Doctrinal Tradition and Teaching Strategies of a Gelukpa Master in Republican China." In *Buddhism Between Tibet and China,* edited by Matthew T. Kapstein, 295–326. Somerville, MA: Wisdom Publications.

Bodiford, William M. 2011. "Zen and Esoteric Buddhism." In *Esoteric Buddhism and the Tantras in East Asia*, edited by Charles D. Orzech, Henrik H. Sørensen, and Richard K. Payne, 924–935. Leiden and Boston: Brill.

Broido, Michael M. 1988. "Killing, Lying, Stealing, and Adultery: A Problem of Interpretation in the Tantras." In *Buddhist Hermeneutics*, edited by Donald S. Lopez, Jr., 71–118. Kuroda Institute Studies in East Asian Buddhism No. 6. Honolulu: University of Hawaii Press.

Brown, Peter. 1970. "Sorcery, Demons, and the Rise of Christianity from Late Antiquity into the Middle Ages." In *Witchcraft, Confessions & Accusations*, edited by Mary Douglas, 17–45. London: Tavistock.

Bubenik, Vit. 2003. "Prākrits and Apabhraṃśa." In *The Indo-Aryan Languages*, edited by George Cardona and Dhanesh Jain, 204–249. London: Routledge.

Bühnemann, Gudrun. 1992. "Some Remarks on the Date of Abhayākaragupta and the Chronology of His Works." *Zeitschrift der Deutschen Morgenländischen Gesellschaft* 142: 120–127.

Buswell, Robert E. 1990. "Prolegomenon to the Study of Buddhist Apocryphal Scriptures." In *Chinese Buddhist Apocrypha*, edited by Robert E. Buswell, 1–30. Honolulu: University of Hawaii Press.

Cabezón, José Ignacio. 2013. *The Buddha's Doctrine and the Nine Vehicles: Rog Bande Sherab's Lamp of the Teachings*. New York: Oxford University Press.

Campbell, John R. B., and Robert A. F. Thurman. 2020. *The Esoteric Community Tantra with the Illuminating Lamp, Volume I: Chapters 1–12*. New York/Somerville, MA: American Institute of Buddhist Studies/Wisdom Publications.

Campbell, June. 1996. *Traveller in Space: In Search of Female Identity in Tibetan Buddhism*. New York: George Braziller.

Cantwell, Cathy. 2020. *Dudjom Rinpoche's Vajrakīlaya Works: A Study in Authoring, Compiling, and Editing Texts in the Tibetan Revelatory Tradition*. Sheffield, UK and Bristol, CT: Equinox.

Cantwell, Cathy, and Robert Mayer. 2012. *A Noble Noose of Methods, the Lotus Garland Synopsis: A Mahāyoga Tantra and Its Commentary*. Wien: Verlag der Österreichische Akademie der Wissenschaften.

Capitanio, Joshua. 2011. "Esoteric Buddhist Elements in Daoist Ritual Manuals of the Song, Yuan, and Ming." In *Esoteric Buddhism and the Tantras in East Asia*, edited by Charles D. Orzech, Henrik H. Sørensen, and Richard K. Payne, 529–535. Leiden and Boston: Brill.

Cassinelli, C. W., and Robert B. Ekvall. 1969. *A Tibetan Principality: The Political System of Sa sKya*. Ithaca, NY: Cornell University Press.

Chan, Elsie. 2000. "Translation of Buddhist Scriptures into Chinese: A Power-Governed Discourse." In *Beyond the Western Tradition*, edited by Marilyn Gaddis Rose, 187–198. Binghamton: State University of New York, Center for Research in Translation.

Chandra, Lokesh. 1984. "Vaipulya Sūtras and the Tantras." In *Tibetan and Buddhist Studies Commemorating the 200th Anniversary of the Birth of Alexander Csoma de Korös*, edited by Louis Ligeti, vol. 2, 99–115. New Delhi: Munshiram Manoharlal Publishers.

Chattopadhyaya, Alaka. 1967. *Atīśa and Tibet*. Reprint, Delhi: Motilal Banarsidass, 1981.

Chattopadhyaya, Brajadulal. 1994. *Making of Early Medieval India*. Delhi: Oxford University Press.

Chaudhuri, Nagendra Narayan, ed. 1935. *Ḍākārṇavaḥ: Studies in the Apabramśa Texts of the Ḍākārṇava (Texts from Nepal 2)*. Calcutta Sanskrit Series No. 10. Calcutta: Metropolitan Printing and Publishing House.

Chen, John K., and Tina T. Chen, ed. *Chinese Medical Herbology and Pharmacology*. City of Industry, CA: Art of Medicine Press, 2004.

Ch'en, Kenneth. 1964. *Buddhism in China: A Historical Survey.* Princeton: Princeton University Press.

Cheung, Martha P. Y. 2005. "'To Translate' Means 'To Exchange'? A New Interpretation of the Earliest Chinese Attempts to Define Translation ('*fanyi*')." *Target* 17.1: 27–48.

Chimpa, Lama, and Alaka Chattopadhyaya, trans. 1990. *Tāranātha's History of Buddhism in India.* [1970]. Reprint, Delhi: Motilal Banarsidass.

Chou, Yi-Liang. 2006. "Tantrism in China." [1945]. Reprinted in *Tantric Buddhism in East Asia,* edited by Richard K. Payne, 33–60. Somerville, MA: Wisdom Publications.

Cicuzza, Claudio. 2001. *The Laghutantraṭīkā by Vajrapāṇi: A Critical Edition of the Sanskrit Text.* Serie Orientale Roma 86. Roma: Istituto Italiano per l'Africa e l'Oriente.

Cleary, Thomas. 1983. *Entry into the Inconceivable: An Introduction to Hua-yen Buddhism.* Honolulu: University of Hawaii Press.

Cleary, Thomas, trans. 1993. *The Flower Ornament Scripture: A Translation of the Avatamsaka Sutra.* Boston: Shambhala Publications.

Collins, Steven. 1990. "On the Very Idea of the Pali Canon." *Journal of the Pali Text Society* 15: 89–126.

Cook, Francis H. 1977. *Hua-yen Buddhism: The Jewel Net of Indra.* University Park: Pennsylvania State University Press.

Cozort, Daniel. 1986. *Highest Yoga Tantra: An Introduction to the Esoteric Buddhism of Tibet.* Ithaca, NY: Snow Lion Publications.

Cozort, Daniel. 1996. *The Sand Mandala of Vajrabhairava.* Ithaca, NY: Snow Lion Publications.

Dalton, Jacob P. 2004a. "The Early Development of the Padmasambhava Legend in Tibet: A Study of IOL Tib J 644 and Pelliot tibetain 307." *Journal of the American Oriental Society* 124.4: 759–772.

Dalton, Jacob P. 2004b. "The Development of Perfection: The Interiorization of Buddhist Ritual in the Eighth and Ninth Centuries." *Journal of Indian Philosophy* 32: 1–30.

Dalton, Jacob P. 2005. "A Crisis of Doxography: How Tibetans Organized Tantra During the 8th–12th Centuries." *Journal of the International Association of Buddhist Studies* 28.1: 115–181.

Dalton, Jacob P. and Sam van Schaik. 2006. *Tibetan Tantric Manuscripts from Dunhuang.* Brill's Tibetan Studies Library vol. 12. Leiden and Boston: Brill.

Dalton, Jacob P. 2011. *The Taming of the Demons: Violence and Liberation in Tibetan Buddhism.* New Haven: Yale University Press.

Dalton, Jacob P. 2016a. "How *Dhāraṇīs* Were Proto-Tantric: Liturgies, Ritual Manuals, and the Origins of the Tantras." In *Tantric Traditions in Transmission and Translation,* edited by David B. Gray and Ryan Richard Overbey, 199–229. New York: Oxford University Press.

Dalton, Jacob P. 2016b. *The Gathering of Intentions: A History of a Tibetan Tantra*. New York: Columbia University Press.

Davidson, Ronald M. 1981. "The Litany of the Names of Mañjuśrī: Text and Translation of the Mañjuśrīnāmasaṅgīti." In *Tantric and Taoist Studies in Honour of R. A. Stein*, edited by Michel Strickmann, 1–69. Mélanges chinois et bouddhiques, vol. 1. Brussels: Institut belge des hautes études chinoises.

Davidson, Ronald M. 1991. "Reflections on the Maheśvara Subjugation Myth: Indic Materials, Sa-skya-pa Apologetics, and the Birth of Heruka." *Journal of the International Association of Buddhist Studies* 14.2: 197–235.

Davidson, Ronald M. 1992. "Preliminary Studies on Hevajra's *Abhisamaya* and the *Lam-'bras Tshogs-bshad*." In *Tibetan Buddhism: Reason and Revelation*, edited by Steven D. Goodman and Ronald M. Davidson, 107–132. Albany: State University of New York Press.

Davidson, Ronald M. 1995. "Atiśa's a Lamp for the Path to Awakening." In *Buddhism in Practice*, edited by Donald Lopez, Jr., 290–301. Princeton: Princeton University Press.

Davidson, Ronald M. 1999. "Masquerading as *Pramāṇa*: Esoteric Buddhism and Epistemological Nomenclature." In *Dharmakīrti's Thought and Its Impact on Indian and Tibetan Philosophy*, edited by Katsura Shoryu, 25–35. Wien: Verlag der Österreichischen Akademie der Wissenschaften.

Davidson, Ronald M. 2002a. *Indian Esoteric Buddhism: A Social History of the Tantric Movement*. New York: Columbia University Press.

Davidson, Ronald M. 2002b. "Gsar ma Apocrypha: The Creation of Orthodoxy, Gray Texts, and the New Revelation." In *The Many Canons of Tibetan Buddhism*, edited by Helmut Eimer and David Germano, 203–224. Leiden and Boston: Brill.

Davidson, Ronald M. 2002c. "Reframing *Sahaja*: Genre, Representation, Ritual and Lineage." *Journal of Indian Philosophy* 30: 45–83.

Davidson, Ronald M. 2005. *Tibetan Renaissance: Tantric Buddhism in the Rebirth of Tibetan Culture*. New York: Columbia University Press.

Davidson, Ronald M. 2009. "Studies in Dhāraṇī Literature I: Revisiting the Meaning of the Term *Dhāraṇī*." *Journal of Indian Philosophy* 37: 97–147.

Dayal, Har. 1932. *The Bodhisattva Doctrine in Buddhist Sanskrit Literature*. London: Routledge & Kegan Paul. Reprint, Delhi: Motilal Banarsidass, 1970.

Decleer, Hubert. 1995. "Atiśa's Journey to Sumatra." In *Buddhism in Practice*, edited by Donald S. Lopez, Jr., 532–540. Princeton: Princeton University Press.

Decleer, Hubert. 1997. "Atiśa's Journey to Tibet." In *Religions of Tibet in Practice*, edited by Donald S. Lopez, Jr., 157–177. Princeton: Princeton University Press.

Dharmacakra Translation Committee. 2020. *The Practice Manual of Noble Tārā Kurukullā*, version 2.42.6. 84000.co. https://read.84000.co/translation/toh437.html (accessed March 28, 2022).

Dharmacakra Translation Committee. 2021. *The Bhūtaḍāmara Tantra,* version 1.0.4. 84000.co. https://read.84000.co/translation/toh747.html (accessed March 15, 2022).

Dharmacakra Translation Committee. 2022. *The Noble Sovereign Ritual of Amoghapāśa,* version 1.0.3. 84000.co. https://read.84000.co/translation/toh686.html (accessed March 16, 2022).

Dolce, Lucia. 2011. "Taimitsu: The Esoteric Buddhism of the Tendai School." In *Esoteric Buddhism and the Tantras in East Asia*, edited by Charles D. Orzech, Henrik H. Sørensen, and Richard K. Payne, 744–767. Leiden and Boston: Brill.

Dotson, Brandon. 2007. "'Emperor' Mu rug btsan and the *'Phang thang ma Catalogue*." *Journal of the International Association of Tibetan Studies* 3: 1–25.

Dowman, Keith, trans. 1984. *Sky Dancer: The Secret Life and Songs of the Lady Yeshe Tsogyel.* London: Routledge & Kegan Paul.

Dudjom Rinpoche. 1991. *The Nyingma School of Tibetan Buddhism, Its Fundamentals and History.* Translated by Gyurme Dorje and Matthew Kapstein. Boston: Wisdom Publications.

Eastman, Elizabeth. 2009. "Incense at a Funeral: The Rise and Fall of an American Shingon Temple." In *TransBuddhism: Transmission, Translation, Transformation*, edited by Nalini Bhushan, Jay L. Garfield, and Abraham Zablocki, 69–85. Amherst: University of Massachusetts Press.

Edgerton, Franklin. 1936. "The Prakrit Underlying Buddhistic Hybrid Sanskrit." *Bulletin of the School of Oriental Studies* 8.2/3: 501–516.

Edgerton, Franklin. 1953. *Buddhist Hybrid Sanskrit Grammar and Dictionary.* 2 vols. Reprint, Delhi: Motilal Banarsidass, 1998.

Elder, George Robert. 1978. *The Saṃpuṭa Tantra: Edition and Translation Chapters I–IV*. Dissertation, Columbia University.

Faure, Bernard. 1991. *The Rhetoric of Immediacy: A Cultural Critique of Chan/Zen Buddhism*. Princeton: Princeton University Press.

Faure, Bernard. 1998. *The Red Thread: Buddhist Approaches to Sexuality.* Princeton: Princeton University Press.

Faure, Bernard. 2003. *The Power of Denial: Buddhism, Purity, and Gender.* Princeton: Princeton University Press.

Filliozat, Jean. 1991. *Religion, Philosophy, Yoga*. Translated by Maurice Shukla. Delhi: Motilal Banarsidass.

Forte, Antonino. 1976. *Political Propaganda and Ideology in China at the End of the Seventh Century*. Napoli: Istituto Universitario Orientale.

Forte, Antonino. 1990. "The Relativity of the Concept of Orthodoxy in Chinese Buddhism: Chih-sheng's Indictment of Shih-li and the Proscription of the *Dharma Mirror Sūtra*." In *Chinese Buddhist Apocrypha*, edited by Robert E. Buswell, 239–249. Honolulu: University of Hawaii Press.

Foxeus, Niklas. 2016. "'I Am the Buddha, the Buddha Is Me': Concentration Meditation and Esoteric Modern Buddhism in Burma/Myanmar." *Numen* 63: 411–445.

Franke, Herbert. 1981. "Tibetans in Yüan China." In *China Under Mongol Rule*, edited by J. D. Langlois, Jr., 296–328. Princeton: Princeton University Press.

Gardner, Alexander. 2021. "The Eleventh Trungpa, Chogyam Trungpa." *The Treasury of Lives*. https://treasuryoflives.org/biographies/view/Eleventh-Trungpa-Chogyam-Trungpa/11231 (accessed April 20, 2022).

Gayley, Holly. 2018. "Revisiting the 'Secret Consort' (*gsang yum*) in Tibetan Buddhism." *Religions* 9.179:1–21. https://doi.org/10.3390/rel9060179.

Gellner, David N. 1991. "Ritualized Devotion, Altruism, and Meditatation: The Offering of the *Guru Maṇḍala* in Newar Buddhism." In *Indo-Iranian Journal* 34.3: 161–197.

George, Christopher S., ed. and trans. 1974. *The Caṇḍamahāroṣaṇa Tantra: Chapters I–VIII: A Critical Edition and English Translation*. American Oriental Series vol. 56. New Haven: American Oriental Society.

Germano, David. 1998. "Re-membering the Dismembered Body of Tibet: Contemporary Tibetan Visionary Movements in the People's Republic of China." In *Buddhism in Contemporary Tibet: Religious Revival and Cultural Identity*, edited by Melvyn C. Goldstein and Matthew T. Kapstein, 53–94. Berkeley: University of California Press.

Giebel, Rolf W. 1995. "The Chin-kang-ting ching yü-ch'ieh shih-pa-hui chih-kuei: An Annotated Translation." *Journal of Naritasan Institute for Buddhist Studies* 18: 107–201.

Giebel, Rolf W. 2011. "*Taishō* Volumes 18–21." In *Esoteric Buddhism and the Tantras in East Asia*, edited by Charles D. Orzech, Henrik H. Sørensen, and Richard K. Payne, 27–36. Leiden and Boston: Brill.

Gnoli, Raniero. 1960. *The Pramāṇavārttikam of Dharmakīrti: The First Chapter with the Autocommentary*. Roma: Istituto Italiana per il Medio ed Estremo Oriente.

Gold, Daniel. 1987. *The Lord as Guru: Hindi Sants in North Indian Tradition*. New York: Oxford University Press.

Gombrich, Richard. 1988. *Theravāda Buddhism: A Social History from Ancient Benares to Modern Colombo*. London: Routledge.

Gómez, Luis, and Paul Harrison, trans. 2022. *Vimalakīrtinirdeśa: The Teaching of Vimalakīrti*. Berkeley, CA: Mangalam Press.

Goodall, Dominic, ed. 2015. *The Niśvāsatattvasaṃhitā: The Earliest Surviving Śaiva Tantra*. Vol. 1. Pondicherry: Institute Français de Pondichéry.

Goodman, Howard L. 1998. *Ts'ao P'i Transcendent: The Political Culture of Dynasty-Founding in China at the End of the Han*. Seattle: Scripta Serica.

Goudriaan, Teun. 1978. *Māyā Divine and Human*. Delhi: Motilal Banarsidass.

Granoff, Phyllis. 2000. "Other People's Rituals: Ritual Eclecticism in Early Medieval Indian Religions." *Journal of Indian Philosophy* 28.4: 399–424.

Gray, David B. 2005a. "Eating the Heart of the Brahmin: Representations of Alterity and the Formation of Identity in Tantric Buddhist Discourse." *History of Religions* 45.1: 45–69.

Gray, David B. 2005b. "Disclosing the Empty Secret: Textuality and Embodiment in the *Cakrasamvara Tantra*." *Numen* 52.4 (2005): 417–444.

Gray, David B. 2007. *The Cakrasamvara Tantra: A Study and Annotated Translation*. New York: AIBS/CBS/THUS [Columbia University Press].

Gray, David B. 2009. "The Influence of the *Kālacakra*: Vajrapāṇi on Consort Meditation." In *As Long as Space Endures: Essays on the Kalacakra Tantra in Honor of His Holiness the Dalai Lama*, edited by Edward A. Arnold, 193–202. Ithaca, NY: Snow Lion Publications.

Gray, David B. 2012. *The Cakrasamvara Tantra: Editions of the Sanskrit and Tibetan Texts*. New York: AIBS/CBS/THUS [Columbia University Press].

Gray, David B. 2013. "Imprints of the 'Great Seal'—On the Expanding Semantic Range of the Term of Mudrā In Eighth Through Eleventh Century Indian Buddhist Literature." *Journal of the International Association of Buddhist Studies* 34.1-2 (2011; published in 2013): 421–481.

Gray, David B. 2017. *Tsong Khapa's Illumination of the Hidden Meaning: Maṇḍala, Mantra, and the Cult of the Yoginīs (An Annotated Translation of Chapters 1–24)*. New York: AIBS/CBS/THUS [Columbia University Press].

Gray, David B. 2019. *Tsong Khapa's Illumination of the Hidden Meaning: Yogic Vows, Conduct, and Ritual Praxis (An Annotated Translation of Chapters 25–51)*. New York: AIBS/CBS/THUS [Columbia University Press].

Gray, David B., and Ryan Richard Overbey, eds. 2016. *Tantric Traditions in Transmission and Translation*. New York: Oxford University Press.

Gray, David B., Olga Serbaeva, Iain Sinclair, and Tsunehiko Sugiki. *The Great Sovereign Mahāyoginītantra Called the Glorious Ocean of Ḍākas*. 84000.co, forthcoming.

Greenwold, Stephen Michael. 1974. "Buddhist Brahmans." *Archives Européennes de Sociologie* 15.1: 101–123.

Groner, Paul. 1984. *Saichō: The Establishment of the Japanese Tendai School*. Berkeley: University of California Press.

Gyatso, Janet. 1992. "Genre, Authorship and Transmission in Visionary Buddhism: The Literary Traditions of Thang-stong rGyal-po." In *Tibetan Buddhism: Reason and Revelation*, edited by Steven D. Goodman and Ronald M. Davidson, 95–106. Albany: State University of New York Press.

Hakeda, Yoshito S. 1972. *Kūkai: Major Works*. New York: Columbia University Press.

Harrison, Paul. M. 1978. "Buddhānusmṛti in the Pratyutpanna-buddha-saṃmukhāvasthita-samādhi-sūtra." *Journal of Indian Philosophy* 9: 35–57.

Harvey, Peter. 2000. *An Introduction to Buddhist Ethics*. Cambridge: Cambridge University Press.

Heesterman, J. C. 1985. *The Inner Conflict of Tradition: Essays in Indian Ritual, Kingship and Society*. Chicago: University of Chicago Press.

Herrmann-Pfandt, Adelheid. 2002. "The Lhan Kar Ma as a Source for the History of Tantric Buddhism." In *The Many Canons of Tibetan Buddhism*, edited by Helmut Eimer and David Germano, 129–149. Leiden: Brill.

Herzog, Werner. 2003. "Wheel of Time." DVD. Werner Herzog Filmproduktion.

Hikosaka, Shu. 1998. "The Potiyil Mountain in Tamil Nadu and the Origin of the Avalokiteśvara Cult." In *Buddhism in Tamil Nadu: Collected Papers*, edited by G. John Samuel and Ār. Śivagaṇēśamūrti, 119–141. Chennai: Institute of Asian Studies.

Hodge, Stephen. 1994. "Considerations on the Dating and Geographic Origins of the *Mahāvairocanābhisaṃbodhi-sūtra*." In *The Buddhist Forum, Volume III: Seminar Papers 1991–1993*, edited by Tadeusz Skorupski and Ulrich Pagel, 57–83. London: School of Oriental and African Studies, University of London.

Hodge, Stephen. 2003. *The Mahā-vairocana-abhisaṃbodhi Tantra, with Buddhaguhya's Commentary*. London: RoutledgeCurzon.

Hopkins, Jeffrey. 1977. *Tantra in Tibet*. London: George, Allen & Unwin. Rev. ed., Ithaca, NY: Snow Lion Publications, 2016.

Huber, Toni. 1999. *The Cult of Pure Crystal Mountain: Popular Pilgrimage and Visionary Landscape in Southeast Tibet*. New York: Oxford University Press.

Hucker, Charles O. *The Censorial System of Ming China*. Stanford: Stanford University Press, 1966.

Hunink, Vincent. 2001. "Apology." In *Apuleius: Rhetorical Works*, edited by Stephen Harrison, 11–121. Oxford and New York: Oxford University Press.

Hurvitz, Leon. 1962. 智顗*Chih-I (538–597): An Introduction to the Life and Ideas of a Chinese Buddhist Monk*. Mélanges chinois et bouddhiques publiés par l'Institute belge des hautes études chinoises, douzième volume 1960–1962. Bruxelles: Juillet.

Hurvitz, Leon, trans. 1976. *Scripture of the Lotus Blossom of the Fine Dharma*. New York: Columbia University Press.

Inden, Ronald. 1990. *Imagining India*. London: Basil Blackwell.

Iyanaga, Nobumi. 1985. "Récits de la soumission de Maheśvara par Trailokyavijaya–d'après les sources chinoises et japonaises." In *Tantric and Taoist Studies in Honour of R.A. Stein*, edited by Michel Strickmann, 633–745. Brussels: Institut belge des hautes études chinoises.

Iyanaga, Nobumi. 1994. "Daikokuten." In *Hōbōgirin*, edited by Adrien Maisonneuve and Jean Maisonneuve, vol. 7, 839–920. Tokyo: Maison Franco-Japonaise.

Iyanaga, Nobumi. 1999. "Dākinī et l'Empereur—Mystique bouddhique de la royaut'e dans le Japon medieval." In *Reconfiguring Cultural Semiotics: The*

Construction of Japanese Identity, edited by Fabio Rambelli and Patrizia Violi, 41–111. Special Issue of *Versus* (*Quaderni di studi semiotici*) 83/84 (May-December 1999).

Iyanaga, Nobumi. 2011. "Tachikawa-Ryū." In *Esoteric Buddhism and the Tantras in East Asia*, edited by Charles D. Orzech, Henrik H. Sørensen, and Richard K. Payne, 803–814. Leiden and Boston: Brill.

Kapferer, Bruce. 1983. *A Celebration of Demons: Exorcism and the Aesthetics of Healing in Sri Lanka*. 2nd ed. Washington, DC: Smithsonian Institution Press, 1991.

Kapstein, Matthew. 1992. "Samantabhadhra and Rudra: Innate Enlightenment and Radical Evil in Tibetan Rnying-ma-pa Buddhism." In *Discourse and Practice*, edited by Frank Reynolds and David Tracy, 51–82. Albany: State University of New York Press.

Kapstein, Matthew T. 2000. *The Tibetan Assimilation of Buddhism: Conversion, Contestation, and Memory*. New York: Oxford University Press.

Kapstein, Matthew T. 2006. *The Tibetans*. Malden, MA: Blackwell.

Kapstein, Matthew T., ed. 2009. *Buddhism between Tibet and China*. Somerville, MA: Wisdom Publications.

Karmay, Samten G. 1980a. "The Ordinance of Lha Bla-ma Ye-shes-'od." In *Tibetan Studies in Honour of Hugh Richardson: Proceedings of the International Seminar of Tibetan Studies, Oxford 1979*, edited by Michael Aris and Aung San Suu Kyi, 150–162. Warminster: Aris & Phillips.

Karmay, Samten G. 1980b. "An Open Letter by the Pho-brang Zhi-ba-'od." *The Tibet Journal* 5: 2–28.

Karmay, Samten G. 1988. *The Great Perfection: A Philosophical and Meditative Teaching of Tibetan Buddhism*. Leiden: Brill.

Kawa Sherab Sangpo. 2013. "Analysis of Tibetan Language Prints Produced During the Yuan Period (hor spar ma)." *Inner Asia* 15.2: 201–224.

Keyworth, George A. 2011. "The Esotericization of Chinese Buddhist Practices." In *Esoteric Buddhism and the Tantras in East Asia*, edited by Charles D. Orzech, Henrik H. Sørensen, and Richard K. Payne, 515–519. Leiden and Boston: Brill.

Khetsun Sangpo. 1996. *Tantric Practice in Nying-ma*. Translated by Jeffrey Hopkins and Anne C. Klein. Ithaca, NY: Snow Lion Publications.

KIMURA Toshihiko. 1999. "A New Chronology of Dharmakirti." In *Dharmakirti's Thought and Its Impact on Indian and Tibetan Philosophy*, edited by Katsura Shoryu, 209–214. Wien: Verlag der Österreichischen Akademie der Wissenschaften.

Kittay, David, and Lobsang Jamspal, trans. 2020. *The Vajra Rosary Tantra (Śrī Vajramāla Tantra) by Vajradhara. An Explanatory Tantra of the Esoteric Community Tantra*. New York/Somerville, MA: American Institute of Buddhist Studies/Wisdom Publications.

Klein, Anne Carolyn, and Geshe Tenzin Wangyal Rinpoche. 2006. *Unbounded Wholeness: Dzogchen, Bon, and the Logic of the Nonconceptual*. Oxford and New York: Oxford University Press.

Kohn, Richard J. 2001. *Lord of the Dance: The Mani Rimdu Festival in Tibet and Nepal*. Albany: State University of New York Press.

KUO Liying. 2003. "Dakini." In *Hōbōgirin*, edited Hubert Durt, vol. 8, 1101. Paris: Librairie d'Amerique et d'Orient Adrien-Maisonneuve.

La Vallée Poussin, Louis de. 1988. Abhidharmakośabhāṣyam. Translated by Leo Pruden. 4 vols. Berkeley, CA: Asian Humanities Press.

Legge, James, trans. 1886. *A Record of Buddhist Kingdoms, Being an Account by the Chinese Monk Fa-Hien of his Travels in India and Ceylon (A.D. 399–414) in Search of the Buddhist Books of Discipline*. Oxford: Clarendon Press. Reprint, Mineola, NY: Dover Press, 1965.

LeVine, Sarah, and David N. Gellner. 2005. *Rebuilding Buddhism: The Theravāda Movement in Twentieth Century Nepal*. Cambridge, MA, and London: Harvard University Press.

Lewis, Mark Edward. 1990. "The Suppression of the Three Stages Sect: Apocrypha as a Political Issue." In *Chinese Buddhist Apocrypha*, edited by Robert E. Buswell, 207–238. Honolulu: University of Hawaii Press.

Lewis, Todd, and Naresh Man Bajracharya. 2016. "Vajrayāna Traditions in Nepal." In *Tantric Traditions in Transmission and Translation*, edited by David B. Gray and Ryan Richard Overbey, 87–198. New York: Oxford University Press.

Li, Rongxi, trans. 1995. *A Biography of the Tripiṭaka Master of the Great Ci'en Monastery of the Great Tang Dynasty*. Berkeley, CA: Numata Center for Buddhist Translation and Research.

Li, Rongxi, trans. 1996. *The Great Tang Dynasty Record of the Western Regions*. Moraga, CA: BDK America.

Lin, Li-Kouang. 1935. "Punyodaya (Na-T'i), un propagateur du tantrisme en Chine et au Cambodge à l'époque de Hiuan-tsang." *Journal Asiatique* 227: 83–100.

Liu, Xinru. 1994. *Ancient India and Ancient China: Trade and Religious Exchanges AD 1–600*. Delhi: Oxford University Press.

Lo Bue, Erberto. 1987. "The Dharmamaṇḍala-Sūtra by Buddhaguhya." In *Orientalia Iosephi Tucci Memoriae Dicata*, edited by G. Gnoli and L. Lanciotti, 787–818. *Serie Orientale Roma* 56.2.

Lopez, Donald S. 1995. "Authority and Orality in the Mahāyāna." *Numen* 42: 21–47.

LU Sheng-yen. 1995. *A Complete and Detailed Exposition on the True Buddha Tantric Dharma*. Translated by Janny Chow. San Bruno, CA: Purple Lotus Society.

Luhrmann, Tanya. 1988. *Persuasions of the Witch's Craft*. London: Blackwell.

Luhrmann, Tanya. 2012. *When God Talks Back*. New York: Vintage Books.

Makransky, John J. 1997. *Buddhahood Embodied: Sources of Controversy in India and Tibet*. Albany: State University of New York Press.

Mather, Richard B. 1968. "Vimalakīrti and Gentry Buddhism." In *History of Religions* 8.1: 60–73.

MATSUNAGA Yukei. 1964. "A Doubt to Authority of the Guhyasamāja-Ākhyāna-Tantras." *Journal of Indian and Buddhist Studies* 12.2: 16–25.

MATSUNAGA Yukei. 1977. "A History of Tantric Buddhism in India with Reference to Chinese Translations." In *Buddhist Thought and Asian Civilization: Essays in Honor of Herbert V. Guenther*, edited by Leslie S. Kawamura and Keith Scott, 167–181. Emeryville, CA: Dharma Publishing.

MATSUNAGA Yukei, ed. 1978. *The Guhyasamāja Tantra*. Osaka: Toho Shuppan.

Mayer, Robert. 1996. *A Scripture of the Ancient Tantra Collection: The Phur-pa bcu-gnyis*. Oxford: Kiscadale Publications.

Mayer, Robert. 2020. "Gter ston and Tradent: Innovation and Conservation in Tibetan Treasure Literature." In *Dudjom Rinpoche's Vajrakīlaya Works: A Study in Authoring, Compiling, and Editing Texts in the Tibetan Revelatory Tradition*, authored and edited by Cathy Cantwell, 30–46. Sheffield, UK, and Bristol, CT: Equinox.

McBride, Richard D. II. 2018. "Wish-Fulfilling Spells and Talismans, Efficacious Resonance, and Trilingual Spell Books: The Mahāpratisarā-dhāraṇī in Chosŏn Buddhism." *Pacific World* 3.20: 55–93.

McMahan, David. 1998. "Orality, Writing, and Authority in South Asian Buddhism: Visionary Literature and the Struggle for Legitimacy in the Mahāyāna." *History of Religions* 37.3: 249–274.

Meinert, Carmen. 2009. "Gangkar Rinpoché Between Tibet and China: A Tibetan Lama Among Ethnic Chinese in the 1930s to 1950s." In *Buddhism Between Tibet and China*, edited by Matthew T. Kapstein, 215–238. Somerville, MA: Wisdom Publications.

Mimaki, Katsumi, and Tōru Tomabechi. 1994. *Pañcakrama: Sanskrit and Tibetan Texts Critically Edited with Verse Index and Facsimile Edition of the Sanskrit Manuscripts*. Bibliotheca Codicum Asiaticorum. Vol. 8. Tokyo: Centre for East Asian Cultural Studies for Unesco, Toyo Bunko.

Mullin, Glenn H. 1996. *Tsongkhapa's Six Yogas of Naropa*. Ithaca, NY: Snow Lion Publications.

Nagao, Gadjin. M. 1991. *Mādhyamika and Yogācāra*. Translated by Leslie S. Kawamura. Albany: State University of New York Press.

Namai, Chishō Mamoru. 1997. "On *Bodhicittabhāvanā* in the Esoteric Buddhist Tradition." In *Tibetan Studies: Proceedings of the Seventh Seminar of the International Association for Tibetan Studies, Graz 1995*, edited by Ernst Steinkellner, vol. 2, 657–668. Wein: Verlag der Österreichischen Akademieder Wissenschaften.

Nanjiu, Bunyiu. 1883. *A Catalogue of the Chinese Translation of the Buddhist Tripiṭaka: The Sacred Canon of the Buddhists in China and Japan*. London: Oxford University Press. Reprint, Onsabrück: Biblio Verlag, 1988.

Newman, John. 1988. "Buddhist Sanskrit in the Kālacakra Tantra." *Journal of the International Association of Buddhist Studies* 11.1: 123–140.

Newman, John. 1998. "The Epoch of the Kālacakra Tantra." *Indo-Iranian Journal* 41.4: 319–349.

Nihom, Max. 1998. "The Maṇḍala of Caṇḍi Gumpung (Sumatra) and the Indo-Tibetan Vajraśekharatantra." *Indo-Iranian Journal* 41.2: 245–254.

Obeyesekere, Gananath. 2012. *The Awakened Ones: Phenomenology of Visionary Experience*. New York: Columbia University Press.

O'Flaherty, Wendy Doniger. 1973. *Asceticism and Eroticism in the Mythology of Śiva*. New York: Oxford University Press.

Orofino, Giacomella. 1994a. "Divination with Mirrors: Observations on a Simile Found in the Kālacakra Literature." In *Tibetan Studies: Proceedings of the 6th Seminar of the International Association of Tibetan Studies. Fagernes 1992*, edited by Per Kvarene, vol. 2, 612–629. Oslo: Institute for Comparative Research in Human Culture.

Orofino, Giacomella. 1994b. *Sekoddeśa: A Critical Edition of the Tibetan Translations*. Serie Orientale Roma. Vol. 72. Roma: Istituto Italiano per il Medio ed Estremo Oriente.

Orzech, Charles. 1995. "Legend of the Iron Stūpa." In *Buddhism in Practice*, edited by Donald S. Lopez, Jr., 314–317. Princeton: Princeton University Press.

Orzech, Charles D. 1996. "Maṇḍalas on the Move: Reflections from Chinese Esoteric Buddhism Circa 800 C. E." *Journal of the International Association of Buddhist Studies* 19.2: 209–243.

Orzech, Charles D. 1998. *Politics and Transcendent Wisdom: The Scripture for Humane Kings in the Creation of Chinese Buddhism*. University Park: Pennsylvania State University Press.

Orzech, Charles D. 2006. "Looking for Bhairava: Exploring the Circulation of Esoteric Texts Produced by the Song Institute for Canonical Translation." *Pacific World* 3.8: 139–166.

Orzech, Charles D. 2011a. "After Amoghavajra: Esoteric Buddhism in the Late Tang." In *Esoteric Buddhism and the Tantras in East Asia*, edited by Charles D. Orzech, Henrik H. Sørensen, and Richard K. Payne, 315–335. Leiden and Boston: Brill.

Orzech, Charles D. 2011b. "Translation of Tantras and Other Esoteric Buddhist Scriptures." In *Esoteric Buddhism and the Tantras in East Asia*, edited by Charles D. Orzech, Henrik H. Sørensen, and Richard K. Payne, 439–450. Leiden and Boston: Brill.

Orzech, Charles D., Richard K. Payne, and Henrik H. Sørensen. 2011. "Introduction: Esoteric Buddhism and the Tantras in East Asia: Some Methodological Considerations." In *Esoteric Buddhism and the Tantras in*

East Asia, edited by Charles D. Orzech, Henrik H. Sørensen, and Richard K. Payne, 3–18. Leiden and Boston: Brill.

Padoux, André. 2002. "What Do We Mean by Tantrism?" In *The Roots of Tantra*, edited by Katherine Anne Harper and Robert L. Brown, 17–24. Albany: State University of New York Press.

Pandey, Janardan Shastri, ed. 2002. *Śrīherukābhidhānam Cakrasamvaratantram with the Vivṛti Commentary of Bhavabhaṭṭa*. Rare Buddhist Texts Series no. 26. 2 vols. Sarnath: Central Institute of Higher Tibetan Studies.

Payne, Richard K. 1991. *The Tantric Ritual of Japan, Feeding the Gods: The Shingon Fire Ritual*. New Delhi: Aditya Prakashan.

Payne, Richard K. 2016. "Fire on the Mountain: The Shugendō *Saitō Goma*." In *Homa Variations: The Study of Ritual Change Across the Longue Durée*, edited by Richard K. Payne and Michael Witzel, 337–370. New York: Oxford University Press.

Payne, Richard K. 2021. "A Pragmatics of Ritual: The Yoshida Goma at the Interface of Shintō and Shingon." *Religions* 12.884: 1–18. https://doi.org/10.3390/rel12100884.

Payne, Richard K., and Michael Witzel, eds. 2016. *Homa Variations: The Study of Ritual Change Across the Longue Durée*. New York: Oxford University Press, 2016.

Petech, Luciano. 1983. "Tibetan Relations with Sung China and with the Mongols." In *China Among Equals: The Middle Kingdom and Its Neighbors, 10th–14th Centuries*, edited by Morris Rossabi, 173–203. Los Angeles: University of California Press.

Petech, Luciano. 1990. "Princely Houses of the Yüan Period Connected with Tibet." In *Indo-Tibetan Studies: Papers in Honour and Appreciation of Professor David L. Snellgrove's Contribution to Indo-Tibetan Studies*, edited by Tadeusz Skorupski, 257–269. Tring, UK: Institute of Buddhist Studies.

Pollock, Sheldon. 2005. "'Tradition' as 'Revelation': Śruti, Smṛti, and the Sanskrit Discourse of Power." In *Boundaries, Dynamics, and Construction of Traditions in South Asia*, edited by Federico Squarcini, 41–61. Florence: Florence University Press.

Pranke, Patrick. 1995. "On Becoming a Buddhist Wizard." In *Buddhism in Practice*, edited by Donald S. Lopez, Jr., 343–358. Princeton: Princeton University Press.

Raphals, Lisa. 1998. *Sharing the Light: Representations of Women and Virtue in Early China*. Albany: State University of New York Press.

Reinders. Eric. 1997. "Ritual Topography: Embodiment and Vertical Space in Buddhist Monastic Practice." *History of Religions* 36.3: 244–264.

Renou, Louis, and Jean Filliozat. 1947. *L'Inde classique: Manuel des études indiennes*. Paris: Payot.

Rerikh, Y. N. 1973. "Mongol Tibetan Relations in the 13th and 14th Centuries." *Tibet Society Bulletin* 6: 40–55.

Rigzin, Tsepak. 1986. *Tibetan-English Dictionary of Buddhist Terminology.* Dharamsala: Library of Tibetan Works and Archives.

Robinson, James B., trans. 1979. *The Buddha's Lions: The Lives of the Eighty-four Siddhas.* Berkeley: Dharma Publishing.

Robouam, Thierry. 2011. "The Sea of Esotericism Is of One Flavor but Has Deep and Shallow Aspects: 'Tantra' and New Age Movements from Agonshū to Asahara Shōkō." In *Esoteric Buddhism and the Tantras in East Asia*, edited by Charles D. Orzech, Henrik H. Sørensen, and Richard K. Payne, 1035–1039. Leiden and Boston: Brill.

Roerich, George N., trans. 1976. *The Blue Annals by gZhon-nu dPal.* 2nd ed. Delhi: Motilal Banarsidass.

Ruegg, David Seyfort. 1966. *The Life of Bu ston Rin po che with the Tibetan Text of the Bu ston rNam thar.* Rome: Istituto Italiano per il Medio ed Estremo Oriente.

Ruegg, David Seyfort. 1991. "*mchod yon, yon mchod* and *mchod gnas/yon gnas*: On the Historiography and Semantics of a Tibetan Religio-Social and Religio-Political Concept." In *Tibetan History and Language: Studies Dedicated to Uray Géza on His Seventieth Birthday*, edited by Ernst Steinkellner, 441–454. Wien: Arbeitskreis für Tibetische und Buddhistische Studien. Universität Wien.

Sakurai Munenobu. 1998. "Cakrasaṃvarābhisamaya no genten kenkyū." *Chizan Gakuho* 47: 1–32.

Salomon, Richard. 2018. *The Buddhist Literature of Ancient Gandhara: An Introduction with Selected Translations.* Somerville, MA: Wisdom Publications.

Samuel, Geoffrey. 1993. *Civilized Shamans: Buddhism in Tibetan Societies.* Washington, DC: Smithsonian Institute Press.

Sanderson, Alexis. 2001. "History Through Textual Criticism in the Study of Śaivism, the Pañcarātra and the Buddhist Yoginītantras." In *Les Source et le temps*, edited by François Grimal, 1–47. Pondicherry: École française d'Extrême Orient.

Sanderson, Alexis. 2009. "The Śaiva Age: The Rise and Dominance of Śaivism During the Early Medieval Period." In *Genesis and Development of Tantrism*, edited by Shingo Einoo, 41–349. Tokyo: Institute of Oriental Culture, University of Tokyo.

Sanderson, Alexis. 2013. "The Impact of Inscriptions on the Interpretation of Early Śaiva Literature." *Indo-Iranian Journal* 56: 211–244.

Sanford, James H. 1991. "The Abominable Tachikawa Skull Ritual." *Monumenta Nipponica* 46.1: 1–20.

Sanford, James H. 2006. "Breath of Life: The Esoteric Nembutsu." In *Tantric Buddhism in East Asia*, edited by Richard K. Payne, 163–189. Somerville, MA: Wisdom Publications.

Śāntarakṣita. 2011. *The Adornment of the Middle Way: Shantarakshita's Madhyamalankara with Commentary by Jamgön Mipham*. Translated by the Padmakara Translation Group. Boston: Shambala Publications.

Śāntideva. 2008. *Bodhicaryāvatāra*. Translated by Kate Crosby and Andrew Skilton. Oxford and New York: Oxford University Press.

Saunders, E. Dale. 1960. *Mudrā: A Study of Symbolic Gestures in Japanese Buddhist Sculpture*. Reprint, Princeton: Princeton University Press, 1985.

Schäffer, Peter. 1992. *The Hidden and Manifest God: Some Major Themes in Early Jewish Mysticism*. Albany: State University of New York Press.

Sen, Tansen. 2002. "The Revival and Failure of Buddhist Translations During the Song Dynasty." *T'oung Pao*, 2nd series, 88.1/3: 27–80.

Sen, Tansen. 2003. *Buddhism, Diplomacy, and Trade: The Realignment of Sino-Indian Relations, 600–1400*. Honolulu: University of Hawaii Press.

Sen, Tansen. 2014. "Buddhism and the Maritime Crossings." In *China and Beyond in the Mediaeval Period: Cultural Crossings and Inter-Regional Connections*, edited by Dorothy C. Wong and Gustav Heldt, 39-62. Amherst/Delhi: Cambria Press/Manohar.

Sen, Tansen. 2015. "The Spread of Buddhism." In *The Cambridge World History, Volume 5: Expanding Webs of Exchange and Conflict, 500CE–1500 CE*, edited by Benjamin Z. Kedar and Merry Wiesner-Hanks, 447–479. Cambridge: Cambridge University Press, 2015.

Sferra, Francesco. 1999. "The Concept of Purification in Some Texts of Late Indian Buddhism." *Journal of Indian Philosophy* 27.1-2: 83–103.

Sharf, Robert H. 2002. *Coming to Terms with Chinese Buddhism: A Reading of the Treasure Store Treatise*. Honolulu: University of Hawaii Press.

Sharrock, Peter D. 2012. "Kīrtipaṇḍita and the Tantras." *Udaya Journal of Khmer Studies* 10: 203–237.

Sharrock, Peter D. 2013. "The Yoginīs of Bayon." In *'Yoginī' in South Asia: Interdisciplinary Approaches*, edited by István Keul, 117–129. London and New York: Routledge.

Sharrock, Peter D., and Emma C. Bunker. 2016. "Seeds of Vajrabodhi: Buddhist Ritual Bronzes from Java and Khorta." In *Esoteric Buddhism in Medieval Maritime Asia: Networks of Masters, Texts, Icons*, edited by Andrea Acri, 237–252. Singapore: ISEAS-Yusaf Ishak Institute.

Shekhar, I. 1960. *Sanskrit Drama: Its Origin and Decline*. Leiden: E. J. Brill.

Shinohara, Koichi. 2014. *Spells, Images, and Maṇḍalas: Tracing the Evolution of Esoteric Rituals*. New York: Columbia University Press.

Siklós, Bulcsu. 1996. *The Vajrabhairava Tantras*. Tring, UK: Institute of Buddhist Studies.

Simmer-Brown, Judith. 2001. *Dakini's Warm Breath: The Feminine Principle in Tibetan Buddhism*. Boston: Shambhala Publications.

Sinclair, Iain. 2016. "Coronation and Liberation According to a Javanese Monk in China: Bianhong's Manual on the *abhiṣeka* of a *cakravartin*." In *Esoteric Buddhism in Medieval Maritime Asia: Networks of Masters, Texts, Icons*, edited by Andrea Acri, 29–66. Singapore: ISEAS-Yusaf Ishak Institute.

Sircar, D. C. 1965. *Select Inscriptions Bearing on Indian History and Civilization*. Vol. 1. 2d ed. Kolkata: University of Calcutta.

Sircar, D. C. 1983. *Problems of Early Indian Social History*. Calcutta Sanskrit College Research Series no. 122. Calcutta: Sanskrit College.

Skilling, Peter. 1992. "The Rakṣā Literature of the Śrāvakayāna." *Journal of the Pali Text Society* 16: 109–182.

Skilling, Peter. 1997. "From bKa' bstan bcos to bKa' 'gyur and bsTan 'gyur." In *Transmission of the Tibetan Canon: Papers Presented at a Panel of the 7th Seminar of the International Association for Tibetan Studies*, edited by Helmut Eimer, 87–111. Wien: Österreichische Akademie Der Wissenschaften.

Skorupski, Tadeusz. 1996. "The *Saṃpuṭa-tantra:* Sanskrit and Tibetan Versions of Chapter One." In *The Buddhist Forum, Volume IV: Seminar Papers 1994–1996*, edited by Tadeusz Skorupski, 191–244. London: School of Oriental and African Studies, University of London.

Slouber, Michael. 2017. *Early Tantric Medicine: Snakebite, Mantras, and Healing in the Gāruḍa Tantras*. New York: Oxford University Press.

Smith, Fredrick M. 2006. *The Self Possessed: Deity and Spirit Possession in South Asian Literature and Civilization*. New York: Columbia University Press.

Snellgrove, David L. 1959a. *The Hevajra Tantra: A Critical Study*. 2 vols. London: Oxford University Press.

Snellgrove, David L. 1959b. "The Notion of Divine Kingship in Tantric Buddhism." In *The Sacral Kingship: Contributions to the Central Theme of the VIIIth International Congress for the History of Religions (Rome, April 1955)*, edited by Carl-Martin Edsman, 204–218. Leiden: Brill.

Snellgrove, David L. 1987. *Indo-Tibetan Buddhism*. London: Serindia Publications.

Snellgrove, David L. 1988. "Categories of Buddhist Tantras." In *Orientalia Iosephi Tucci Memoriae Dicata 3*, edited by G. Gnoli and L. Lanciotti, 1353–1384. *Serie Orientale Roma* 56.3. Roma: Istituto italiano per il Medio ed Estremo Oriente.

Sobisch, Jan-Ulrich. 2008. *Hevajra and Lam 'bras Literature of India and Tibet as Seen Through the Eyes of A-mes-zhabs*. Wiesbaden: Dr. Ludwig Reichert Verlag.

Sørensen, Henrik H. 2006a. "Esoteric Buddhism in Korea." In *Tantric Buddhism in East Asia*, edited by Richard K. Payne, 61–77. Somerville, MA: Wisdom Publications.

Sørensen, Henrik H. 2006b. "Esoteric Buddhism in Korean Sŏn Buddhism During the Chosŏn Period." In *Tantric Buddhism in East Asia*, edited by Richard K. Payne, 78–98. Somerville, MA: Wisdom Publications.

Sørensen, Henrik H. 2011a. "Textual Material Relating to Esoteric Buddhism in China Outside the Taishō, Vols. 18–21." In *Esoteric Buddhism and the Tantras in East Asia*, edited by Charles D. Orzech, Henrik H. Sørensen, and Richard K. Payne, 37–67. Leiden and Boston: Brill.

Sørensen, Henrik H. 2011b. "Early Esoteric Buddhism in Korea: Three Kingdoms and Unified Silla (ca. 600–918)." In *Esoteric Buddhism and the Tantras in East Asia*, edited by Charles D. Orzech, Henrik H. Sørensen, and Richard K. Payne, 575–596. Leiden and Boston: Brill.

Sørensen, Henrik H. 2011c. "Esoteric Buddhism Under the Koryŏ (918-1392)." In *Esoteric Buddhism and the Tantras in East Asia*, edited by Charles D. Orzech, Henrik H. Sørensen and Richard K. Payne, 597–615. Leiden and Boston: Brill.

Sørensen, Henrik H. 2011d. "Esoteric Buddhism Under the Chosŏn." In *Esoteric Buddhism and the Tantras in East Asia*, edited by Charles D. Orzech, Henrik H. Sørensen and Richard K. Payne, 616–657. Leiden and Boston: Brill.

Sperling, Elliot. 1994. "Rtsa-mi Lo-tsā-ba Sangs-rgyas grags and the Tangut Background to Early Mongol-Tibetan Relations." In *Tibetan Studies: Proceedings of the 6th Seminar of the International Association of Tibetan Studies. Fagernes 1992 Volume 2*, edited by Per Kvaerne, 801–824. Oslo: Institute for Comparative Research in Human Culture.

Sundberg, Jeffrey Roger. 2003. "A Buddhist Mantra Recovered from the Ratu Baka Plateau: A Preliminary Study of Its Implications for Sailendra-Era Java." *Bijdragen tot de Taal-, Land- en Volkenkunde* 159.1: 163–188.

Sundberg, Jeffrey Roger. 2004. "The Wilderness Monks of the Abhayagirivihāra and the Origins of Sino-Javanese Esoteric Buddhism." *Bijdragen tot de Taal-, Land- en Volkenkunde* 160.1: 95–123.

Sundberg, Jeffrey Roger, and Rolf Giebel. 2011. "The Life of the Tang Court Monk Vajrabodhi as Chronicled by Lü Xiang (呂向): South Indian and Śrī Laṅkān Antecedents to the Arrival of the Buddhist Vajrayāna in Eighth-Century Java and China." *Pacific World* 3.13: 129–222.

Stanley, D. Phillip. 2005. "The Tibetan Buddhist Canon: The Kangyur (Bka' 'gyur) and Tengyur (Bstan 'gyur)." The Tibetan and Himalayan Digital Library (THDL). http://www.thlib.org/encyclopedias/literary/canons/index.php#essay=/stanley/tibcanons/.

Stearns, Cyrus. 2010. *The Buddha from Dolpo: A Study of the Life and Thought of the Tibetan Master Dolpopa Sherab Gyaltsen*. Rev. ed. Ithaca, NY: Snow Lion Publications.

Strong, John S. 1992. *The Legend and Cult of Upagupta: Sanskrit Buddhism in North India and Southeast Asia*. Princeton: Princeton University Press.

Sugiki, Tsunehiko. 2001. "On the Making of the *Śrīcakrasaṃvaratantra*, with a Critical Sanskrit Text of Jayabhadra's *Śrīcakrasaṃvarapañjikā*." *Chisan Gakuhō* (智山学報) 50: 91–141.

Sugiki, Tsunehiko. 2002. "A Critical Study of the Vajraḍākamahātantrarāja (I) Chapter 1 and 42." *Chisan Gakuhō* (智山学報) 51: 81–111.

Suzuki, Daisetz Teitaro, trans. 1932. *The Lankavatara Sutra: A Mahayana Text*. Reprint, Delhi: Motilal Banarsidass, 1999.

Takakusu, Junjirō, trans. 1896. *A Record of the Buddhist Religion as Practiced in India and the Malay Archipelago (A. D. 671–695) By I-Tsing*. Oxford: Clarendon Press.

Taupier, Richard. 2015. "The Western Mongolia Clear Script and the Making of a Buddhist State." In *Buddhism in Mongolian History, Culture, and Society*, edited by Vesna A. Wallace, 23–36. Oxford and New York: Oxford University Press.

Templeman, David. 1989. *Tāranātha's Life of Kṛṣṇācārya/Kāṇha*. Dharamsala: Library of Tibetan Works and Archives.

Templeman, David. 1995. *The Origin of the Tārā Tantra, Jo Nang Tāranātha*. Rev ed. Dharamsala: Library of Tibetan Works and Archives.

Thurman, Robert A. F. 1976. *The Holy Teaching of Vimalakīrti: A Mahāyāna Scripture*. University Park: Pennsylvania State University Press.

Thurman, Robert A. F. 1988. "Vajra Hermeneutics." In *Buddhist Hermeneutics*, edited by Donald S. Lopez, Jr., 119–148. Honolulu: University of Hawaii Press.

Tinsley, Elizabeth. 2011. "Kūkai and the Development of Shingon Buddhism." In *Esoteric Buddhism and the Tantras in East Asia*, edited by Charles D. Orzech, Henrik H. Sørensen, and Richard K. Payne, 691–708. Leiden and Boston: Brill.

Tucci, Giuseppe. 1949. *Tibetan Painted Scrolls*. Kyoto: Rinsen Book.

Türstig, Hans-Georg. 1985. "The Indian Sorcery Called Abhicāra." *Wiener Zeitschrift für die Kunde Südasiens und Archive für Indische Philosophie* 29: 69–117.

Tuttle, Gray. 2005. *Tibetan Buddhists in the Making of Modern China*. New York: Columbia University Press.

Tuttle, Gray. 2009. "Translating Buddhism from Tibetan to Chinese in Early-Twentieth Century China (1931–1951)." In *Buddhism Between Tibet and China*, edited by Matthew T. Kapstein, 241–294. Somerville, MA: Wisdom Publications.

Urban, Hugh B. 2003. *Tantra: Sex, Secrecy, Politics, and Power in the Study of Religion*. Berkeley: University of California Press.

Urubshurow, David. 2013. "From Russia with Love: The Untold Story of How Tibetan Buddhism First Came to America." *Tricycle*, Winter issue. https://tricycle.org/magazine/geshe-ngawang-wangyal/ (accessed April 20, 2020).

Vaidya, P. L., ed. 1963. *Saddharmalaṅkāvatārasūtram*. Buddhist Sanskrit Texts no. 3. Darbhanga: Mithila Institute.

Van der Kuijp, Leonard W. J. 1991. "On the Life and Political Career of T'ai-si-tu Byang-chub rGyal-mtshan (1302–?1364)." In *Tibetan History and Language: Studies Dedicated to Uray Géza on His Seventieth Birthday*, edited by Ernst Steinkellner, 277–327. Wien: Arbeitskreis für Tibetische und Buddhistische Studien. Universität Wien.

Van der Kuijp, Leonard W. J. 1992. "Notes Apropos of the Transmission of the Sarvadurgatipariśodhanatantra in Tibet." *Studien zur Indologie und Iranistik* 16: 109–125.

Van Gulik, R. H. 1961. *Sexual Life in Ancient China: A Preliminary Survey of Chinese Sex and Society from ca. 1500 B.C. till 1644 A.D.* Leiden: Brill. Reprint, New York: Barnes and Noble, 1996.

Van Schaik, Sam. 2013. *Tibet: A History*. New Haven: Yale University Press.

Van Schaik, Sam. 2020. *Buddhist Magic: Divination, Healing, and Enchantment Through the Ages*. Boulder, CO: Shambhala Publications.

Verardi, Giovanni. 1994. *Homa and Other Fire Rituals in Gandhāra*. Napoli: Istituto Universitario Orientale.

Verardi, Giovanni. 2011. *Hardships and Downfall of Buddhism in India*. Delhi: ManoharPublications.

Vose, Kevin A. 2009. *Resurrecting Candrakīrti: Disputes in the Tibetan Creation of Prāsaṅgika*. Somerville, MA: Wisdom Publications.

Wallace, Vesna A. 2001. *The Inner Kālacakratantra: A Buddhist Tantric View of the Individual*. Oxford and New York: Oxford University Press.

Wallace, Vesna A. 2004. *The Kālacakratantra: The Chapter on the Individual Together with the Vimalaprabhā*. New York: American Institute of Buddhist Studies and Columbia University Press.

Wallace, Vesna A. 2010. *The Kālacakratantra: The Chapter on Sādhana Together with the Vimalaprabhā Commentary*. New York: American Institute of Buddhist Studies and Columbia University Press.

Wallace, Vesna A. 2011. "A Brief Exploration of Late Indian Buddhist Exegeses of the 'Mantrayāna' and 'Mantranaya.'" *Pacific World* 3.11: 95–111.

Wallace, Vesna A., and Christine Murphy. 2017. "Contemporary Mongolian Buddhism." In *The Oxford Handbook of Contemporary Buddhism*, edited by Michael Jerryson, 161–174. New York: Oxford University Press.

Wallis, Christopher. 2008. "The Descent of Power: Possession, Mysticism, and Initiation in the Śaiva Theology of Abhinavagupta. *Journal of Indian Philosophy* 36.2: 247–295.

Wallis, Glenn. 2002. *Mediating the Power of the Buddhas: Ritual in the Mañjuśrīmūlakalpa*. Albany: State University of New York Press.

Walser, Joseph. 2005. *Nāgārjuna in Context: Mahāyāna Buddhism & Early Indian Culture*. New York: Columbia University Press.

Walter, Michael L. 2009. *Buddhism and Empire: The Political and Religious Culture of Early Tibet.* Leiden and Boston: Brill.

Waugh, Teresia, trans. 1984. *The Travels of Marco Polo.* London: Sidgwick & Jackson.

Wayman, Alex. 1977. *The Yoga of the Guhyasamājatantra: The Arcane Lore of Forty Verses.* Delhi: Motilal Banarsidass.

Wechsler, Howard J. 1985. *Offerings of Jade and Silk: Ritual and Symbol in the Legitimation of the T'ang Dynasty.* New Haven: Yale University Press.

Wedemeyer, Christian K. 2002. "Antinomianism and Gradualism: The Contextualization of the Practices of Sensual Enjoyment (*Caryā*) in the Guhyasamāja Ārya Tradition." *The Indian International Journal of Buddhist Studies* 10.3: 181–195.

Wedemeyer, Christian K. 2006. "Tantalizing Traces of the Labours of the Lotsāwas: Alternate Translations of Sanskrit Sources in the Writings of rJe Tsong kha pa." In *Tibetan Buddhist Literature and Praxis: Studies in its Formative Period 900–1400*, edited by Ronald M. Davidson and Christian K. Wedemeyer, 149–182. Leiden and Boston: Brill.

Wedemeyer, Christian K. 2007. *Āryadeva's Lamp That Integrates the Practices, Caryāmelāpakapradīpa, the Gradual Path of Vajrayāna Buddhism According to the Esoteric Community Noble Tradition.* New York: AIBS/CBS/THUS [Columbia University Press].

Weinstein, Stanley. 1987. *Buddhism under the T'ang.* Cambridge: Cambridge University Press.

White, David Gordon. 1996. *The Alchemical Body: Siddha Traditions in Medieval India.* Chicago: University of Chicago Press.

White, David Gordon. 2003. *Kiss of the Yoginī: "Tantric Sex" in Its South Asian Contexts.* Chicago: University of Chicago Press.

Willemen, Charles. 1983. *The Chinese Hevajratantra: The Scriptural Text of the Ritual of the Great King of the Teaching, the Adamantine One with Great Compassion and Knowledge of the Void.* Orientalia Gandensia. Vol. 8. Leuven, Belgium: Uitgeverij Peeters.

Wolff, Kurt H., trans. 1950. *The Sociology of Georg Simmel.* Glencoe, IL: Free Press.

Wu, Jiang. 2018. "The Rule of Marginality: Hypothesizing the Transmission of the Mengshan Rite for Feeding the Hungry Ghosts in Late Imperial China." *Pacific World* 3.20: 131–167.

Wujastyk, Dominic. 2003. *The Roots of Ayurveda.* Rev. ed. New York: Penguin Books.

Yamada, Isshi. 1981. *Sarva-tathāgata-tattva-saṅgraha: A Critical Edition Based on a Sanskrit Manuscript and Chinese and Tibetan Translations.* Śata-piṭaka Series, Indo-Asian Literatures. Vol. 262. Delhi: Jayyed Press.

Yang, Zeng. 2018. *A Biographical Study on Bukong 不空 (aka. Amoghavajra, 705–774): Networks, Institutions, and Identities.* Doctoral disseration,

University of British Columbia. https://open.library.ubc.ca/collections/ubctheses/24/items/1.0363332 (accessed March 29, 2023) .

Yee, Wan Ko. 2008. *H. H. Dorje Chang Buddha III: A Treasury of True Buddha-dharma.* 多杰羌佛第三世：正法寶典。 Vancouver, WA: World Buddhism Publications.

Yeshe Tsogyal. 1978. *The Life and Liberation of Padmasambhava.* Translated by Gustave-Charles Toussaint, Kenneth Douglas, and Gwendolyn Bays. 2 vols. Berkeley: Dharma Publishing.

Zablocki, Abraham. 2009a. "The Taiwanese Connection: Politics, Piety, and Patronage in Transnational Tibetan Buddhism." In *Buddhism Between Tibet and China*, edited by Matthew T. Kapstein, 379–414. Somerville, MA: Wisdom Publications.

Zablocki, Abraham. 2009b. "Transnational *Tulkus:* The Globalization of Tibetan Buddhist Reincarnation." In *TransBuddhism: Transmission, Translation, Transformation*, edited by Nalini Bhushan, Jay L. Garfield, and Abraham Zablocki, 43–53. Amherst: University of Massachusetts Press.

Index

For the benefit of digital users, indexed terms that span two pages (e.g., 52-53) may, on occasion, appear on only one of those pages.

Abé, R., 120, 158
Abhayākaragupta, 203, 204–5
Abhidhānottaratantra, 79, 87–89, 91–92, 143–45
Abhidharma, 25–26, 149
ācārya, 12, 86, 93, 97–98, 99–100, 102–3, 172–73, 185–86. *See also* vajrācārya
Adamantine Path. *See* Vajrayāna
Adamantine Pinnacle Collection. *See* Assembly of the Eighteen Adamantine Pinnacle Yoga Scriptures
Akṣobhya, 85, 195–96
Amitābha, 131–32, 159, 196–97
Amoghavajra (不空金刚), 13–14, 28, 29, 109–11, 113, 117, 118, 119, 123, 168, 170–71, 180, 194–95
appendix tantra, 33–34, 61–62, 143–44
Āryāḍākinīvajrapañjara Tantra, 82
Āryadeva, 146–47
Āryāmoghapāśakalparāja, 58
Ārya school, 190, 197–98
Āryatārākurukullākalpa, 106
Āryavidyottama-mahātantra, 44
Asaṅga, 56, 84–85
Assembly of the Eighteen Adamantine Pinnacle Yoga Scriptures, 28–29, 39–40, 59–60, 146, 160, 162–63, 171
Atiśa Dīpaṅkaraśrījñāna, 101–2, 126–27, 154–55, 175, 179, 188, 202, 203
Attaining Enlightenment in This Very Existence, 79–80
The Attainment of Divine Vision in the Mantra-Vajrayāna, 75–76
Avalokiteśvara, 58, 59, 120–21, 146–47
Avataṃsaka Sūtra, 57, 79
awakened speech, 8, 48, 57–58, 65–66, 141–42, 145–46, 164, 191–92
Awakening of Mahāvairocana Tantra. *See* Mahāvairocanābhis aṃbodhi Tantra

Bhavabhaṭṭa, 181
Bhāvaviveka, 72–73
Bhūtaḍāmara Tantra, 83–84
Bodhipathapradīpa, 202
Brahmins, 50, 104, 114–15
Buddhaguhya, 148–49, 150–51
Buddhajñāna, 205
buddha nature, 68, 72–73, 78, 80–81, 82, 185–86
Buddhapālita, 72–73
buddhavacana. *See* awakened speech
buddha yoga. *See* deity yoga
Buddhist tantric traditions (definition of), 8–9

Butön Rinchendrup (bu ston rin chen grub), 145, 165, 173–74

Cakrasaṃvarābhisamaya, 102
Cakrasaṃvara Tantra, 18–19, 32–34, 39–40, 61, 62–63, 64–66, 67, 69–70, 71–72, 86–87, 99–100, 104–5, 116, 126, 136–37, 142–45, 180–81
Candrakīrti, 72–73, 144, 200–2
Cantwell, C., 18–19, 164
celibacy, 3–4, 5, 20–21, 167–68, 202–3, 204, 207
censorship, 168–69, 172, 173–76, 183, 187–88
central channel (avadhūti), 91–92, 102
Chan [Mahayana Buddhist tradition], 73, 130–32
Chang-an, 37, 109–10, 111, 117, 119
coded language (sandhyā-bhāṣa), 26–27, 50–51, 69–70, 71
Commentary on the Glorious Binding of the Wheels King of Tantras Called the Assembly of Supreme Bliss, 39–42
Commentary on the Method of the Perfection of Wisdom in 150 Stanzas, 29–30, 111–13
completion stage. *See* perfection stage (niṣpannakrama)
concentration (samādhi), 40–42, 55, 79, 80–81, 156–57, 193, 195, 198, 199
Confucianism, 183, 188
consort observance (*vidyāvrata*), 19–21
creation stage (*utpattikrama*), 90–91, 133–34, 157, 207
cyclic existence, 25–26, 78

Daizong emperor (代宗), 110–11, 113, 117
Ḍākārṇava Tantra, 33–34, 63, 68
ḍākinī, 9–10, 33–34, 35–36, 38–39, 45, 94–95, 154, 199
ḍākinī mantra, 37–39
ḍākinī tantras, 10, 35–36, 94–95
Dalton, J., 12, 152
Dānapāla, 180, 183–84, 185, 186–87
Daoism, 25–26, 110–11, 123, 138
Daolin (道琳), 21–24, 25, 26
Davidson, R., 14, 69, 71, 146–47, 172
deity yoga, 77–79, 80–81, 82, 85, 86, 87, 89, 90, 101–2, 152, 155–57, 201, 207
Detailed Commentary on the Awakening of Mahāvairocana Tantra, 148–50
Detailed Exegesis of the Import of the Sarvabuddhasamāyogaḍākinījālasamvara Tantra, 31, 156–57
dhāraṇī, 12, 41–42, 103–4, 124, 130–32, 159–60, 162–63, 174–75
dhāraṇī collections, 8, 13
dharmakāya. *See* reality body
Dharmakīrti, 10, 35–36, 94–95
Dharmapāla, 180, 187–88
Ḍombipa, 146–47
Dunhuang, 122, 124–25, 162–63
Dvikramatattvabhāvana-nāma-mukhāgama, 205–6

emptiness, 72–75, 77–78, 79, 81, 82–83, 87, 112–13
Esoteric Achievement. *See* Guhyasiddhi
Explanation of the Secret Meaning of Glorious Vajrasattva, 156
explanatory tantras, 32–34, 87, 143, 144–46, 147, 200
Exposition of the Guru's Oral Instructions on the Background Verse of the Glorious Esoteric Community Tantra, 190–92

Franke, H., 128, 129
fury fire (caṇḍālī, gtum mo), 91–92

Gaṅgdhār, 9–10

Gathering of Intentions Sutra, 64–65
Geluk [Tibetan Buddhist tradition], 127, 129–30, 135–37
Generation stage. *See* creation stage (*utpattikrama*)
Ghaṇṭāpāda, 147
Goryeo Dynasty, 124, 130–31
great adept, 8–9, 24, 30–31, 102, 115, 121–22, 128, 146–47
Greater Path. *See* Mahayana
Guhyasamāja Tantra, 20, 29–30, 59–61, 63, 74, 99–100, 136–37, 142–43, 144, 152–53, 162–63, 171, 175–76, 179, 180, 183–85, 190, 192–94, 195–96, 197–98, 200, 207
Guhyasiddhi, 19, 20–21
Gupta Dynasty, 6, 14, 151
guru, 8–9, 19–20, 46, 50, 52, 88, 102, 114–15, 116, 125, 128, 137, 142–43, 205–6

Harṣa Śīlāditya, 15–16
Hayagrīva, 45
Heian era, 120, 160
Heruka, 43, 45, 86–87, 89, 101–2, 143–44
Hevajra Tantra, 50–51, 61, 68–69, 70, 128–29, 134, 142–43, 146–47, 152–53, 162–63, 165, 175–76, 180, 187
Hinduism, 2, 5, 7, 9, 11, 14, 15, 44, 45, 46, 50, 54, 79, 104, 151
  See also Śaiva [Hindu tradition]
homa fire sacrifice, 104, 131–32, 147, 151, 152, 162–63, 170–71, 172, 182, 186–87
Huiguo (惠果), 111, 119, 158, 159, 160, 162

Illumination of the Hidden Meaning, 104–5
Index of the Adamantine Pinnacle Scripture Yoga in Eighteen Sections, 180, 194–95
Indrabhūti (king), 24, 29–30, 111–12, 115–16, 121–22
Indrabhūti (commentator), 39–40, 147
Indranāla, 31, 32, 156, 157
initiation, 6–7, 12–13, 19–20, 50–51, 52, 82, 86, 92–94, 96–103, 110–11, 114, 116–17, 118–19, 128–29, 133–34, 147, 156–57, 162–63, 167, 187–88, 202–3, 205
Interpretation of the Lotus Sūtra, 159–60
Introduction to the Mahāvairocana Sūtra, 27
Introductory Summary of the Import of the Unexcelled Yoga Tantras, 152–54

Jainism, 7, 46, 63–64
Jayabhadra, 61, 62, 65–66, 67, 100–1
Jñānamitrā, 29, 30, 111, 113
Jñānapāda school, 197–98, 205
Jñānatilaka-yoginītantrarāja-paramamahādbhuta, 42

Kagyü [Tibetan Buddhist tradition], 127, 129, 130
Kālacakra Tantra, 47, 63, 64–65, 66, 67, 72–73, 74–75, 77–78, 136–37, 142–43, 146–47
Kambala, 147
Kāṇha. *See* Kṛṣṇācarya
Kanmu Emperor (桓武), 118–19
Kāpālika [Hindu tradition], 14, 16–17, 35, 94–95
Kapstein, M., 123, 175
Kashmir, 24, 46, 126, 188–89
Kathmandu, 114–15, 121–22, 134–35, 161, 188–89
Kaula Hindu tradition, 66
Khubilai Khan, 128–29, 134, 135–36
Kṛṣṇācarya, 146–47

Kṛṣṇayamāri Tantra. *See* Sarvatathāgatakāyavākcitta-kṛṣṇayamāri Tantra
Kūkai (空海), 27–28, 36–37, 79, 111, 118–20, 158, 159–60, 162
Kukurāja, 156

Lalitavajra, 31
lāmā [goddesses], 70
Laṅkāvatāra Sūtra, 36–37
Lha-lama Yéshé-ö (lha bla ma ye shes 'od), 125, 126, 127, 175
Locanā, 20–21
Lotus Sūtra, 54–55, 118
Lūipa, 102, 147

magical practices, 2–3, 6, 10–12, 29, 36–37, 38–39, 48, 57–58, 83–84, 89, 95–96, 97, 99, 102–6, 129, 143, 157, 160–61, 168, 170–71, 173, 176, 180–81, 182–83
Mahākāla, 38–39, 45, 97–98, 128–29
Mahāmāyā Tantra, 142–43
Mahāpratisarā-dhāraṇī, 103–4
mahāsiddha. *See* great adept
Mahāvairocana. *See* Vairocana
Mahāvairocanābhisaṃbodhi Tantra, 11, 16–17, 27, 36–37, 117–18, 150–51, 160, 162–63
Mahāvajradhara. *See* Vajradhara
Mahāyāna, 1, 11, 12, 13, 17–18, 23, 25, 28, 36, 51–52, 53–54, 55, 56–57, 58–59, 64–65, 72–74, 75, 77, 79, 82, 83, 84–85, 104, 106, 109, 114, 118–19, 121, 131–32, 134, 138–39, 149, 151, 158, 159, 162, 183, 184, 185–86, 194, 197, 201–2
Mahāyānasūtrālaṃkāra, 56
mahāyoga tantras, 29, 75, 122, 148, 152–53, 154, 171, 174, 188, 191
mandala, 2, 4, 13, 19–20, 24, 26–27, 32, 52, 61, 75–78, 81, 82, 83–85, 86–87, 88, 89, 92–95, 96, 97–98, 100–1, 102, 103, 109, 111, 112–13, 114, 115, 116, 117, 129, 130–31, 147, 152, 154, 156–57, 172, 195–97, 203, 205–6
Mañjuśrī, 59
Mañjuśrīmūlakalpa, 84–85
Mañjuśrīnāmasaṃgīti, 61
mantra, 1, 10–12, 19–20, 32, 36–37, 38–39, 41–42, 45, 46–47, 50, 81, 83, 87, 89, 92, 93, 94, 96–98, 100–1, 103, 104–5, 106, 130–31, 143, 153, 159–60, 170–71, 174–75, 181, 195, 201, 205–6
  Mantra School (*see* Shingon School [真言宗])
  See also ḍākinī mantra
Mantranaya, 1, 160–61
Mantrayāna, 1, 83, 147, 153, 160–61
Mantric Method. *See* Mantranaya
Mantric Path. *See* Mantrayāna
maritime trade, 13–14, 107–8
Māyājāla Tantra, 162–63
Mayer, R., 17, 18–19, 164
McMahon, D., 53, 55
meditation manual. *See* sādhana
monasticism, 5, 11–12, 19, 49–50
mother tantras. *See* yoginītantras
mudrā (consort), 94, 96–97, 99, 101–2, 156–57, 190–91, 201, 203–4
mudrā (gesture), 23–24, 26–27, 69–70, 83, 94, 95–96, 153, 195
mudrā (insignia), 87
mūlatantra. *See* root tantra
myth, 12, 15, 20–21, 25, 26, 27–28, 29–31, 32–33, 34–36, 37, 39–42, 43–46, 154

Nāgabuddhi, 85
Nāgārjuna, 23–24, 25, 27–28, 30–31, 72–73, 144, 146–47
Nālandā Monastery, 15–17, 21–22, 23, 24, 26–27, 35, 71–72, 108–9, 114–15, 119, 121, 126
Nara era, 117–19

Nāropa, 146–47
Nayatrayapradīpa, 78–79
nirvana, 41–42, 78
nondual gnosis, 76, 79, 82, 91, 102
Northern Song Dynasty, 113, 123, 124, 131–33, 162–63, 168–69, 170, 175–76, 178–79, 180, 186–87, 188
Nyingma [Tibetan Buddhist tradition], 6, 17, 30, 45, 47, 64–65, 75, 121–22, 127, 138, 148, 155, 157–58, 164, 165–66

Oḍiyāna, 24, 30, 31, 39–40, 43–44, 115
Orissa, 15–16
Orzech, C., 6, 103

Padmasambhava, 24, 121–22, 127, 138
Padmavajra, 19, 20–21
Pāśupata [Hindu tradition], 14
perfection stage (niṣpannakrama), 91, 102, 152, 199–200
possession (*āveśa*), 93–96
Pradīpoddyotana, 144, 200, 201
protective formula (*rakṣā*), 11–12, 104
Puṇḍarīka, 66, 67, 146–47

Qing Dynasty, 134–37

Ratnākaraśānti. *See* Śāntipa
reality body, 29, 40, 90, 93, 158–59
Rinchen Zangpo (rin chen bzang po), 125–26, 152–53, 175
Rongzom Chökyi Zangbo (Rong-zom Chos-kyi bZang-po), 75, 76
root tantra, 12, 32, 33–34, 87, 141–46, 201–2
Running Commentary on the Awakening of Mahāvairocana Sūtra, 37–39, 92–93

sādhana, 32, 87, 144–45, 147
Saichō (最澄), 118–19
Śaiva [Hindu tradition], 2, 7, 9, 10, 11–12, 14–15, 16–17, 19, 20–21, 35, 39, 44, 46, 47, 48, 66, 69–70, 71–72, 94–95, 97, 98–99, 104, 154, 157
Śākta [Hindu tradition], 94–95
Sakya [Tibetan Buddhist tradition], 127–28, 146–47, 165
Śākyamuni Buddha, 6, 13, 16, 25, 28–29, 30, 48, 53, 54–55, 57, 58, 59–60, 63–64, 159, 191–92
Sakya Paṇḍita Kunga Gyaltsen (sa skya paṇ ḍi ta kun dga' rgyal mtshan), 128
Samājasādhanavyavasthāna, 85
Sampuṭa Tantra, 61
Sampuṭatilaka Tantra, 31
saṃsāra. *See* cyclic existence
Samye Monastery, 121–22
Sanderson, A., 10, 47, 69–70, 94–95
Sandhivyākaraṇa Tantra, 82, 145, 200
Sanskrit, 1–2, 4, 7–8, 22–24, 32–33, 63–68, 70, 83–84, 107–8, 119, 133–34, 161, 169–70, 172–73, 176–81, 183–84, 185, 187–88, 189, 192
Śāntarakṣita, 121–22
Śāntipa, 146–47
Sarvabuddhasamāyoga-ḍākinījālasaṃvara Tantra, 29–30, 31, 32, 61, 62, 69, 78, 95, 99–100, 112, 155–56
Sarvabuddhasamāyoga Tantra. *See* Sarvabuddhasamāyoga-ḍākinījālasaṃvara Tantra
Sarvanivaraṇaviskambhin, 192, 194
Sarvatathāgatakāyavākcitta-kṛṣṇayamāri Tantra, 31, 155
Sarvatathāgata-tattvasaṃgraha-nāma-Mahayana-Sūtra, 39–40, 58–59, 96–97, 98–99, 113, 149–50, 156, 167, 171

Sarvarahasya-nāma-tantrarāja, 81–82
Śatasāhasrikā Prajñāpāramitā Sūtra, 26
Saunders, D., 95–96
secrecy, 1, 6–7, 8, 9, 13, 26–27, 42–43, 50–52, 61, 62, 63, 65–66, 70, 73, 82, 83, 91–92, 94, 96–97, 99, 102, 115, 119, 133–34, 140, 151, 153, 157, 159, 160, 174–75, 177, 180, 181, 183, 185–86, 195, 196, 199–200, 205, 206
sexual abuse, 140, 206
sexual practices, 3–4, 5, 10, 16–17, 20–21, 25, 93–94, 98–101, 125, 129, 130–31, 132–33, 140, 152, 157, 167, 171, 181, 184, 185, 186–87, 191, 194, 196–98, 199–200, 201, 202–3, 204–6
Shingon School (真言宗), 110–11, 117, 119, 120, 124, 131–33, 139, 160
Shintō, 131–32, 139
Śiva, 2, 7, 19–20, 44, 97
  Śiva as Hara, 46
  Śiva as Īśvara, 37–38, 39, 44, 58
  Śiva as Mahādeva, 40–42
  Śiva as Maheśvara, 38–39, 41, 44, 45, 58
  Śiva as Rudra, 45
skillful means, 8, 35, 40–41, 54, 60, 62, 66, 77, 82, 150–51, 153, 154, 158–59, 195
Songtsen Gampo (srong bstan sgam po), 120–21
spells. *See* dhāraṇī, mantra, vidyā
Śraddhākaravarma, 152–54
Śrīguhyagarbhatattvaviniścaya, 45
Sri Lanka, 22, 109
Śrīparamādya-mantrakalpakhaṇḍa, 93–94
Śrīparamādya-nāma-mahāyānakalparāja, 97–98
Śrīsaṃvarakhasama Tantra, 77
Śrī-Tattvapradīpa, 115–16
Śrī-Vajrabhairava Tantra, 136–37, 175–76, 182–83, 186–87
Śrīvajramālābhidhānamahāyogatantra, 60–61, 63, 197–99
Śrīvijaya, 107–8, 109
Subāhuparipṛcchā Tantra, 167, 172
Śubhakarasiṃha (善无畏), 37, 39–40, 45, 92, 109–11, 117–18, 124, 167, 172–94
subtle body (sukṣmakāya), 91, 152, 206
Susiddhikara Sūtra, 149–50, 162–63

Tāmralipti, 22, 107–8
Tang Dynasty, 110–11, 120–21, 123, 170, 173, 178–79
Tantra (definition of), 7–8
Tantra on the Adamantine Womb King of Wealth, 113–14
tantric feast (gaṇacakra), 68–69
Tārā, 106
Tāranātha, 34–35
Tendai School. *See* Tiantai (天台) school
Theravāda, 57, 63–64, 133–34
three levels of embodiment (trikāya), 71–72, 201–2
Tiantai (天台) school, 118–19, 131–33
treasure texts (gter ma), 17, 18–19, 121–22, 164
Tridé Songtsen (khri de srong btsan), 174–75
Tripiṭakamāla, 78
Tri Songdetsen (khri srong lde btsan), 121–22
Tsongkhapa (tsong kha pa), 83
Two Fascicle Lexicon, 174–75

Ūmā, 41–42, 44
unexcelled yoga tantras (niruttarayogatantra), 91–92, 99–100, 123, 148, 152–53, 162–63, 165, 167, 175–76, 188–89

Union of All Buddhas. *See* Sarvabuddhasamāyoga Tantra
Uttaratantra, 143–44, 153–54
uttaratantra [genre of tantras]. *See* appendix tantra

Vairocana, 38–39, 40–41, 45, 59, 190–91, 196–97
Vajrabhairava, 182
Vajrabhairava Tantra. *See* Śrī-Vajrabhairava Tantra
Vajrabuddhi (金刚智), 13–14, 28–29, 108, 109–11, 124, 171–72, 195
vajrācārya, 49, 71, 83, 111, 114–15, 117, 161, 182–83
Vajraḍāka, 63, 144–45
Vajradhara, 30–31, 32, 40–41, 43, 44, 62, 63, 78, 138–39, 156–57
Vajragarbha, 61, 146–47
Vajraghaṇṭa. *See* Ghaṇṭāpāda
Vajrahūṃkara, 89
Vajrakīlaya, 18
Vajrapāṇi, 29–31, 40–42, 43–44, 59, 63, 114, 115–16
Vajrasattva, 63, 112–13, 155–57
Vajrāvalī, 203–4
Vajravārāhī, 63, 101–2, 147
Vajrayāna, 1, 42, 71, 75, 76, 138, 153, 157–58, 160–61
Vajrayoginī, 147
Vedas, 104
Vibhūticandra, 74–75
vidyā as "consort"
  See also consort observance (*vidyāvrata*)
vidyā as "spell," 12, 23–24, 37–38
vidyādhara, 23, 25–26, 112–13, 133–34, 182–83
Vidyādharapiṭaka, 21–22, 23–24, 25–27, 48, 149–50, 160–61
Vikramaśīla Monastery, 71–72, 114–15, 126, 203
Vilāsavajra, 150–51, 190, 191–92, 197–98, 199–200, 205
Vimalakīrtinirdeśa Sūtra, 79, 138–39, 178
Vimalaprabhā, 66–67, 146–47
vinaya, 11–12, 22, 25–26, 133–34, 149, 204
Vīravajra, 33–34
Vīrupa, 146–47
visualization, 13, 18, 20–21, 46–47, 74, 79, 80, 83–84, 85, 87–88, 92, 96, 101–2, 118, 131–32, 133–34, 150, 151, 152, 157, 181, 196–97, 203, 204–5, 206
  See also deity yoga
vyākhyātantra. *See* explanatory tantra

White, D., 16–17, 45, 47, 49
wizard. *See* vidyādhara
Wizardry Collection. *See* Vidyādharapiṭaka
Wuxing (無行), 10–11
Wuzong emperor (武宗), 117, 122–23

Xuanzang (玄奘), 15–16, 108, 178

Yijing (義淨), 10–11, 21–22, 24, 25, 26–27, 28, 45, 107–8
Yixing (一行), 37, 39–40
yogatantras, 148, 150–51, 152, 153, 154, 165
yoginī, 68, 69–70, 79, 88, 94–95, 134, 154, 206
yoginītantras, 68, 132–33, 154, 175–76, 188
Yuan dynasty, 128–31, 135–37, 164

Zahor, 29–30, 112–13
Zen. *See* Chan [Mahayana Buddhist tradition]

www.ingramcontent.com/pod-product-compliance
Ingram Content Group UK Ltd.
Pitfield, Milton Keynes, MK11 3LW, UK
UKHW021841190326
469119UK00020B/246

9 780197 623848